I REMEMBER

I REMEMBER

by **DAN RATHER**

with *Peter Wyden*

LITTLE, BROWN AND COMPANY

BOSTON   TORONTO   LONDON

First Edition

Library of Congress Cataloging-in-Publication Data
Rather, Dan.
    I remember / Dan Rather with Peter Wyden. — 1st ed.
      p. cm.
   ISBN 0-316-73440-3
   1. Rather, Dan. 2. Journalists — United States — Biography.
I. Wyden, Peter. II. Title.
PN4874.R28A3 1991
070.4'092 — dc20
[B]
                                 91-21773

10 9 8 7 6 5 4 3 2 1

RRD VA

*Published simultaneously in Canada
by Little, Brown & Company (Canada) Limited*

PRINTED IN THE UNITED STATES OF AMERICA

To my brother, Don, and my sister, Patricia,
who have dedicated their lives
to teaching what we were taught

Contents

Acknowledgments

One of the joys in writing this book has been the opportunity to remember and to acknowledge that my lifelong heroes are my mother and father, and to tell why.

The fact that both crossed the river long ago hasn't faded my admiration and appreciation of them. Indeed, in my mind and in my heart, they loom larger, not smaller, and memories of them grow stronger, not dimmer.

I now live and work in environments where some people view it as unfashionable to acknowledge such things. Thank God, I have finally reached an age and stage where what such people think no longer matters.

What matters are the lessons and the love.

My wife, Jean Grace Goebel Rather, contributed mightily to this book, as she has to every other good and decent thing with which I have been associated for most of my adult life.

Our children, Robin and Dan, helped in ways large and small and, as always, have been constant in their support and encouragement.

Many people at CBS helped. I thank them all, including those whose names for one reason or another may not be mentioned here.

Among those in and out of CBS who made direct and important contributions to this book and to whom I am especially indebted are: Sims McCutchan of the Houston Public Library System, Eve Bartlett of the Wharton County Museum, Robert Gottlieb of Boston University, David and Susan Buksbaum, Richard and Carole Leibner, Martin Eisenstein, Ethel Goldstein, Nancy Kay, Allen Zelon, Stuart Witt, Cynthia Pulis, Vince Gonzales, Donna Dees, Bill Madison, Tom and Claire Bettag, Ann Hodges, Toby Wertheim, and the Heights Association of Houston.

Special thanks are due the anonymous authors of the WPA guide to Texas. This book was written during the Depression as part of a project to keep writers out of poverty. The formal title is *Texas—A Guide to the Lone Star State*. From it, I picked up or confirmed much detail. Fortuitously, it was published in 1940, which placed it at the center of my period of recollections.

Fredrica S. Friedman, Vice President, Executive Editor, and Associate Publisher of Little, Brown and Company, has been superb in taking this book from dream to reality. So has my book agent, Bill Adler. Peter Wyden contributed not only his talent, experience, and expertise, but also his gift for having a good time while working.

Many people have helped me along the way in life. Some of them are written about in this book. To all of them I owe more than can ever be repaid or acknowledged. But I remember.

In the woods, along the river
New York State, June 11, 1991

I REMEMBER

1

The "Rags" Rathers of Texas

MY BEST FRIENDS still call me "Rags." That was my name when I was growing up in the oil country outside Houston, Texas—Rags and Danny. But even some of my buddies can't remember that my father was also called Rags, never anything else, and so was the forefather who begat the tradition, my grandfather Rather.

There is a point to this family confession, although it's hardly a headline item. The point is that in our family, the same as in the news business, not everything is necessarily what it seems to be. At least not what it appears to be up front, right now. There's always a story in back of the story; I learned that as a boy. It's fun, and sometimes even useful if you want to stay humble, to look back on beginnings, how it all started. That's what I propose to do in these recollections.

There'll be no earthquakes here, no encounters with presidents or dictators, just a series of freeze-frames of my own small-town America and its vanishing life-style of fifty years back, an eternity.

I almost titled this book *The Winter of '41*, because that's when this story reached its climax, at least in my mind. December 7, 1941, to be exact, when the Japanese attacked Pearl Harbor. The Great Depression was beginning to ebb, our great war was building toward its crest.

This is a book about these times and the people. It's about how much has changed:

standards of living	medicine
morals	authority
respect	jobs
ditch digging	street fighting
parenting	religion
air-conditioning	

And much more. Such as "bettering oneself." You'll meet my parents and grandparents along the way. They and all the other people in these pages, the people of my youth, believed in progress. They were all believers in something we called the American dream.

Conservatives were people who believed in conserving the Constitution, including the Bill of Rights; liberals were those who believed in a continuing, self-renewing American Revolution. Both sides believed that America was the only truly revolutionary country in the world, that the Constitution and the concept of freedom embodied in it were sacred.

When they sang "America, the Beautiful," the line that goes, "Long may our land be bright with freedom's holy light," they knew what it meant and believed in it.

The people in this book, Americans who beat the Depression and won the war, differed and fought each other over what directions the country should take. But few ever questioned anyone else's patriotism. It just wasn't done.

I remember.

For context and perspective, for gaining even the most rudimentary sense of time and place, I need to tug the calendar back mightily for a moment. A clichéd reminder that the country has undergone gigantic change in half a century won't do. A close-up glance at a few baselines yields pictures of two nations, America then and America now—so much the same, yet bafflingly different.

It's like leafing through the family photo album and finding myself suddenly confronted, simultaneously, with the image of the boy Danny Rather on the unpaved streets of the Heights Annex and of Dan Rather, anchorman, navy blue pinstripes and all.

We were about half the size in population back in 1940. There were 131 million Americans then, 250 million of us now. My hometown, Houston, where we moved from Wharton, Texas, when I was less than a year old, has quintupled in size, from 386,000 to 1.9 million. Hitler was the villain back then and it appeared that he might actually win World War II. Franklin Delano Roosevelt occupied the White House. Big was beautiful and so much cheaper. We of the Depression generation remember the commercial jingle for Pepsi-Cola:

> Pepsi-Cola hits the spot,
> Twelve full ounces that's a lot,
> Twice as much for a nickel, too,
> Pepsi-Cola is the drink for you.

Among the latest hit tunes we were humming were "Roll Out the Barrel," "You Are My Sunshine," "Chattanooga Choo-Choo," and (yup!) "Deep in the Heart of Texas." The big new movies included *Gone with the Wind* and *The Wizard of Oz* with pigtailed little Judy Garland. Ernest Hemingway exulted that his latest bestseller, *For Whom the Bell Tolls,* about love in the soon-to-be-forgotten Spanish Civil War, was still going like "frozen daiquiris in hell." The ultimate wrinkle in cars was automatic transmission, and it made a hit although it was an $825 extra. Oldsmobile was trumpeting, "See at firsthand what it's like to drive for hours on end without ever shifting gears." (You could buy a standard-shift Oldsmobile, loaded, for about two thousand dollars.)

More arresting than what we did have were all the things we didn't. To mention a small selection: frozen foods, credit cards (and all other forms of plastic), penicillin, split atoms, panty hose, yogurt, dishwashers, pizza. And "made in Japan" was synonymous with junk.

Baby isn't the only one who's come a long way.

It's hard to believe I'm old enough for this assignment, but I was born October 31, 1931, and maybe I qualify because I don't remember a soul in those years before and after Pearl Harbor who owned a new bicycle, much less a new car. My mind does brim over with memories of rafting down Buffalo Bayou, dreaming as boys will; running everywhere barefoot for nine months a year; and being barred from the privilege of using our eight-party line, the only phone on the street.

Those weren't easy or lazy times for me and for my favorite (and least-loved) people. Some days were grim, full of pain. But you'll not hear me complain that life was dull or, on balance, unhappy. At least not once you looked beyond surface appearances.

The "Rags" nickname makes a neat little example. We Rathers were not so-called because the family had failed to rise from rags to riches like the downtown oil millionaires. Quite the contrary. The nickname got going because my grandfather Rather was something of a dandy.

Grandfather worked as a "pipeliner," a layer of pipe, for the oil fields. So, for most of his life, did my father, Daniel Irvin Rather, formally named Irvin. So, for a spell, did I, baptized Dan Irvin Rather (everybody hated "Junior"). I worked in the oil fields in my teens and early twenties, before my fantasies of adventure chased me out of the oil business.

I expect that more than a few readers may be in for some surprises here. At least I've met people in New York who go into absolute disbelief when they question me about my way-back past.

I can understand why. I've been on television for a long time and take not a little pride in having survived in my enthusiastically chosen profession. That means that people think of me as mostly sitting at the anchor desk, looking formal and maybe a bit overwhelming, unless I happen to be covering a war or some other outdoors tragedy.

Strangers are entitled to think of me as an eastern elitist, and many do. They know I've been headquartered with CBS in New York nearly forever.

"What part of New York are you from?" they'll inquire.

"I'm from and of Texas," I'll tell them. "Wharton, a bend in the river."

The usual response is: "You're kidding me!" And maybe they think my father was a businessman.

I always say Father dug ditches, which is accurate and brief. It also makes me a victim of the sound-bite communications style common to television. Actually, the pipe that he put down brought the nation's rapidly expanding industry its lifeblood, oil—the precious energizer that was also the boon of Texas. And there was a whole lot more than ditch digging to Father's work as a member of a pipeliner gang, but I don't want to get ahead of my stories.

Nor do I want to doll up the facts. Pipelining was grinding, filthy, sweaty physical labor. Much of it was indeed digging ditches to lower oil pipe into, slowly, gently, and sometimes onto a pipeliner's foot. And nobody climbed onto the crew truck at 7:00 A.M. in navy pinstripes. Khakis—wrinkled, often threadbare—were the uniform of that workplace.

Not for Grandfather, though. My grandmother Rather saw to it that her young husband left home in well-ironed, well-mended work clothes every morning. Sometimes she even put a little starch in the shirts. And Grandfather always had a fresh red or blue bandanna sticking out of his hip pocket. For the time and place he looked quaint, perhaps even ridiculous. The other pipeliners would hoot and often somebody hollered, *"Look at them rags!"* Hence the name.

It's somewhat misleading because Grandfather's co-workers really liked him and were essentially pleased that he would trouble to put on such a snappy getup to perform their rather basic tasks. He knew he wasn't being subjected to a put-down. He wore his nickname with pride—like a well-pressed, lightly starched battle dress. So did my father wear the name, and so do I. I guess all three of us family men realized early in our careers that we were accepted, accepted as good hands. We were intensely, perhaps naively, proud of that accomplishment because in our raw, fiercely indepen-dent universe there was no compliment higher than, "He's a good hand."

To me, there still isn't. I suspect that's because of the way I look back on my roots—my family, my Texas. I mean it when I make a point of saying that I'm *of* Texas, not merely *from* it. But here I go, getting ahead of my stories again.

2

Where I Come From

NOBODY KNOWS the place where I come from. This improbable claim is almost literally true and I can prove it. I'm from the Heights Annex, not from the adjoining Heights, and in my family this has always been considered a significant distinction. Both communities have been part of Houston, Texas, for decades, but the district called the Heights is alive and tolerably well, whereas the Annex is terra incognita. When I asked a friend not long ago to check with the city archivist's office for information on its origins, the folks there dug through their files and could find no trace of my home grounds. The place had been sucked up by its surroundings as if it were a puddle.

If this carries hints of Lower Ruritania, that impression is accurate. The suggestion that I'm from a Houston suburb also is fanciful, quite aside from the fact that nobody I grew up with ever heard of the word "suburb." Our Annex was so isolated from the real world that we might as well have been roosting in the most rural piney woods. Although we lived only about seven miles or so from downtown as the crow flies, I knew neighbors who'd never been there. And I didn't drink up the bright lights of Houston until I was nine years old.

My sister, Pat, possesses a document showing that the Heights Annex was a real estate promotion that the Magnolia Loan and Building Company began to flog in 1916 in what was then a downtrodden rural Dogpatch northwest of town. It extended from Thirteenth to Nineteenth Street and was four blocks deep. The map on Pat's document suggests a bustling municipal district. Actually, when I was a boy the Annex was still pretty much a real estate developer's primal vision. We were surrounded by not a few vacant lots, the streets were unpaved all the way to Shepherd Drive, and some houses on our block of Prince Street (we lived at number 1432) as yet lacked indoor plumbing. Running water was not universal.

While our house was small, I take pride in reporting that it was somewhat too big to qualify as a "shotgun house," such as the one that was home to us back in my birthplace, Wharton. Shotgun houses are a cut above shacks and have nothing to do with shotgun weddings. I'm not positive about the meaning of the term. Some think that such homes were called "shotgun" because they tended to be long and lineal, like what they call "railroad flats" in New York. My preferred theory is that they're so named because they're so small that you can hit everybody in the place with one shotgun blast.

Truth to tell, the Heights Annex as an entity was a presence mostly in my father's mind and therefore in mine. Father had grown up in the neighborhood when the Annex consisted mostly of tents and lean-tos. It was a haven for have-nots, families who couldn't afford houses in the Heights. Still, Father took great pride in the Annex, as he did in all things that he considered his own. He had a right to feel possessive about the Heights Annex; he had been present at the creation.

Our links to the world at large could hardly have been more tenuous when I was small. To get to the nearest bus connection you had to walk one and a half miles. The streetcar was three miles distant. To get to Weingarten's, the nearest market, Mother had to hike three miles round-trip. Shopping carts were unknown. She generally went with another woman or two from the neighborhood. They made frequent rest stops with their grocery bags, so such an expedition consumed about half a day.

The nearest bank, of course, was even farther distant, there being rarely enough money at hand to warrant safekeeping.

Self-sufficiency was taken for granted. We kept a cow down the street, chickens out in back, and grew most of our own vegetables on an empty lot. "Shade tree mechanics" tinkered their own jalopies into working condition on weekends.

It wasn't quite like living in Erskine Caldwell's territory, but his *Tobacco Road* wasn't all that different.

The only accessible place of business was Putney's. Mr. and Mrs. Putney ran this establishment right in back of their house. It was a grocery store of sorts and they survived in business because they sold on credit. I guess they could make their economics work because their overhead was so low and there were so many things they didn't sell. They also didn't have to worry about spoilage since they carried no fresh food of any kind.

I patronized Putney's for "sody pop," which I fished from the icy water of a big cooler. Vending machines didn't exist yet. You opened the bottle yourself and put your nickel on the counter. Most items in the store that were of interest to me cost a nickel except for those that were priced at a penny, like many of the candies. I favored "jawbreakers"—large, round pieces of gum encased in hard candy.

My father, when he wasn't working on Saturday, often would walk his little family—my mother, me, my brother,

Don, and sister, Patricia—down to Putney's late Saturday afternoon for cold pop and conversation. There would be neighbors gathered around, inside and out. Sometimes Dad would sit down for a game of dominoes while Mother talked with the other women and the children played. We whiled away many a Saturday twilight this way.

The Annex was home to one remarkably cosmopolitan link with the Great Outside. It was with us in wintertime only. Walking past a vacant lot on our way to school early in the morning we would come across the Flying Valentis practicing in their long tights and tank tops. They were a troupe of circus acrobats, a local family who were pros of national standing. They played the Shrine Circus downtown and the Houston Fat Stock Show, and most of the year they toured around the country.

Although we were used to their art, the Flying Valentis never ceased being the wonder of the neighborhood. Every morning it was like getting invited to a great show without having to buy a ticket. They did triple somersaults above their practice nets and caught each other by the forearms while swinging from the trapeze. We'd gasp when they missed connections and fell into their nets.

From this hard-working family with its specialized brand of togetherness we learned that even life in the limelight was no cakewalk. When we traipsed back from school in the afternoon the Valentis were still swinging away from their nets, and when they returned from tour looking banged up and limping and with limbs in casts we could see that a price had to be paid for fame. Their vicissitudes would have been good preparation for survival in the acrobatics of network television.

The Heights—the next-door neighborhood whose poor relations we in the Heights Annex were—had considerably more to recommend it. For one thing, it had a history.

Although it, too, began life as a real estate promotion, its very birth in 1892 was classy.

The area had ever been known as the Heights because it was seventy-five feet above sea level and twenty-three feet above downtown Houston, which made it the early-day equivalent of a resort area. During the yellow-fever epidemics that struck Houston periodically in the last century, many citizens fled to the Heights and camped in its healthful air until the siege subsided. And while the Allen brothers, the founders of our town, paid one dollar per acre for the six-hundred acre tract in 1836, the developers had to pony up forty-five dollars an acre some fifty years later.

Press-agent hoopla entered the act even then. A local composer wrote the "Houston Heights Polka" and the sheet music was published. The cover showed off a fancy drawing of a projected hotel. The developers, the Omaha and South Texas Land Company, eventually did build a hotel, but the picture on the sheet music was, well, idealized. Its many spires and towers would have done a Rhine castle proud. It just happened that they were not part of the true architectural plans.

From the start there was evidence that the grandiosity of the founders did not exist on paper alone. The pioneers planned and actually built the Heights Boulevard, and it was a main drag with a difference. When I grew up, the boulevard was still ground zero, the center of civilization, our Champs Elysées and Kurfuerstendamm. It runs twenty blocks, from what is now called Interstate 10 to Twentieth Street, straight as a ruler, its lanes separated by a grassy median sixty feet wide shaded by palm trees and huge gnarled oaks. Two bandstands gave it a small-town feeling that might have come out of Thornton Wilder's *Our Town*.

Yessir, Heights Boulevard was a spread to be proud of, and magazines raved about its beauty even in recent years. Mostly I think our prize thoroughfare stood out because its picturesque and generous style was so totally unexpectable in a place like the Heights as I first encountered it and in subsequent years.

It looked grand to me, though not to old-timers. Many of the huge, stately Victorian mansions on their generous lots along the boulevard needed paint. The hotel was gone and so was the old Opera House and the local newspaper. Less-affluent families, in search of reasonably priced housing, had moved in.

One relic of past splendor was the Heights Theater at Ashland and Nineteenth, my roistering place on Saturday afternoons. Tickets were five cents. I would be given eight cents, however, so I could splurge on a large bag of popcorn as well. And for your nickel ticket you got pummeled with so hefty an extravaganza that you could barely totter away from the theater when it finally let out after two and a half hours.

First came a "short"—a heart-in-your-throat action serial that would leave off in a cliff-hanging scene, somewhat in the manner of *Indiana Jones*. While you caught your breath, a tag line on the screen would flash: "to be continued." Then followed a cartoon; the newsreel; previews of coming attractions (which were even more shamelessly juiced-up than they are nowadays); and a shoot-'em-up main feature: Tom Mix or Hopalong Cassidy or Roy Rogers or William S. Hart, in his enormously tall cowboy hat. He was my father's favorite and his movies were later more or less remade as the TV series *Gunsmoke*.

I guess my own predilection was for Gene Autry because he proclaimed the cowboy credo that I took to my heart. He also did his own trick riding and cow roping, which were the finest and truest things a man could do. Our hoots and hollers accompanied the action and all Black Hats took an eardrum-shattering beating from our young vocal cords.

On rare occasions my parents handed out an extra nickel, in which case I'd rush after the show, with my appetite aroused beyond tolerance, to Miz Bender's across the street. There, for a nickel, yes, a nickel, they made huge, juicy hamburgers.

This was how my dream Saturday afternoon unreeled when I was small. By the time I was in junior high, the Heights Theater was already replaced for me by the ornate "Majestic," or "Loews," downtown, where my parents took me to see first-run pictures; and by then Heights Boulevard had become largely deserted and its empty expanses were used for drag races.

The Heights never deteriorated into hardscrabble poverty; it was a faded senior citizen in reduced circumstances, a premature suburb, way ahead of its time. The up-and-coming families pushed farther out, much farther, to the north and west where there was plenty of space. Even more than most American cities, Houston was, as we used to say, "on the grow." The Heights got left behind.

And it got tougher. And tougher. I was doing what came naturally when, by way of just one example, I had to fight for my corner to sell newspapers. "There wasn't all that much crime in our section," remembers one of our most famous Heights alumni, "it's just that the people were tough there. Super tough. You either learned to take care of yourself or you got the shit beat out of you."

So reported the autobiography of A. J. (Tony) Foyt, five years younger than myself, whose father, a virtuoso of a mechanic, ran the B&F garage. My father had his car repaired there, once we had one. That was no small sign of confidence. Young "A.J." began driving gas-powered miniature racing cars when he was four and rose to great fame. He became the nation's greatest big-horsepower track racer, winning the Indianapolis 500 four times. A.J. did us proud.

I knew other alumni to remember, neighbors who also dug themselves out of the big ditch that was the Heights. In my mental scrapbook are images of two boys who were about my age and whom I used to know in school. Bobby Waltrip was whispered about. He was an OK boy, but the other kids muttered, unfairly, that there had to be something a little different about Bobby.

He had a lot of dealings with corpses, his grandfather having founded the Heights Funeral Home in 1926. Bobby grew up with his parents in an apartment above the business. In the evenings and on weekends he helped out with funerals, and when he became old enough to drive he used to chauffeur the hearse.

This is an upbeat story with a very American ending. By the 1980s, Bobby was chairman, president, and CEO of Service Corporation International, the nation's largest undertaker. Everybody now called him "Bob." His company was called the McDonald's of its industry. It was a Fortune 500 company that owned 347 funeral homes, 88 cemeteries, 61 flower shops, and several funeral-supply companies. Its sales ran nearly $400 million a year.

"Racehorse" Haynes was another Heights kid who made it on the outside. His real name was Richard. Never mind. Even today everybody still calls him "Racehorse" although he is one of the country's foremost criminal defense attorneys, celebrated in movies and best-selling books. He got the nickname because his football coach at Hamilton Junior High liked his speed.

Racehorse's daddy was a plasterer and, like me, this boy had an influential grandmother. She taught him to read and write early on and she ingrained in him the habit of paying close attention to meaningful little details and casual remarks. When he was eight and, like me, an eager library patron, his idol was Sherlock Holmes because the great sleuth lived largely on his powers of observation. Racehorse promptly began to practice by memorizing the number of steps in front of his home and between each floor in school.

He gained prominence in his youth by succeeding at a specialty widely and competitively practiced in the Heights.

Racehorse was an outstanding street fighter, and he was famous for two moves that served him particularly well.

A shady character, occupying a drugstore stool next to Racehorse, would utter a negative remark. Racehorse would grasp the back of the tough guy's head and yank it full-face toward his own skull. Simultaneously, Racehorse would be lowering his head. Then he would smash the top of it into the offender's nose. His research had told him that noses could be broken by the hardness of the tops of heads, and occasionally they were.

Another Racehorse move began from a standing position, facing an opponent. Racehorse would grab his victim's shoulders quickly and firmly, spin him around, then grab the man's jacket at the top, lift it up, and pull it down over the shoulders, trapping the opponent's arms. The bad guy would then be spun around again, with his arms pinned by the pulled-down jacket, to face a now fast-punching Racehorse. Creativity such as this made Haynes a street-fighting legend.

Haynes's legal legend was built upon courtroom acquittals for defendants in dire difficulty, such as the Fort Worth multimillionaire T. Cullen Davis, charged with having murdered his wife, stepdaughter, and the wife's boyfriend; and the Houston plastic surgeon Dr. John Hill, who was alleged to have done away with his wife by feeding her poisoned French pastries (the case became the subject of Thomas Thompson's bestseller *Blood and Murder*).

To Racehorse, characteristically, even if a client was charged with murder most foul, a suspect was not a "defendant." He was "the citizen accused," a taxpayer like the rest of us, innocent unless convicted, which Racehorse's clients rarely were.

His success had a lot to do with his boyhood in the Heights, and this is not my own parochial conclusion but an observation of independent legal professionals. Watching

Haynes's courtroom work, they noticed his uncanny understanding of people.

"It tells the story of a special brand of courtroom law-
yering, one that found its genesis in Haynes' blue-collar
youth, when he learned not only how to talk to people—how
to reach out and persuade them—but also how to hear
them, and how to understand their thinking and motivation." So wrote Emily Couric in her 1988 book, *The Trial
Lawyers.*

Still more pointedly, one of Racehorse's peers figured
out why Haynes never talked down to a jury. It "comes from
growing up in a place where people talk down to you," said
this attorney.

There is a phrase that describes the way Racehorse
turned his humble origins to his advantage. It's called "making lemonade out of lemons."

Another Heights boy who milked fame and fortune
from this hat trick was Red Adair, the super-champ of oil-
fire fighters, whose troops were among the first to be called
in for help with the mother of oil conflagrations in the Gulf
War. Red is older than I am, born 1915 in a shotgun house,
too, and the landmarks of his youth resemble mine remarkably. He also swam in Buffalo Bayou, bought nickel hamburgers at Miz Bender's, loved the movies at the Heights
Theater, and graduated from John H. Reagan High School,
where the coach (then Pop Adams) was one of his revered
role models.

I have tried to develop some skill myself at the art of
converting liabilities into assets. And if my father possessed
this dexterity only to a limited degree, he made up for it in
his own ways of showing *pride*, pride in the Heights Annex,
pride in the Heights, pride in his native Houston and its
breathtaking growth. The city's population almost doubled
just between the years 1930 and 1940, from 292,000 to
386,000, and I remember when Dad exulted, "Some day it'll
be over a million!" Its current population of 1.9 million

probably wouldn't have surprised him. Nor would he have taken much time to mourn the passing of his beloved Annex. He didn't have much patience for past or present and I can hear him snap, as always, "Turn a card!" accompanied by the flip of the hand that meant, "Move along, move along! We've got a long way to go."

3

When Might Makes Right

OUR PART OF TOWN was overwhelmingly white and thought of itself as tough but peaceful. A kind of "don't tread on me" spirit was pervasive and a point of pride, yet few of the people who lived in the Heights thought of it as really violent.

Yes, there were beatings and killings and street brawls and family fights. Nevertheless, the general belief in the community was pretty much: These things happen nearly everywhere, they're just part of life.

Other people in some other parts of town had a different opinion. They thought it was a bad neighborhood. Maybe not the worst, but bad.

Not everybody realized it then, but as the urbanization of America, including even Texas, began to gather momentum and then the Depression descended, the whole country became more violent. In neighborhoods such as ours you could see it and hear it more often than in most.

*   *   *

We happened to be passing the corner of Studewood and
Eleventh one night, Homer Bredehoeft and I, when the
savagery of life in the Heights unreeled before us in a scene
that could have come out of an Edward G. Robinson mob-
ster movie.

Two cars had met in a collision. The accident had obviously occurred only moments before because the usual
crowd of kibitzers was still collecting. The drivers of the
damaged vehicles were performing in the traditional mode.
They were yelling at each other and waving their arms
around.

Abruptly, as if the intersection were being visited by a
thunderclap, the atmosphere darkened. Out of nowhere,
four wrecking trucks pulled up in quick succession and
squealed to a halt, surrounding the wreckage like vultures
diving on defenseless prey. Burly men tumbled out of the
cab of each truck, whooping.

Homer and I got out of there, running, scared as hell.
The scene was familiar. Most likely, iron pipes, chains, tire
irons, guns, and knives would be flashed within moments,
and we knew that bullets would not distinguish between
participants and bystanders. Our parents had taught us
from earliest childhood never to linger around the battleground of turf wars.

The incident is worth noting only because it was so very
commonplace. Violence was often around me even on Prince
Street while I was fighting off rheumatic fever, peaceably
studying life as a nonparticipant month after month out of
the window where my parents had moved my bed. Usually
I'd spot nothing bloodier than a hawk swooping down on a
screeching chicken, until one afternoon I heard a fierce
male voice yelling and then female screams, both from down
the block. A man was beating up his wife and doing an
extensive job of it.

The fighting started on the screened porch and moved

into the front yard when the woman ran to escape, the man pursuing in total rage and dragging her into the house by her hair.

Shocked and a little frightened, I asked Mother later why people could be so awful to each other.

"You just forget you saw that," Mother instructed. "We don't stick our noses into other people's business. And don't be asking your father about it."

That startled me further. Why this conspiracy of silence over an outrageous act that everyone could have seen in public and broad daylight? We spoke freely in my family, so at first I thought that maybe Mother only wanted to protect Father from bad news when he came home exhausted from work. That was probably part of it, but it couldn't be the entire story. It had to be that we were not supposed to encroach on other people's privacy. Furthermore, when Texans were in a bad temper you never knew when bullets, perhaps just stray bullets, might start flying as in a collision of piratical car wrecker crews.

Confirmation of my theories came sometime subsequently when shots were fired two and a half blocks away from us, near Thirteenth and Roderick, around nine o'clock one night. It developed that a husband had gotten into an argument with his wife. The lady had several brothers and they came running, all bearing handguns.

I ventured that it might be interesting to see what the fuss was about. Father set me straight firmly along the anticipated lines. We were not going to stick our noses into other folks' business or risk becoming targets of gunplay.

I'm willing to wager that nobody called the police that night. I was raised in a gun culture and guns were like pieces of furniture. I didn't know of a male adult who didn't have one or, usually, many more than one.

My father, who never fired a shot in anger, owned a single-shot break-over .410 shotgun that he inherited from his father; a 12-gauge pump duck gun that he shared with his brother, my uncle John; a Winchester 30-30 deer rifle; and an old octagon-barreled .22 rifle.

"I love the outdoors and I like to hunt, makes me feel in touch with my ancestors," was his explanation for his fire-arms.

He rarely owned handguns because he thought they were mostly useless. Once when he was traveling more than usual he traded some tools for a small .38 revolver and gave it to my mother: "For home protection, just in case." He wanted a revolver instead of an automatic because he considered revolvers more dependable: "No jams and fewer mis-fires."

Mother hated the thing. She viewed it as far too dangerous to have around a house with children. Farm girl that she was, she had grown up around long guns. Indeed, her older sister, my aunt Lolo, was a crack shot and regularly won shooting contests at the Bloomington County Fair. So Mother already knew how to load and fire rifles and shotguns. But she often said that she could not imagine shooting another human, with the possible exception of someone threatening her children. In that case, she said, she believed she could shoot with more accuracy and knock-down power by using a shotgun.

Mostly Mother just didn't want to think about all this. She wasn't about to have anything to do with the revolver. She would sooner have slept with a tarantula at her bedside than with that revolver.

The collection of rifles and shotguns was kept in Father's clothes closet, which was not locked up. However, all weaponry was administered according to certain unbreakable house rules. No gun ever was stored with ammunition in it. Shells and bullets were never kept in the same place with the guns; Father stored them in a box on a high shelf away from the closet.

"Never, ever assume a gun is unloaded," was another of his commandments. "You check it, then check it again."

The importance of never pointing a gun at anybody and never looking down the barrel of one was also emphasized. Safety rules were taught and retaught over the years. And since guns were valuable, they were subject to regular ritualistic cleaning and polishing—a procedure almost as loving as the petting of puppies.

So much for our department of hunting. What about the fellow half a block from us on Prince Street who invariably packed a revolver while he washed his car? I'm not certain that I ever gave this sight any special thought when I was young. If I had, I might have said that the man was generally feeling threatened and insecure; that maybe he liked to impress people; and that he didn't want to be defenseless if someone came at him with a firearm—which was more likely in Texas than in other places.

Rituals ruled the decision on when it was OK to shoot. The act was both deliberate and casual. When our neighbor Mr. Sikes fired at rabbits or squirrels with his .22 from his back porch, it was understood that his targets were supposed to be hit in the head. Anything less precise was considered poor form.

To explain the roots of the Texas gun worship isn't easy. In his lively history of Texas, T. R. Fehrenbach, whose ancestors helped to settle our state, points to our affinity for the past: "The great difference between Texas and every other American state in the twentieth century was that Texas had a history," he wrote in 1968. "Other American regions merely had records of development."

When I was a boy we had not yet quite freed ourselves from the struggle of surviving the time when we were still woodsmen primitives. Consider: We were the great-grandsons of shooters not long out of the wilderness, not far away from the 1830s Texas War for Independence against the Mexicans. In 1895, Indians—partly in self-defense— were still scalping our relatives in a kill-or-be-killed slaughter. That wasn't so long ago.

"The horse, the pistol, and the unwritten code of the West were not laughable in their day," Fehrenbach wrote. "They left an impress that lingers still. . . . The taking of life could not and did not develop the stigma in Texas it already had in the more sedate regions of America, because the Texans were at war. . . . Like the gentleman's sword in Europe and Ireland, the pistol lingered very long after it had ceased to be a necessary tool."

On my own mini-frontier during World War II, fighting began early. I not only had to scrap for my corner to sell Sunday papers. When I was in grade school, we punched each other for the best seats down in front in the Heights Theater. After class in junior high school, I watched epic combat almost every afternoon in the alley behind Weingarten's supermarket. Some bouts lasted for hours. We witnessed the Heights version of the European duel ("If you do that again . . ."). We saw manhoods made and broken. Occasionally, girls fought each other, too, and they tended to be even more vicious than the boys.

Here was the precursor of *West Side Story* and today's more intensely troubled youth. We had no drugs. We did have boys about to become predator dropouts, extorting money from younger kids, hustling girls, graduating not with high school diplomas but with the skills to survive the streets.

I don't want to suggest that we were a latter-day Dodge City. In our neighborhood, nobody locked house or car doors. I don't remember a single burglary, and no woman needed to be in fear when she got off the shuttle bus late at night. And yet, undeniably, there was a special Texas brand of affinity for murder. Something deeply embedded could quickly wipe away neighborliness when a Texan felt angered or threatened, and—pop!—he would be "going to the iron."

The proof is in the corpses. In 1938, we had 757 murders in Texas. In New York there were 427, in California there were 355. The trend held steady, with Houston doing more than its share of killing. The city's Junior Chamber of Commerce actually appointed a "Murdertown Committee" in the 1950s and sent observers to Chicago to study crime prevention.

Local students of violence blamed the trend on our Texas past and, in consequence, the cavalier attitude of grand juries in handing up indictments and the custom of judges to go easy on killers.

"I don't understand Texas justice," an eastern lawyer allegedly told an old Texas judge. "You'll suspend sentence of a convicted murderer, but you'll hang a horse thief."

"Sonny," the old judge is supposed to have replied, "I reckon that's 'cause we got men that need killin' but we ain't got no hosses that need stealin'."

Funny? I never thought so.

Close to my immediate neighborhood, around Nicholson Street near the railroad tracks, roamed a gang of future murderers, young marauders who liked to beat up kids, preferably younger ones, including me and Homer Bredehoeft, my frequent partner on adventures in Buffalo Bayou and other hangouts. Homer complained to his mother, who complained to his father, who decided that we should defend ourselves by learning how to box. My mother wasn't crazy about the idea but went along with it. She knew about the menace of Nicholson Street.

Mr. Bredehoeft was an intriguing character who worked more regularly than most of the fathers I knew. He rotated a bewildering number of jobs, usually at night. Mostly, I think, he loaded cans at the dairy. With a bulldog tenacity that I admired, he scrambled for enough money to take flying lessons, a breathtaking leap out of the pedestrian ways of the Heights Annex. Some Sundays he buzzed the neighborhood from an altitude of maybe three hundred feet. And he knew a lot about boxing.

I watched with trepidation as he paced off the dimensions of a boxing ring under a live oak tree in his backyard, hung some tired rope, and produced two sets of severely wrinkled and ripped boxing gloves that were many sizes too big for boys. First Mr. Bredehoeft taught his older son, Bobby. Bobby was a miniature Marciano, an innate scrapper who would become a honky-tonk bouncer at age sixteen. Homer later boxed extensively as an amateur and still later as a professional. I was his partner and more of a problem student.

Never a natural combatant, I was interested all right but also impressed by the downside of the proceedings. One could get hurt, and I sometimes got banged around quite a bit. But I learned. I picked up how to put one's front foot sideways for better anchorage, and my confidence grew as it became apparent that one didn't have to be the most powerful puncher to survive. All three Bredehoefts were good at teaching the "stick and run" method of keeping attackers away. I learned how to keep jabbing, the left flicking out all the time, and then to dance away fast.

It was Mr. Bredehoeft who first taught me the necessity of getting up after you get knocked down to the ground or canvas, and how to do it: "In a boxing match, roll to your knees, watch the count, stay down until your head clears or for as long as you can trying to clear it. But in a street fight, Danny, get up quickly, never stay down."

After completing my education in the makeshift ring behind the Bredehoeft's house, I fared somewhat better with the tough guys from Nicholson Street. Since then I haven't always done what Mr. Bredehoeft taught, but I've never forgotten his patience or his lessons.

Once, years later, in my brief and undistinguished time as a private in the marines, I found myself boxing in a Saturday-night unofficial "Non-Commissioned Officer's Club Smoker." Bouts were supposed to have been arranged to pit boxers of roughly the same weight and experience against one another. Instead, I found myself in the ring with a bruiser who outweighed me by forty pounds and had all the moves of an experienced club fighter. He knocked me down twice in the first round.

On the stool between rounds my ears were ringing, but I could hear the small crowd shouting. I could also hear Mr. Bredehoeft. I was saying to myself, "I'll try to stick and run, but if this guy decks me again I have to consider staying down."

In the second round he quickly floored me with a thunderous right. My head luckily cleared enough to decide that valor and pride were not the issue, common sense was. I could have gotten up. I didn't. Mr. Bredehoeft would have understood. I still try to subscribe to the creed, "In your heart you should be a get-up fighter." But that night helped to teach me that sometimes what your head tells you should balance what your heart says.

In subsequent years my attitude about guns and hunting also changed. Persuaded more by the beauty of animals than by anything else, I gave up hunting. (I still love to fish but release what I catch.) About others who still like to hunt I do not sit in judgment. I understand. But for me the killing of anything ceased to have appeal. I wanted to move myself away from it as far as the nastiness of the world would permit.

If I'm not ideally constructed to be an aggressive questioner or scrapper, this begs a question: How did I, of all reporters, become the object of occasional personal attack by high priests of the political Establishment, or at least a segment thereof? Sometimes it seems as if I've turned into a symbol of what's been called the effete eastern media, the honor coming mostly by appointment of Senator Jesse Helms of North Carolina.

On first thought this is puzzling. I can't recall ever having aired a nasty word about the Senator. He, on the other hand, seems to have Dan Rather near the top of his mind. In the flush of his election victory last November he stepped to the microphone and congratulated himself on having defeated a noncandidate, me. On other occasions the Senator participated in hostile moves to take over CBS so, he said, he could become "Dan Rather's boss."

On second thought, this oratory isn't mysterious. My job is to be accurate and fair, an honest broker of information. Period. It is a job that automatically puts me down in places Senator Helms dislikes. In the early 1960s I was the point man of CBS News on many of the most controversial civil rights stories. During the Watergate scandals, it was my job as White House correspondent to ask President Nixon questions that he didn't want to be asked. These are "crimes" that many big-money political contributors don't forgive or forget, and Senator Helms likes to remind them of me because he gets money from them.

So be it. It isn't my role to fight back and I've tried not to do so. No constituency elected me to any office. I do think it's hilarious that in my later years I've become a red herring, or better, a red blanket, to be waved in front of fat cats. Still, if Senator Helms or anybody else can use me to legally sucker people into sending them money, they're entitled.

What have I learned from my encounters with violence and controversy? A lot. For one thing, there's invariably somebody tougher than you are. How many of them are lined up against you? Well, if you step outside and start a fight you'll find out and next thing you're hospitalized. For another thing, I try to keep in mind that trouble is the easiest thing in the world to find. And for still another, when you practice daily journalism you are constantly humbled by how often you can be wrong.

4

Life with Father

FATHER RULED the family and work ruled Father, as it would come to rule me. That's no casual commonplace. There was nothing common about work—a job—when I was growing up. At home along Prince Street, Father was considered something of an aristocrat because all through the Great Depression he always had a job. A job was a treasure.

His work as a pipeliner stamped Father inside and out. He was no giant—five feet eleven—but he was tough as iron. His shoulders were broad; his chest was thick; his forearms bulged. The grip of his large, callused hands was a vise. The deeply tanned, leathery face, with its dark eyes and dark, wavy hair, rarely broke into a smile. Not that Father was dour; far from it. He was simply a bit embarrassed about the two gold teeth in the upper center of his mouth. One of his real teeth had been knocked out by a horse, the other when he and his gang momentarily lost control of a length of oil pipe.

Father did not limp, however, as did many of his colleagues. Toes were often mangled under the men's safety-toed boots when pipe slipped to the ground. Father was nimble and always stepped aside in time.

He was my hero and I knew exactly why. I got the message through personal experience.

He worked stripped to the waist almost the year around, and my most enduring childhood memory of him is seeing him in the ditch, digging, drenched in sweat—sweating as if water were pouring off him—when he first took me along to his job, riding in the "bear trap." I was five or six and he wanted to bond with his firstborn son. This was his no-nonsense way.

Pipeliners were proud professionals with work habits codified into rituals, much as in a church service. Father was never late. Indeed, punctuality was his eleventh commandment. He saw lateness as a signal to the boss that you didn't care about your job, a potentially suicidal misstep. "If you're to be there at seven," he lectured me, "you be there at six forty-five. And you don't go to the water bucket more than once an hour." You also don't fuss with your clothes on company time.

I considered it anything but a disgrace that Father was hauled around to various work sites by way of a "bear trap," a contraption also known in the oil industry as a "doghouse." Dad's company would winch this little wooden shed, seven or eight feet tall, with windows and a slightly gabled roof, onto a flatbed truck for mobility. Inside was room for maybe ten men, their tools, and some pretty good poker games. Elsewhere, folks might have recoiled from going to work in a bear trap or a doghouse. Not in Texas in the Great Depression. If you were traveling by bear trap that meant you had work, and work was king.

Actually, nobody considered any aspect of pipelining to be anything other than inviting. Father often came home and said that he'd seen a hundred hands at the gate that morning to apply for twenty-five jobs that had opened up at under a dollar an hour.

By 9:00 A.M. it was time for a "chaw." Everybody chewed tobacco: Beech-Nut, Day's Work, or Red Man. It was the custom. It was also because you weren't allowed to smoke, as nearly every man (and more and more women) used to do constantly in those days before we knew that tars could cause cancer.

Which reminds me to explain why the raw limbs of men like Father—usually his hands were covered to the forearm by White Mule work gloves—were vital to industry. Technology was not yet much with us. Horses were just going out; cars were barely beginning to come in as mass transportation. Most major machinery was also novel. Much less of it existed than we see nowadays and it wasn't nearly so sophisticated. The human back and hands were pivotal tools.

Management was an elementary function then. Father's foreman, I remember, had an enormous beer belly. He spit hard from a huge chaw lumped in one cheek, and he was the only hand not stripped to the waist.

"OK, boys," he'd shout when the gang needed to locate a leak in the pipeline, "gimme a big bell hole."

He was calling for a bell-shaped excavation, and this required the hands to use their "sharpshooters." I had heard Father put down another man privately at our house by saying, "He wouldn't know a shovel from a sharpshooter." I couldn't understand that. Why would pipeliners use guns? The answer was that they of course didn't. At the ditch I could see for myself that a sharpshooter was a short-handled narrow shovel for breaking ground during the first stage of the job. Longer-handled regular shovels were used later to scoop dirt out.

The banter and camaraderie that passed between the hands, who worked in crews of seven to ten, was reassuring to me when I was little. It softened some of the day's hard edges. Sometimes the men hummed or sang, and Father knew how to rope me into the adult circle.

"Bring me a medium crescent wrench," he'd command and I was eager to hop to it.

The removal of a defective length of pipe was delicate surgery and the foreman called upon the female anatomy to get the operation moving.

"Heist 'er leg, boys," he'd yell, and the sick pipe would come swinging out of the ground.

"That was a good day's work," said Father, looking pleased, when we climbed back in the bear trap.

It had also been a fairly light day. Sometimes he worked so hard and his muscles ached so severely that mother had to help him out of bed in the morning as if he were crippled.

So it's understandable that Father was our center and our unquestioned leader. You would have known this from watching the family at supper time ("dinner" was what we nowadays call lunch). The meal always awaited Father's arrival. Nobody would dream of being late or inattentive. If Father's face told me he had had a bad day, I tended to speak little, even though I was a natural-born chatterbox. Anyway, Father had the first and last word at the table. One interrupted him only at one's peril.

Grace was always said, at breakfast, too: "Come, Lord Jesus, be our guest. . . ." It's a practice that I continued with my kids and still follow at our table today.

After Father said grace he'd turn first to Mother and ask about her day, and she'd report the doings of the neighborhood: "The lower part of the field caught on fire, but it burned itself out" . . . "Mrs. Sikes says she heard the preacher is looking for another church" . . . "Mr. _____ left home. . . ."

"He'll be back," Father said, and the AWOL husband was—within three days.

After Mother's report, I got my turn, then my younger brother and sister. Supper was our big family occasion, not a time for kids to lobby for special privileges. "I'm really working on my handwriting," I would report. Or, "We started softball." Sightings of fresh phenomena, such as a brand-new truck, were headline items. Our rituals taught me that the Rathers were a family unit, that we belonged together, did things together, that we were close. No closer than most other families we knew, but close.

It was at supper that I also learned—by family practice, not from lecturing—that we were not poor. Not the Rathers, no sir, definitely not. I knew any number of fathers along Prince Street who hunted vainly for work, year after year, perhaps getting a job here and there, briefly, followed by long layoffs. Layoffs seemed as unavoidable as colds.

Not for my father, though. His work was steady and we never once experienced going hungry. We even had meat on the table a couple of times a week, most weeks, and meat was a measure of well-being then, not a source of risky animal fats.

Sometimes we even had a little food to spare, which is how I met up with people who were truly poor, of whom there seemed to be an awful lot. Looking like the homeless of today, they shyly approached our screened back porch around supper time. I guess I soaked up events graphically even then, because I remember these fairly regular scenes precisely.

They always came in families. The wife and children would linger in the background. The husband would take off his hat—men used to wear hats when embarked on a serious mission—and knock. Mother went out. The ensuing dialogue was always much the same.

"Excuse me, ma'am. Is the man of the house in?"

This was man-to-man business. The supplicant would be too embarrassed to bare his need to a woman. Besides, the wife would not have parted with food without authority from her husband. It was too important a family decision.

Father would go out and look the people over. He was

shrewd at sizing up strangers and wanted to form an impression of the callers. He knew in advance what they would want. Were they legitimate and really in need? He seemed to sense these things.

The stranger at the door would never admit explicitly that he was hungry. He had his pride and tried to save face.

"I wonder," he'd ask, "if you have enough extra after supper? Can we stick around or can we come back?"

When we had leftovers, my father would usually say OK and my mother would wrap up a little food. Some weeks, too many families came calling at our back door and we quickly ran out. Quite often, we had nothing extra to give to begin with.

"Tonight's not a good night," Father would say regretfully. "Let me call my brother up the street." And he would phone my uncle John. If Uncle John had nothing, Father might try the Snyder house and then perhaps still another neighbor.

This was how people got along. Relatively few "went on the dole," which meant going on public welfare. Instead, they bartered, they borrowed, they made do, they postponed. If they had to beg, they begged.

Finding work was the goal always. I don't remember anybody ever losing sight and giving up on that target: work, any kind of labor. When my uncle John wasn't working, which was much of the time, he went out to look for a job each and every day, maybe driving a hundred miles to follow up an erroneous rumor ("They're hiring in Beaumont").

I don't recall that the hungry families at our doorstep made me feel embarrassed or smug or guilty. I really don't think they did. I realized that a lot of good people were simply down on their luck through no fault of their own. This is the way it went for ordinary folks before the country headed into World War II and better economic weather.

As far as the Rathers were concerned, the relevant

point was hammered home to me by Father with some frequency. We *gave* charity. We didn't *take* it. And we shared whatever we had, especially time and muscle.

I remember the time when my special friend Georgie Hoyt's mother, across the street, was pregnant with his sister, Ellen. Mr. Hoyt didn't find work too often and the family had no running water. Father decided that this wasn't right, what with the baby coming on. So one Sunday he and another neighbor laid a water pipeline from our house over to the Hoyts, and Father paid their water bill.

That's how things got done in the spirit of the old motto: God helps those who help themselves.

Father fortunately possessed the skills to help quite a bit. When my sister followed my brother and our family burst the seams of our house, he and Uncle John took five Sundays to put up the frame of an additional room—and forever to finish it.

Oil, the stuff in Father's pipelines, was our greatest good fortune. It kept us afloat, along with much of our area, and we were grateful for it.

Paradoxically—and every Texas schoolboy knows this story—oil started out as a nuisance in our state. In the last century, people who were digging for desperately needed water would find their wells invaded and spoiled when oil seeped into them. And there still weren't enough oil-hungry machines in use to make for much of a market.

Oil became "black gold" on January 10, 1901, when "Spindletop" blew in a bit east of us near the Gulf around Beaumont. It was one of the great gushers of all time. Its advent was also a remarkably fortuitous coincidence of nature: It created supply just as demand began to skyrocket.

The boom-and-bust cycles of Texas oil were born. A wild speculator, "Bet a Million" Gates, who made his first millions with the production of barbed wire, founded the Texas Company, later known as Texaco. The Gulf and Humble companies also got their starts on Spindletop leases. This was the yeasty and romantic stuff that made *Giant*, Edna Ferber's novel and the movie that followed.

I still watch that film on late-night TV. It's something of a caricature, but pretty much on the money. Those forests of oil derricks were considered humongous even in Texas.

Just sixty-five years after the Allen brothers, Augustus and John, New York real estate promoters who were spiritual forefathers of "Bet a Million" Gates, paddled up Buffalo Bayou and proclaimed the founding of a swampy spot called Houston, their megalomania was vindicated. Houston had it all—everything to become the godfather of an oil (and later petrochemical) empire: the flatlands for laying pipelines to get the oil to the ports; the ship channel for locating refineries and getting their product shipped; a climate away from hard winters; and the people, above all, the people—the bankers willing to make high-risk loans, the promoters, the wildcatters, the crazies, and steady hands like my grandfather and my father to put down some down-to-earth foundations to make the dreams work.

The Rathers were very lucky to be in on this new frontier, especially because the oil boom expanded even during the Great Depression and was in place to feed the war economy with its appetite for fuel, the ships Texas was building by then, and the muscle of willing workers.

Oil determined where we lived and dictated where I was born: Wharton, Texas, a town of around twenty-six hundred people some fifty-five miles southwest of Houston. Wharton had good people and a good location on the river but not a lot else in those days. I lived there less than six months, my parents about a year. Wharton was a base camp for the Houston Pipeline Company and Father's work. Until my arrival on the scene, he migrated periodically with the growth of the pipeline network. Not long before I was born, my parents had also resided briefly in El Campo and Refugio. These were hot oil areas at the time. That's where the work was. And as I've mentioned, work was what life was mostly about.

5

"If They're Gonna Chunk, I Ain't Goin'!"

"**F**EEL IT," said Grandma Page. "Feel how rich it is."

She picked up a handful of soil from her loamy blacklands and I took it with both hands because I was very little, maybe five or six years old; I can't remember exactly.

I felt the soil in my fingers and it was a fact: I could feel how rich it was.

And so were all the Rathers. We were on one of our visits to my mother's mother on the farm my grandparents rented at Bloomington, Texas, about 160 miles southwest of Houston, and these were invariably gloriously satisfying days, among the best in all my life, surely among the most fondly remembered.

Of course my grandparents weren't really rich. They lived in a two-and-a-half-room shotgun house with a water pump on the back porch and, out back, an "outhouse" (toilet), dozens of chickens, several horses, a few scraggly cows, and a goat. On one side was a large fig tree under which a variety of snakes nested. On the other was a small vegetable garden.

My grandparents chopped and picked cotton, and since they got paid by the pound they often started working before dawn and toiled into the first burst of cool air after sunset. In later years, I'd help on the fields at harvest time, stuffing cotton into long white sacks. On that remembered afternoon, after Grandma Page had suspended work for a few minutes so we could take our midday meal right there, and she then got me to appreciate my native soil, I whiled away the time simply luxuriating, relaxing.

Bloomington, Texas, would seem to be too basic a place to allow time for loafing. It had maybe fifteen people, mostly relatives of ours. It had a feed store, a post office, a road in and out, and not much else, not even a church. It did have Grandma's thick black soil and the limitless Texas sky. Both are among the strongest of my earliest memories. I marvel today that I was conscious of these verities of my environment. I do recall that I was powerfully aware of them.

Not only did we feel and smell the land with pleasure. Since kids wore shoes only between December and February we were quite literally connected to the soil, and the palpable feel of this link made me feel good. My memory of the Texas sky seems to reach back even a little further and touches the primordial. In Bloomington the blueness loomed especially enormous and benign and inviting. I lay on my back in the fields often and long, taking in the expanse from horizon to horizon and thinking vague thoughts of my freedom: no restraint, unrestricted permission to run and explore any-where throughout the uncurbed place where my mother grew up and to which she still felt much attached.

A family trek to Bloomington was pure adventure. We usually went by train or bus because Father's Oldsmobile, which he purchased in its senior years, was too feeble for such a major outing. And major it certainly was on my pleasure scale. I remember the square dancing, the corn on the cob fresh from the field, and, most particularly, Grandma Page's tapioca pudding.

These, however, were not the main attractions that were so special about our trips to her house. I'm not sure what made these holidays so magical to me. It could have been no more than the excitement from a change of scene and routine, the sheer exuberance set off by a trip, any trip, in that undemanding age. Today we have the all-inclusive but blasé saying, "What a trip!" When I was small, all expeditions away from home required so much time and preparation that I felt a little like Robinson Crusoe. We weren't as itinerant and as impatient as we've since become.

Living in relative isolation and with few distractions could thus be an advantage. The seemingly unlimited availability of time was another wonder. Security of any kind was lacking, yet unlike today, there was always time for everything. Grandmother Page chopped cotton, raised a family, kept the house spotless, did a lot of reading, made tapioca pudding—yet she was never hurried and ever accessible. She was short, broad, big-bosomed, with a leathery wagontrain face—the quintessential babushka.

If her life was one of drudgery, which it was, I didn't experience it as such. Did folks then know secrets of life that we've forgotten? I remember Grandma Page showing me how to seize and wring the neck of a screeching chicken in time for supper. She showed me how to grab the chicken's neck firmly with one hand, knuckles on top, hold on to the back with the other hand, and give a very quick combination twist and jerk—all in one motion.

That lesson, too, was imparted to me with good humor and as a natural circumstance of farm life. If you wanted chicken on the table, how else would it get there?

I am told that I was the first of the Pages or Rathers to make it through college, and I've given some thought to how I got *there*.

There was no worship of learning in our tribe, as existed in Jewish families, for example. There was worship of work. Work and land. We came through the Cumberland Gap after Daniel Boone's time as homesteaders, driven by the promise of acres. We settled in Indiana and Ohio. Sometime in the nineteenth century rumors were heard there of better land and a more temperate climate in Texas. It was supposed to be a marvelously inviting place.

My people dispatched a scouting party and word headed back that the reports were true. The richest black land stretched out and on down in Texas, lots of it, and ordinary people could own some of it, although our wagons would get there too late for us to be given a section by the government at no cost, as had the earlier arrivals. That's why we were renters.

Our matriarch, Grandmother Page, was of that wagon breed, a big woman of unsurpassed energy. She was up at three-thirty or four o'clock in the morning to bake and churn and get ready for the fields. At night, along with the cooking and sewing, there was energy left for her reading.

I doubt that Grandma Page went beyond the sixth grade in school, and hers was not a home filled with books. Sitting by her coal lamp, she read aloud to Mother from her precious copy of the Sears Roebuck catalog about garden seed and other items of home interest. Mother was the youngest of her children and considered the brightest. Eventually she would finish high school, the only one in the family to have done so up to that point.

By the time I came along, not much had changed except the edition of the catalog. Grandmother Page read me page after page from it. I don't remember that she ever ordered anything. The Sears catalog was her dream book. Its content wasn't about garden seed. It was about her dreams.

I also believe she thought that the act of reading was important for deepening a child's interests. Grandma all but revered reading.

"Come, Danny, I'll read to you," she would say. That was enough to make me come running. It meant story time and story time most often was Bible time. The Bible was quite literally an open book for all the Rathers. You would rarely see a closed Bible in any of our homes. An open Bible meant that the good book was alive and well and had been lately in use. This was no pretense.

Grandma Page was well aware of my favorite Bible stories and catered to my taste for the great deeds it recorded, especially those of Joshua at the Battle of Jericho. Meaning no disrespect for Grandma's religious beliefs, I should clarify that her Bible offerings were meant less to serve the cause of piety than our need for entertainment. Joshua was my Sylvester Stallone, I guess. Grandma's house lacked electricity, so it had no radio (the very word "television" was of course not heard for more than another decade). And since radio was the standard source of diversion, we had to reach out for pretty simple forms of fun in Bloomington, Texas.

We all had a feel for music, fortunately. My grandparents were the owners of a hand-cranked Victrola and even now I can hear Grandma play and replay her favorite record. I think it was also her only one, and it was called "Strawberry Roan." It celebrated a little horse with pink ears, and its impecunious bronco rider creaked out a story with which we could all empathize:

> I wuz just layin' around town,
> Just wastin' my time,
> Out of a job
> And not makin' a dime . . .

Grandfather Mark, a lanky, Lincolnesque figure with sunken cheeks, spoke so little that people thought he must know a lot more than he did. He actually was knowledgeable in quite a few matters. In addition to planting, raising, chopping, and picking cotton, he was a blacksmith and shoed a lot of horses. He also was an amateur veterinarian of repute. I recall us all getting rousted out one 3:00 A.M. by a farmer who needed help with what I suppose was the calf equivalent of a breech birth.

In spring and summer, Bloomington became the occasional stop for a spectacular extravaganza, the traveling revival tent. Although this was the showcase for a circuit-riding fundamentalist preacher to emit hellfire and brimstone, we considered the experience less religious than entertaining. Up to a point, that is.

The tent was open, the floor was sawdust. Typically, fewer than a hundred people were gathered. The preacher was usually from Tennessee and the buildup of his message came at a slow pace. His point was unmistakable and highly personal. He wanted me to worry about my status in my next life. He questioned the strength of my faith, no small accusation.

I remember an occasion when I sat on the wooden bench in the revival tent next to my grandparents and the preacher had worked himself up to a furious pitch about our shaky loyalty to the Lord. At the height of his emotion he reached into a trunk behind him, produced two snakes, and threw them into the crowd.

This was an unprecedented feature of the revival service, at least for us. The snakes didn't land too close to our row, but nobody could figure out whether they were poisonous, and so the shrieking and the general rush out of the tent were a sight to behold.

"You see," thundered the preacher triumphantly, "your faith is fragile!"

I couldn't figure out what the snakes were supposed to have to do with my religious faith, which was and is in fine shape, I think. I received the stunt with a mixture of fear and amusement and a touch of admiration for such unrestrained showmanship.

Grandma Page reacted negatively to the snake tossing. When we used to talk about throwing, as in baseball, we'd call it "chunking." After the snake incident, whenever Grandma was told that a revival tent was coming to town, she'd frown and demand, "Is they gonna chunk?" Then she'd say with finality, "If they're gonna chunk, I ain't goin'."

She never did, and this struck me as reasonable. Showmanship should have its limits in exploiting shock for the sake of shocking, at least by a man of the cloth.

This was the world of my mother until she left home at seventeen to look for a job.

Mother had been saving a little money because she wanted to go to college. Her yearning for self-improvement was every bit as developed as my father's, and her esteem of a college education was stronger. One time when I was small we had a visitor, and when he left, my mother said to me with admiration, "He's a college man, you know." I've long forgotten who the caller was; I never forgot Mother's words or her reverent tone of voice. Would I ever get to be a college man?

6

Family: "Call, Raise, or Get the Sandwiches!"

DIVORCE. It was a nonsubject when and where I was growing up. It wasn't done. Not in our neighborhood, not among folks we knew. That isn't to say there weren't plenty of marriage problems and problem marriages. There were.

In Texas and many other places if a man and a woman lived together "as man and wife"—that is, together, for six months or more—they were deemed, by law, to be legally married. And the law was enforced. We had more than a few "common-law marriages" in our all-white part of town. So did people in other parts, white, black, Mexican, and mixed.

Yet: Whether they were married in a church or synagogue, in a civil service, or by "common law," couples mostly stayed together and had children if they could. That was the norm. In the 1990s, only one American family out of four lives in the "traditional" family configuration: two parents with two children. In the 1930s and early forties, divorce was not only seldom talked about, it was hell to get, nearly impossible if there were children.

In Texas and in the nation as a whole we simply had not
yet felt the sledgehammer impact of family breakups encouraged by a single event: World War II with its long sep-
aration between marriage partners, women moving into the
work force, and other trends of liberation, good and ill.

Talk about the increase in the divorce rate! In 1945 it
stood at 1.7 per one thousand population. In 1945 it had
doubled to 3.5. By 1985 it had about tripled to 5.0.

On reflection, divorce also wasn't practical when I was
young. Where in the world would you go as a divorced
person? You'd have to have a second home, and most folks
found it barely feasible to maintain one.

Mother was a working woman. It would be erroneous, however, to think that we were a two-career family in the way
this term is commonly understood these days. If you had
asked Veda Byrl Rather (called Byrl) straight out whether
she considered herself a career woman, my bet is that she
would have chuckled and said, "Oh no, I'm just helping
out."

And that she did. Did she ever! I know I cannot give a
full list of all the jobs she held when I was small. I remember
that she sold hardware for a while. Another time she ped-
dled encyclopedias door-to-door. She did sewing in a small
factory. She waited on tables in restaurants. She answered the
phone in a construction office. Mostly, though, she worked at
home sewing.

Mother was a happy, open person and blessed with
inexhaustible energy. Sewing cheered her particularly and
that was obvious. It set her to humming and she'd show a
little smile around the eyes. It was the best of all her worlds:
being home and bringing in extra money at the same time.
She sewed upholstery and slipcovers. She turned out work
shirts and sport shirts and cut her own patterns for them.
Other women would come to her with pictures from the
Sears catalog and ask, "Can you do this?" Mother always said

she could. Not all of her creations came out to perfection, but she succeeded often enough.

Sometimes she sewed things by hand, using only needle and thread. Mostly she sewed them on a contraption known as a "treadle machine." This was a sewing machine powered by feet; you pumped your foot forward and backward on a pedal at the bottom of the machine. The pedal was connected to a set of wheels and belts that transferred the foot power into power to make the sewing machine needle go up and down fast. Mother could make it sing.

Why did Mother work, often outside the home, when my father brought home a regular paycheck? Well, the paycheck wasn't that much. Mother worked to make ends meet, also so we could have things we couldn't otherwise get. She, as many other mothers in that time and place, burned with a hot, hard flame to make things better, to "have better things," "have a better life," and—most of all—to make sure her children had a better life. She had grown up on the farm with a deep hard-work ethic. And there was her remarkable energy.

What kind of job she had was no big deal for Mother. She didn't need any ego building, and since times were as they were, she lost so many jobs all the time that no stigma was attached to the innumerable occasions when she did lose one.

What interested her passionately was her family; being a full and equal partner to Father; being a steady presence for her children; and striving, striving, striving to improve our lot through countless schemes of self-improvement.

She waited on tables so much of the time because this didn't require too many hours away from home. Usually she worked from eleven to two and again from five-thirty to seven-thirty. I can't remember a time when she wasn't home for supper. I do recall going along to work with her on Saturday nights in a restaurant where the customers' finances didn't allow tipping. Everybody seemed to like her a lot in the place, however, and she returned the favor.

*   *   *

I guess it's fitting that Mother met Father while she was doing similar work in the busy Travelers Hotel at the railroad tracks in Victoria, Texas, when both were nineteen (they were also born in the same month, October, as was I). She had come in search of work a year or so before, all by herself, from her parents' tenant farm. That was in Bloomington, down the road, where there was nothing for Mother to do but continue to pick cotton, as she had done since she was eleven or twelve. In Victoria she rented a room in a family's home near the hotel; she could eat at the restaurant and earn enough to send money regularly to her folks, who needed it badly.

Father's work as an oil pipeliner happened to bring him into the neighborhood for a time, and so he appeared in the hotel dining room with a gang of his co-workers. Mother brought him his supper—and they were married the following year. Father displayed an excellent sense of humor, an adroit way with words, and he knew how to spin a yarn that measured a yard wide and miles long.

Mother saw him as a hero figure, as I did. He was her Humphrey Bogart, as she put it. Certainly Father was as intense, as taciturn, and as darkly handsome as Bogie. Like Bogie, he smoked incessantly, a pack and a half or sometimes two packs of cigarettes a day, which wasn't at all unusual in those times, and Father held a cigarette precisely as Bogart did.

In turn, Dad always said that Mother reminded him of the beautiful actress Carole Lombard, who died in a 1942 plane crash. Ms. Lombard had smooth golden hair while Mother's hair was dark; nevertheless, I can see the resemblance: the delicate features, the flawless skin, the graceful manner of moving. Like Ms. Lombard, Mother reflected an appealing combination of strength and vulnerability. These women were gentle but not weak. They had backbone.

To me, Father was a hero because he was strong, respected by all, never boring, never bored, almost never at a loss, a man of dignity and style, with one enthusiastic eye ever on the lookout for a future so brimming with exciting novelty that he could hardly wait for it. His ditch-digging was dangerous—cave-ins and other accidents were not uncommon. The work required prodigious stamina, and he was good at it.

All my life I've admired true professionals, all professionals, and Father was a pro. You'd never find my dad downgraded to doing "doping," which was the lowest, dirtiest job of pipelining. It consisted of smearing filthy creosote on pipe leaks and was reserved for dunces and pipeliners who showed up late for work.

Furthermore, his obsession with advancement and anything technological placed him at any number of cutting edges. He was first to learn about rods that were dropped into oil tanks to gauge the contents, and he knew how to repair these instruments. Holding forth on his vision of future tank farms that would require no human hands at all, he sounded like a computer engineer long before computers existed. When he could no longer delay acquiring a slide rule, knowing that it would cause him endless trouble, he gave one of his beloved hunting guns for it in trade.

Dad let me know that he was aware of being too often an absentee father, and he looked for every chance to take me hunting or fishing on Saturdays. These were cherished times for privacy, exchanges of confidences, and learning outdoor skills from my father, the teacher. He could read sky and wind, and he was good at anticipating weather changes. He knew the significance of cloudy water, sensing where fish would hide. He lectured on their movements and habitats and on the differences between redfish, catfish, sunfish, and speckled trout. He walked with his head up to gauge wind and perhaps to stop cold for a deer or a covey of quail.

Father had what I later, in Vietnam, came to know as "jungle eye"—the ability to see tiny movements, frame by frame, even to follow insects.

The quiet hours of such a day, a world away from people and pressures, produced indescribable euphoria in us both. I had this liberating sense of running free. I was conscious of Father's chest expanding, the triangle around his eyes opening up to relax, the sense of camaraderie between us. Spotting a run of speckled trout, he'd light up and display a look of sheer joy.

He truly had the makings of a fine teacher on an astonishing number of subjects more advanced than duck hunting. He instructed me on how to look for work. When I was old enough to make the rounds of the department stores at Christmas, he lectured on the importance of shined shoes, a fresh shirt, and a bushy-tailed attitude.

"Everybody is looking for someone who can do," he said, so I tended to nod with enthusiasm pretty much whenever a potential boss asked me whether I had mastered this skill or that.

I like to believe I've inherited some of Father's talent at teaching. It's crucial for me in my television role not to come across as preaching, much less hectoring. I do think of myself not only as a deliverer of news but as an explainer, which I suppose is pretty close to being a teacher.

I'm in good company. My hero Ed Murrow called television "The biggest classroom in the world." And my mentor Eric Sevareid of CBS called himself a champion of "elucidation, not advocacy." Well and elegantly stated.

True, I've had complaints that I sometimes overexplain, and there may be merit in this criticism. Still, I suspect Dad would rather have me explain too much than too little.

Horton Foote captured this and more in his movie *On Valentine's Day*. Foote's is not a glitzy name, although two of his screenplays have won him Academy Awards. Famous or not, I admire him inordinately. Not the least reason is that he hails from the flyspeck where I was born, Wharton, Texas, and in more than half a century of producing play after play and film after film, Foote has rarely written about anything other than our birthplace and the people in it.

This time I was in for a stunning and very intimate surprise. *On Valentine's Day* is set in 1917 and unreels the first year in the marriage of Horace and Elizabeth Robedaux, whom Foote had fashioned from the memories of his own parents.

Within minutes, I rose off my seat. Horace Robedaux of Wharton, Texas, was a handsome, most earnest, proud, and dignified young man with surprisingly graceful, fluid movements, dirt-poor but endowed with an irrepressible sense of independence—the very picture of my own father! Both Dad and Horace might have carried picket signs warning, "Don't tread on me!" Dad was a shade more assertive than Horace, but otherwise the two men were uncanny carbon copies of each other, down to their easy, appealing ways of showing unobtrusive physical affection for their wives.

Besides being so eerily evocative of my father, the film also rendered time and place and people with unsettling authenticity: the economic hardships endured, the ability of ordinary folks to carry on . . . and on.

"Much of Foote's writing is of individual resilience in the face of heartbreak," wrote Samuel G. Freedman in a moving *New York Times Magazine* profile about Foote and his work when *On Valentine's Day* came out.

Resilience—a perfect word for my father. And in the same article I found still more to unite Foote and his father with my father and me.

"I believe very deeply in the human spirit, and I have a sense of awe about it," Foote told Freedman. "I'm always measuring myself: could I do that? Could I take that?"

Father was a sucker for strays, and I mean human adult strays. I can't count how many times he brought home from work, without warning, one "Junior" Shaw, or another crony or two, to have supper with us. I do remember Mother's face whenever Junior, a hulking pipeliner in his thirties, appeared and gave her a shy smile. Her face dropped and her temperature rose visibly.

"This has got to stop," I heard her pronounce later. "We're not a hotel."

It was one battle she couldn't win. Father's strays kept materializing at her table, and more often than not they were total strangers, hitchhikers picked up by Dad on his many long, dull drives when he was promoted to troubleshooting for his oil outfit. He was a compassionate man and he liked company.

Not all too many cars traveled on the Texas backroads, and lonely, broke people were always looking to thumb rides. Picking them up was not the no-no it would become in later years. Everybody picked up almost anybody. For years it was the way I traveled between home and college.

Hitchhiking being a fairly safe charity, Mother didn't object to Father making friends on the road. When he brought his strays home, she was invariably polite and poker-faced as she set another place at the table. However, I could recognize her discreet way of mentally rolling her eyes. Junior Shaw and his fellow strays never failed to set her silent protest in motion. And when she pushed her complaints, out loud later on, Father's neck would swell and he'd state that ultimately his word was law in our house, which would make Mother subside—until the next time.

As anybody knows who has ever so much as heard about Houston, its heat is the stuff of legend and misery. In summer, daytime temperatures under a hundred degrees constitute a cool spell. As I was to learn in my traveling correspondent days, the climate is literally the same as in Calcutta. The air hangs heavy as drapery. You get soaking wet just from sitting down and doing nothing. Air-conditioning was unknown in my neighborhood when I was a boy, and attic fans didn't become common until after the war. At the Heights Theater they did "condition" the air; they left the doors open.

Our sweaty woe was a challenge that appealed to Father's appetite for building things to help improve our lives, especially whenever a project involved electricity. Everything about electricity fascinated Father.

Among his favorite reading matter was a how-to magazine, I think it was *Mechanics Illustrated*, and one issue told how to build and install an attic fan, a fairly new invention when I was around ten years old. Eureka! What a grand idea for easing the summer suffering of the Rather family!

Father understood the gadget's limitations. It wouldn't cool anything and it was helpless against humidity—the scourge that used to bring jungle hardship pay to foreign diplomats stationed among us. But the new device would break up the air that hung over us so heavily; it would stir up a blessed breeze. Such a payoff was worth a pile of trouble, and that's exactly what it became, though never enough to dampen Father's creativity.

His timing was excellent. He was taking an International Correspondence School course that was teaching him how to build an electric motor of about three to five horsepower. It was too large to fit the fan's capacity, but who was counting? The excitement generated by the act of construction was of itself more powerful. It was also infectious.

"Rags is building an electric motor," was the word spread through our torpid little neighborhood like a call to arms, and on Sundays, the principal time available for spectator sport, friends and neighbors congregated to watch—and comment on—Father's slow but steady progress in our backyard. I was allowed to fetch him tools out of the toolbox he had built for himself. He and I were the stars of the operation and relished the attention.

The project required far too much space to fit inside our house, which was just as well because indoors was Mother's domain and Mother viewed the fan-in-progress with suspicion. At first she tried to have Father give the monster up. It took too much of his almost nonexistent spare time. She had other chores waiting for him.

She should have known better. Father never gave up on anything, and he certainly would not stop when he was having fun and learning a lot at the same time.

Inevitably, the project had to be moved indoors and Mother's sense of foreboding escalated. Fruitlessly, she protested against the dirt Father stirred up when he cut an opening into the ceiling of our minuscule hallway. It looked like an enormous hole to her and to me. Nevertheless, it had to be enlarged because it was too small to accommodate the motor when Father wanted to anchor it to a crossbeam.

The wiring caused Mother further anguish. Father had learned all about this art from his correspondence course, and he trusted his professors, "the Institute boys." Mother didn't. She feared for her husband's life, which caused my parents to bicker even in front of me, and that was very rare.

"Don't electrocute yourself!" Mother kept commanding.

"Don't bother me, Byrl," he bellowed back.

After months of Sundays, the deed was done. The mammoth motor was poised in its hole. Vents had been cut into both ends of the attic. Father had done it all except for consulting Mr. Bredehoeft, the only aviator in our neighborhood, about the configuration of the propeller-like beaverboard blades.

The Sunday of the fan's inauguration was an event of scope, a large memory of my formative years. The house and backyard were crowded with maybe thirty expectant eyewitnesses from several blocks around. If the fan worked, they might get one, too. Beer was served. The size of the installation caused murmurs. It was piping hot and got even hotter when I helped close the windows along one side of the house to beef up the fan's effectiveness.

Father turned the switch. Would the monster work?

Did it ever! The blades picked up speed slowly but very powerfully, whirling faster and faster. While it didn't twirl any people, the machine quickly sucked two bubbles into Mother's favorite wallpaper, light blue with a delicate flower pattern. One patch was pulled off the middle, another near the top of the wall. Her foreboding had proved justified.

"Shut that thing off!" she yelled into the storm, and Father did.

On balance, the crowd was impressed. Not Mother. She wanted the monster out, out of the house. Father calmed her down by promising immediate engineering adjustments. By late that afternoon he had learned to open all doors and windows all the way to dissipate some of his handiwork's mighty pull. Subsequently he slowed down the motor.

The changes helped, although the gadget always drew too much air through our tiny house. It was like living in a mini-tornado. We sure didn't have to suffer from stagnant air any longer.

I got to help my father replace the wallpaper and never forgot that if your talent makes you a public spectacle, no matter how good you are, you can wind up with wallpaper all over your face.

While my parents would have been puzzled by the term "conflict resolution," they were pretty good at practicing it.

Their fights over money, a nuclear agenda in so many marriages, were rare and relatively mild. Mother was the treasurer. She held the purse strings and paid the bills. Dad handed her his paycheck and she usually gave him whatever cash he asked for. Special expenditures were often subject to postponement. If he wanted a new pair of khakis, she might say, "Not this month, we're kinda close," and that would settle it.

Tempers occasionally erupted because Father believed that Mother wasn't quite as organized as she might be. He'd demand, "Where's the receipt for _____" and if Mother couldn't produce the wanted piece of paper at once, Dad would scowl and then, sometimes, growl. Blowups would be reserved for such occasions as when Mother, having juggled to rob too many Peters to pay too many Pauls, found that she couldn't cover the electric bill at the end of the month and Father came home to a dark house. That did happen and he didn't handle it all that quietly.

Withal, their battles were rather civil. "Shut up" was not in the family lexicon. The strongest that I might hear out of Dad would be, "Don't give me that again!" or "I don't want to hear any more of that!"

Mother held her own. Sometimes Father got a bit carried away by his patriarchal authority, and she knew how to deflate this flexing of male ego.

"Let's get busy on these ducks," I once heard him command Mother with some show of bristle. He and his cronies had dragged in more freshly shot ducks than any one person could possibly clean quickly, and the men were lounging around the kitchen enjoying a nip of whiskey to ease the cold.

Faced with such an ultimatum, I could detect Mother's counter-bristle. I could all but see her neck swell.

"I'm gonna need a lot of help," she said.

She shot Dad a strong look, and he took the hint.

"OK, boys," he said to his entourage, "let's get out a couple of tubs of water," and they got to work.

The maddest I ever saw Mother was the time Dad was determined to take our 1938 Oldsmobile about three hundred miles south to hunt deer. Mother was dead set against the project. She didn't need to point out that the Olds was so rusted out that it had holes all along one side. The frailty of its internal organs was equally deplorable, merely less apparent. Everybody knew about the Olds. It was an unwell car even for much shorter distances.

Father decided that Mother was too much of a worrywart. He and the ubiquitous Junior Shaw and a couple of other pipeliners would not be deterred from heading south for the deer. Mother mentioned that there were plenty of deer to be hunted quite close by. Father said that the deer were much more plentiful where he was going. They were also bigger and therefore better.

Well, the outing turned into a disaster, as Mother had predicted. Somewhere below the old oil town of Beeville, the Oldsmobile stopped the hunters by driving a rod through the block. They had to hitchhike home. Father arrived well after midnight, bedraggled in a driving rain and faced with another storm in our house.

Mother really let him have it this time. Part of her tirade was delivered right in front of me, which was rare. My parents liked to show a united front before their kids.

"Dammit," she yelled in the ancient manner of wives when they've been ignored, "I *told* you! You don't *listen* to me!"

I don't recall what Dad said. Probably not much.

Mother kept up her drumfire for several nights running, and later, when the Olds was towed back with the hole in its intestines, she started all over again. Father never showed that he was truly contrite, if indeed he was. He had Foyt's garage fix a brass plate over the breach in the engine, which made the car sound like a concrete mixer, but he drove it doggedly for many more years.

The battle over the deer hunt was notable for more than its decibel level. Its tenor of hostility was out of keeping with one of the more reassuring rules I grew up with, which dealt with the importance of making up.

"We don't go to sleep feeling bad about one another," I was instructed, and I enjoyed life under a white flag.

Even at the height of the deer-hunt wars I never picked up a sense that anybody would stomp out of the house. Both of my parents knew that it took hard work to keep a family stable, and they kept everlastingly at the task. Besides, there was no point in leaving the house. As I've said, where would you go? And in the case of my parents, who would want to?

Late one night when I was five or six years old and had long been put to bed, I woke up and heard music being played in the kitchen. This was unusual for such an advanced hour, so I got up, cracked my door open quietly, and peeked to see what was going on.

They didn't see me, but I glimpsed what looked to me like a magical sight. I didn't want to disrupt it. My parents were dancing.

They danced for a long time, maybe an hour, off and on, sometimes stopping to fine-tune the radio through the static, trying to bring in one of the outlaw stations across the Mexican border, the ones that carried slow and fast tunes. These outlets were also home to "Doc" John R. Brinkley, once candidate for governor of Kansas, who promised rejuvenation with a "goat gland" treatment that cost $750, which made us laugh our heads off. He was our Johnny Carson.

Doc Brinkley was not on the air that night, so Mother and Father danced through the static, ballads, and all other kinds of music, and they were plainly happier than I'd ever seen them. Mother hummed along much of the time and both were smiling a lot. It was especially sweet and remarkable to see the delight on my father's face. The pressures of the workday had been lifted from his features; I remember that distinctly.

They never did spot me and I never asked them why they chose to go dancing in the kitchen that night. I suspect they felt an urge to relive their courtship years. They also must have felt safe, which was important, for as I grew older I learned that even the most respectable dancing was still somewhat controversial in Texas when I was very little, although it was becoming acceptable.

Accounts by the Sage of Lampasas, Stanley Walker, the old-time editor, tell us that only a few years earlier dancing was not considered clean fun. It was for sinners only. Preachers fanned the belief that the dance floor was the way straight to hell. In truth, dances tended to be large, unruly shindigs that were often tuned up with a lot of drinking. These events tended to attract juvenile and not-so-juvenile delinquents. Brawls were common and blood would flow with the whiskey. These were not good places for family folk. In one of our man-to-man talks, Father cautioned me never to give my real name in such a place.

By the mid-1930s, Texas was becoming less puritanical. My parents mentioned a dance hall operating four or five miles northwest of the Heights Annex, although they were not specific about ever having actually gone there. On holiday trips to Bloomington, way out in the country, we sometimes did go to outdoor events where the music ran to waltzes, polkas, and square dancing, along with current tunes to which one did the "Texas two-step," also known as the "cowboy stomp."

These were sedate Saturday-night family affairs. My parents and I would attend together with Aunt June and Uncle Corbin and some other "younger folks." Sometimes Grandma Page would go too, and there were other entire clans present, including toddlers. Less enterprising and more religious people were still staying away from such frivolity, but the veil of sin had largely lifted.

By the time I was in the eighth grade, a boy was supposed to be able to dance if he wanted to keep in step socially. I still didn't know how, and the day of a major school dance was at hand. I didn't feel like going. Mother thought I should. I reminded her of my ineptitude at dancing.

"Come on," she said, "I'll show you." And off we went on her prized kitchen linoleum, waltzing to the radio, one-two-three, one-two-three. I didn't get it and felt uncomfortable. Mother didn't give up. When the radio delivered a standard two-step tune we tried that, and eventually I got the hang of it.

"See?" Mother coaxed. "It's not hard." I said I guessed it really wasn't, once you knew how.

It helped them in managing their kids that my parents suffered from no inhibitions about displaying physical affection. Mother was a great hugger, especially before I left for school and just before I went to sleep. On an affection scale of ten, I'd rate her at a seven at least, maybe an eight. Father was a respectable six. On the same scale, Grandma Page was an eleven.

In their joint struggles against the adversities that ruled so much of their lives, Mother and Father brought to bear distinctly different styles. These seemed to complement each other at least a good bit of the time, although I'm not sure I understood why. Mother clung to the bottom line that love conquers all. Father was questioning of this view; it didn't gibe with his experience. Listening to one idealist and one realist, I guess I figured that I couldn't lose.

To Mother, the family failures weren't failures. They were setbacks, perhaps heavy losses, disappointments, but temporary. She never forgot that she and Dad were immeasurably better off than their parents had been. Anyway, right or wrong, thick or thin, Father was her star, deserving of nonstop praise for his unflagging efforts.

Father was not an unforgiving person, but he sometimes had a difficult time trying to forgive himself. The record in his head kept playing, "I shoulda" this, or "I coulda" that. . . .

Mother let him talk it all out, usually at the supper table after the dishes were cleared away. She made sure that the house was his sanctuary. If money was even more acutely short than usual, she'd assure him that she'd cut back here and there; it could be done. And if he persisted in blaming himself for something gone wrong, she'd hoist him by his own motto and tell him to turn a card. Not that she'd use the words; they were *his* property.

"That's yesterday," she'd say. "What's done is done."

Mother invented no-fault insurance long before the insurance companies did. And she did one better. She led a no-fault life and tried to get Dad to do the same—and at the same snappy pace.

To turn a card. I'm pretty sure that the phrase originated in my parents' regular poker games at home. They'd have some other couples over and would play for chips, rarely for money, not even small change. Poker was the house game; I didn't hear about bridge until after college. Mother and Father made good poker partners. Both liked to keep the proceedings moving. Years later, in the marines, I learned the maxim "Lead, follow, or get out of the way." At our home poker games, it was either Father telling ditherers to turn a card and flipping a hand in a matching motion, or it was Mother snapping out her own version: "Call, raise, or get the sandwiches!"

The tradition plays on. When my own children get edgy, they don't ask me to turn a card. They just move a hand in the flipping gesture.

One role assignment that hasn't changed with the decades is the motherly portfolio as the family physician in residence. When I see TV commercials showing a mother dispensing medicine as "Dr. Mom," I have to smile because my mother, too, performed such jobs with gusto and considerable good sense.

Besides her faith in the curative powers of fresh air and hot baths, she supported the American passion for "being regular." Heaven knows the origin (or psychological meaning) of our national preoccupation with bowel movements, to be accomplished more or less by the clock; Mother was a devout believer.

She extolled "roughage," which meant that we were

supposed to eat oranges with the peels. When fiber a few years ago became an article of our daily incantations, I recognized mother's roughage all over again. She also held firm to her faith in the health benefits of Texas "ruby red" grapefruit; peaches raised by our relatives in East Texas; and the pecans that we couldn't afford to buy but which luckily grew on trees near the creek bottom.

It goes without saying that we couldn't afford mineral water. I doubt that we'd ever heard of *digestifs* like the then popular Pluto Water ("When Nature Won't, Pluto Will") or the laxative Serutan ("Nature Spelled Backwards"). When any of us reported serious constipation, Mother dispensed very cheap mineral oil. I remember the stuff vividly. It smelled and tasted as if it came from the car's crankcase.

To call our house small would be to enlarge it. "Tiny" would make a better fit. I guess everybody has heard the ancient gag about the house that was so small you had to go outside to change your mind. Well, our bungalow on Prince Street was so small that if we had any guests for dinner, we had to eat in relays. Truly.

During the research for this book, I hunted hard for a paper trail that might reveal the origins of our house. I found none and concluded that none exists. As best I figure it, Father and Uncle John put up the main frame with the possible help of a carpenter friend. The inside was forever— as they say in the literary world—a work in progress. I do recall that when we sold the place in 1956 it brought about $1,600. Even then that was pretty cheap. Our next house, in Garden Oaks, was a well-used structure that we acquired on a thirty-year loan for $6,100. It did sit on an extra-deep lot.

My homestead was white clapboard, and sometime after my father built it around 1932 he added an open front porch barely big enough for a swing. Walking inside, you were right in the living room (which measured maybe fifteen by seventeen feet), and right behind it was the kitchen, with our only table for eating and the floor that was Mother's showpiece because of the genuine linoleum. To the right of the living room was my parents' bedroom and behind it was another bedroom of around twelve by ten feet for me and my brother, Don, who is six years younger than I, and, for quite a while, also for my sister, Pat, eight years younger. And that was it.

Everyone today thinks children need to have their own rooms and privacy. It may be better that way, but no one around our house could afford to think that. Outside of the very best section of town, River Oaks, we had never heard of anyone who thought so.

Mother didn't on the farm. Father didn't, when he was brought up on the outskirts of town. Don and I slept in the same bed for many years, then in twin beds, closely side-by-side, and always in the same small room until I left home for college. The two of us slept in that same room with Pat until about the time she started school. That's when my father and Uncle John built the small room onto the back of the house.

None of this was unusual. We had it better than some in our neighborhood because our family was smaller. Large houses and apartments with more than two bedrooms and more than one bathroom were not common anywhere in the country during the 1930s. And they were highly unusual where I lived.

Father coined one of his bon mots to describe the style of our furniture. He called it "early oil field."

My parents' pride in their mini-castle was nonetheless palpable and meticulously catered to. On Prince Street, unless a family was truly down and out, the peeling of paint on the outside of houses was rarely sanctioned, and so you could infer quite a bit about a family's fortunes from the look of their home.

"They're too poor to paint, too proud to whitewash," my father would diagnose.

We hovered somewhere above the middle of our street's economic range and we'd usually compromise: paint the house and then whitewash the garage (once Dad built one). He and I would get out the steel brush and start scraping at least the front of the house, if not all of it, every two and a half or three years, depending on Mother's verdict after her inspections. Of the three grades of available paint, Father would usually select the middle kind, the decision coming down only after thorough discussion between both parents.

The upkeep of our house on the inside fell in Mother's purview alone, and in the light of our finances her ardor for wallpapering must be considered mildly extravagant. We wallpapered more often than any family in sight. Mother liked cheer and change, and wallpaper was her principal outlet, her way of indulging in both.

"Irvin, I want to rewallpaper the bathroom" was her typical tactic for introducing the subject every year and a half or two. The selection of some happy new design was up to her. I got to mix the paste. Father muttered only quietly and infrequently to himself, except when it came to slapping the wallpaper on ceilings, which was mandatory. He hated that a lot. Still, pressured as he always was for free time, he never went on strike against Mother's papering binges. He knew that fresh wallpaper had a tonic effect upon her, the way jewelry soothes the women of the rich, and he loved to please her when the world permitted him to do so.

Guided by her maxim that nobody is too poor to plant a flower, Mother led the neighborhood in her unrelenting campaign for outdoor beautification. She was happy whenever she had time to get her hands in soil, surely a throwback to the farm days of her childhood in Bloomington.

Her floral enthusiasms were many. She had a soft spot for camellias, fragile and hard to raise; azaleas, also fragile but a lot easier to deal with; peat moss, which she studied by way of a special book she got from the library; and the thick carpets of Saint Augustine grass, which was very laborious to plant but lit up Prince Street by coming up a very rich shade of green. It was deeply rooted, with a matty texture. Some say it came from Saint Augustine, Florida; I believe it originated in San Augustine, Texas.

We were the first in the neighborhood to grow this grass. It spread from corner to corner. Mother talked somebody out of a few strands, and once we planted these on one end of the yard and the other, the grass would expand if it got nearly drowned in water. Mother and Father were crazy about this grass, and I guess I loved it, too, although it was a mighty pain for me to water twice a day. Sprinklers? They weren't known.

It was all part of Mother's campaign for self-improvement, for bettering our lot by putting a greener face on it, and for setting a morale-building example for neighbors all around. We always had the prize-winning lawn, and its "manicuring" was something of a neighborhood joke.

Her yellow roses were another of Mother's passions, and magnolias cornered still another special place in the luxuriating garden of her mind. When I played along Buffalo Bayou in season, I'd look for magnolia blossoms and bring them home. Mother would put them in a bowl and have them on the supper table as a centerpiece.

Somehow she also found time to become a founder of the Shepherd Drive Garden Club. It's a bit of an effort to believe that Mother had anything in common with the ample club ladies in ample hats who fussed with flowers in the old *New Yorker* cartoons by Helen Hokinson, and yet she did. Her club became a centerpiece, too, a hotbed of female socializing and backyard coziness. And it lasted. Just the other day Pat told me she returned to our old neighborhood for a club reunion that brought back times when thumbs somehow seemed greener than now.

*   *   *

My own role within the tight fabric of our family unit was much determined by the accident of my having been the firstborn child. I used to think that this simply made me more available as auxiliary manpower. Of course we had never heard of the psychological implications of what the researchers call "birth order."

In recent years I've seen some of the literature on this learned subject and discovered that we early arrivals are supposedly perfectionists, driven, organized, logical, aggressive, and we're said to be leaders.

Hmm. I do remember helping my parents in minding my little brother and sister while Mother did the supper dishes and Father was hitting his books for his correspondence course in electricity. Don, who is a high school principal in Klein, a Houston suburb, is generous in his memories. He remembers that I taught him rewarding tricks for football, baseball, and knocking down attackers on the street and that I made up a system of stars to encourage his good behavior. I hope I wasn't too terribly patronizing.

About the childhood of Pat, now a Houston-area teacher, I remember singing her to sleep with my rendition of "South of the Border." I guess I *was* a little driven, even then, because I remember how badly I wanted her to go to sleep before Mother would come in to check on us. Ah, birth order. Perhaps viewers who watch me cover wars occasionally notice fallout from this happenstance.

7

Tom Sawyer Days

FRIENDSHIPS WERE true friendships then.

My best friend from the age of three was Georgie Hoyt, who lived across Prince Street from us. He was a year older, tall and beefy, a powerhouse. Georgie was my leader and protector. I always felt safe when he was around. Besides, he was stimulating company. Georgie was muscular beyond his years. He had dark, wavy hair, languid movements, and spoke with deliberation.

We could talk to each other about anything at all, and, heavens, how we did talk! Mostly we convened on the flat extension of the corrugated tin roof over the barn where, as I recall, the Fahey family or some other neighbors kept a cow and horses. A chinaberry tree was our ladder and also the provider of much-needed shade. (The tree's marble-sized chinaberries had a soft center and made excellent bullets for shooting boys suspected of hostile intentions. Instead of guns, we used shooters made of hollowed-out chinaberry tree limbs about ten inches long.)

Georgie and I perched on the roof, jabbering and dreaming on and on, often from the time school let out until after sunset. Time was limitless and we never, never ran out of things to talk about. Or to pretend.

Our pretend games dealt mostly with sports. We played football against each other up on that roof, spinning out game after game, in blow-by-blow detail, usually with Georgie starring in the role of his hero, "Jarring Jawhn" Kimbrough, the bruising Texas A&M fullback.

Trust was an important need, then as now, and we trusted each other enough to trade thoughts on intimate family matters. Georgie's father was chronically in search of work. He rarely found a job, and when he did it never lasted long. Georgie poured out his soul about the family's hand-to-mouth existence, and I guess it was his yearning for security that eventually led him to a lifetime career in the navy.

Georgie's reaching out for the navy, much like my dream to be a reporter of news, stemmed from other motivations as well. We had itchy feet. Though we felt at home in the Heights Annex, we knew that there were better places, and so we looked to move three ways: on, out, and up.

The yen for adventure was another strong magnet. The wanderlust bug bit us kids early in the form of a universal passion for trains. Yes, trains. Kids raised on the distant vapor trails of jet travel tend to have difficulty in believing the romantic, lusty pull of locomotives and rail cars. Planes are impersonal technology, mere containers. Trains are a promise.

Surely there is nothing more seductive than the whistle of a train puffing past you toward far-off destinations. It's why Georgie and I were drawn to the Sam Houston Zephyr almost as if it had been a shrine.

The Zephyr, a streamliner sleek and silvery, ran from Houston to Dallas. The Sunset Limited went to New Orleans. Both traveled on tracks more than four miles away through our woods. Georgie and I hiked to the roadbed with some frequency, just to watch the Zephyr whoosh past and to fantasize about the people lucky enough to sit in those trains and what they were going to do when they got to Dallas or New Orleans. New Orleans! I'm not sure we'd heard of anybody who'd ever been there.

We never knew when the Zephyr would come to pass us by, and it didn't occur to us that there were timetables. When thoughts of remote places moved us, we just hit out into the woods and lounged around the tracks for hours, if necessary, until we were galvanized by the sounds of the Zephyr's approach. Ah, what a spectacle of motion! And what sounds! Everybody at some time has listened to train whistles, but the Zephyr had a horn. It didn't whistle. It thundered out a deep "Waaa-UMP! Wa-ah-waaa-UMP!" I can hear the magic sound in my ear now.

Our most satisfying adventures required very little fantasizing. We staged these enterprises around Buffalo Bayou and in the adjoining marshy woods that lay one vacant field and five hundred yards beyond Prince Street. And our capers were real.

Buffalo Bayou was our Mississippi, and I guess today Georgie and I might be cast by some TV miniseries as Tom Sawyer and Huck Finn. The resemblance never occurred to us because Ol' Man River was much too far north and Mark Twain's famous boy adventurers were fictions, creations of books in the library, old books at that.

Buffalo Bayou was nature here and now, like a jungle annex of the Heights Annex, and its history was at the heart of Houston's authentic past, our past, which was drilled into us at school early and often, with violins and trumpets.

We knew that our city's very own founders, the two New York real estate sharpies John and Augustus Allen, had paddled up Buffalo Bayou fifty miles from Galveston in 1836 to stake out nonexistent Houston on 6,642 swampy acres slightly south of here. Why, we were still swatting the descendants of the same mosquitoes that needled the flesh of the pioneers!

We camped under the stars in these woods (no tents). We swung off grapevines, imagining we were Tarzan. We'd seen Tarzan movies and they inspired us to considerable heights of speculation. Why did he swing from trees? Presumably to dodge the lions, tigers, and giraffes, of course. Do they bite? Sure they do! One would have to be stealthy.

Where do lions live, anyway? In the jungle, in Africa. That sounded inviting, especially to Georgie, who faced more pressure at home than I.

Life away, away from supervision, seemed sweet, and we decided we should make off for Africa. How would we get there? By boat, naturally, and so we made our preparations.

The Indian-style canoes that we fashioned by hollowing out tree trunks would invariably capsize, but we thought that the rafts we assembled from tree limbs and grapevines were gratifyingly seaworthy. Once, in fact, we were going to steer them toward the Gulf through what had long ago been widened to become the oceangoing Houston Ship Channel. We didn't make it to the Gulf, much less to Africa. After one night of "polling" we had made so little progress—and were so hungry—that we turned back, grateful to get home.

I still think we could have made it at least to the coast. I wish we had, because down along the Gulf I wanted to explore for traces of the long-gone Karankawa Indians that we'd heard so much about. These fellows spent most of the daytime hours in leafy treetops and came to ground at night to eat their settler neighbors. This habit came to them naturally because they were cannibals. Gnawed human bones were found in their refuse piles, and when they got angry at another of my local heroes, Jean Lafitte, the buccaneer, they polished off four of his tasty men at one meal.

In our neck of Buffalo Bayou, a branch called White Oak Bayou, the adventuring was actually more fun because there was never anybody else in sight. We were as cut off as if on the Amazon. The water was forever dirty brown, from twelve to maybe forty feet wide, up to thirty feet deep after a heavy rain, more normally around five to six feet. Great overhanging live oak, hickory trees, magnolias up to eighty feet high, and much thick brush shrouded our wilderness for permanent privacy. Even Tom Sawyer didn't have a more exclusive playground.

When we weren't skinny-dipping we assumed the accustomed roles for our favorite scenarios. Remembering the Alamo, Georgie usually became Davy Crockett, and I was Jim Bowie. Floating along on our rafts, we became Stephen F. Austin, the first colonizer of Texas Anglos and the true father of our state; and René-Robert Cavelier, better known as Sieur de La Salle, the great French explorer who seized and named Louisiana and wound up murdered, west of us, by his own men in a mutiny.

We never lacked for extra parts to play when Homer Bredehoeft came with us. And it was Homer, scouting the sights from a thirty-foot cliff by the water, who spotted the great soft-shelled turtle, gray-green and surprisingly speedy, that set us, excited and ranting, on a memorable chase for the better part of the day. Sometimes on the surface, sometimes hidden in the water, Mr. Turtle gave us a rampaging run. Nearly three feet in diameter, he measured over a foot high and looked mean. Shouting and wielding big sticks, we stalked him as if he were the world's biggest whale—remaining careful to stay ashore because none of us was a strong swimmer and we'd been told that sometimes people had been drowned in the Bayou.

Time after time the turtle outwitted us. We were getting pretty worn out and discussed whether we should just let him go. But no! Mr. Turtle was a challenge and he wasn't going to get the better of us. He was devious. We were persistent and we'd win out.

Homer continued his job as lookout. The turtle ducked and scampered. I helped Georgie, our leader, and Georgie finally developed a plan. We would block Mr. Turtle with a big wood block at a shallow spot where we knew the Bayou split.

It worked. Our prey was trapped! We were scared that he would snap at us. We'd only pursued armadillos in the past. They looked ferocious, but we knew they were docile. Huge turtles were beyond our hunting experience. Twice the great beast slipped away from us. He didn't snap, however, and that was his undoing.

We thought we were engaged in a heroic feat. Actually, Mr. Turtle proved pretty tame, once caught. We flipped him on his back, cuffed him tightly in vines of muscadine grape, heaved him up the bank, and built a stretcher of two sticks and more vines. Whereupon we hauled him off to captivity on Prince Street.

It was getting dark when we made it home, swaggering like intrepid bushmen with a conquered lion. Victory! Nobody could have been prouder when we released Mr. Turtle into a washtub. We thought we'd hang on to him as a pet and as a reminder of our courage.

Mr. Turtle made a sensation around the neighborhood. Homer's father came over to congratulate us and lots of other neighbors arrived to crowd around the tub and watch the great turtle splash about in his prison cell.

I was waiting for Father's praise, and when he finally made it home from work he didn't let me down. He complimented us all roundly on a significant achievement, admired Mr. Turtle, and, after supper, gently led us into a discussion of his future.

We boy hunters advanced our idea of turning him into a pet, perhaps training him to come with us on our rounds, like a puppy.

Father laughed and guided us back to reality. The great creature was unlikely to survive in tap water. He'd miss his muddy Bayou home and would probably not survive being deprived of his freedom. That made sense, and so that very night we wrapped Mr. Turtle in vines again, placed him back on his stretcher, and followed Father through the dark in a mournful procession to the Bayou, where we let our prisoner scamper off into his watery domicile.

It was an anticlimax to a triumphant day and I was sad to see our erstwhile adversary go. Still, we'd made our point when we didn't let him outwit us, and by releasing him we had become benefactors of the environment. Father had arranged a charitable and face-saving deal. It was a negotiation I wouldn't forget.

Why didn't I identify with Tom Sawyer in those times? Maybe it was because I lacked Tom Sawyer's guile. That little scamp was always getting away with some pretty underhanded pranks. Remember when he sweet-talked a string of his buddies into painting his aunt Polly's fence for him while he sat out his assigned chore, relaxing under a shade tree? Tom lived to brag about his trickery. If I'd pulled such a caper, I'd have felt my father's belt upon my backside mighty promptly. For whatever reason, I lacked Tom Sawyer's talent for getting away with dubious practices.

Not that I didn't launch any number of silly stunts. My birthday coincides with Halloween, and one year my friends and I were in particularly pesty spirits. The practice of "tricking" adults was well entrenched; the paying of ransom in the form of "treating" was not.

We chased around, turning over a couple of outhouses and switching some chairs on porches. Then we decided to punish a bachelor who lived three blocks down the street for some unremembered, supposedly unfriendly (and probably imaginary) behavior.

Wrapped in bed sheets, we hid in some weeds by his house, and when he emerged I hauled a brick half at him. It turned out that he sustained a slight gash to the head and that our security was poor. Pretty soon our victim turned up at my house, and Father's beating of my butt with his belt was not slight.

We held a stupid grudge against another man who lived alone, this one on the fourteen hundred block of Nashua Street, around the corner. I think he drove a bread route because he slept during the day. He was essentially a good guy and a noted shade-tree mechanic. I remember watching him grind valves on Sundays, with the engine of his car raised on a block and tackle.

Anyway, this hardworking soul had the temerity to grouch and growl at Georgie and me and we decided to mete out revenge.

Our victim had a small tree of muscadine grapes, sour and hard skinned. We got hold of some thick roofing tacks with big heads, stuck them into some grapes, placed them behind the wheels of his car, and hid in the bushes.

Eventually the poor fellow got in his car, failed to notice the grapes—naturally—and drove himself quickly into two flat tires. When he got out of the car, cursing, we were enchanted and exchanged a secret handshake in our hiding place.

Tracked down almost immediately, we didn't lie but tried to brazen out the confrontation by looking innocent. When this didn't work, we confessed and Father's belt went to work again.

This time, Father insisted that I go to see the victim, apologize, and work off the punishment by raking and cleaning up his yard with Georgie's help. It was a vast yard and poorly kept, but we realized that we'd done real damage and had to make amends. Georgie's father collaborated fully with mine, and Georgie got a licking too.

Acute rudeness could suffice to set my parents' disciplinary wheels moving. One time Mother received a tip from a neighbor lady who had overheard me being "disrespectful" to another woman down the block. That was enough for Dad.

He put on his jumper—we didn't call it a jacket—and marched over to the lady's house. On the way, he told me: "You *will* knock on the door. You *will* apologize. You *will* say that you'll never do such a thing again. And you *won't*."

I did what I was told, whereupon Dad walked me to the toolshed behind our garage and took off his leather belt. It didn't hurt very much, but I cried because my dignity was offended. Dad said quietly, "Don't cry." Boys were not supposed to cry. Boys were supposed to mind their parents and respect their elders.

The sin that launched this little morality play was hardly grave. My friends and I had been playing football on the street in front of the lady's house. Several times the ball landed in her zinnias. Several times she came out and told us to move the game. We didn't. Finally, when she came out once more, young Danny Rather said "Shut up!" And that, in our family, simply was not done, never allowed.

The mention of tears gives me an opportunity to have my say about a contemporary subject that should be a nonissue. My father was of a very old school on this one. Standards have changed, I'm happy to see. I refer to the respectability of showing emotion in public, an alleged weakness that some pseudosophisticates have ridiculed in connection with my on-camera reporting of the Gulf War, the bombing of our marine barracks in Beirut, the explosion of the Challenger, and other heartbreaks, fortunately rare.

In critiques of my delivery on some such occasions I've been described as "teary," "watery-eyed," "weird," and "Rather strange."

I find it not one bit strange for an adult male occasionally to be seen with water brimming in his eyes. To the contrary, in my value system the strange ones among us are the few who prefer robots, the would-be highbrows who want us to be zombies frozen into stoicism every time our hearts are hit hard. Or, worse, they don't feel anything at all. Manhattan Island accounts for more than its share of such fellow citizens.

My acceptance of openly reflecting authentic emotion on appropriate occasions is rooted in the values of that special country called Texas. In our scheme of acceptable behavior it wasn't considered unmanly (or unwomanly) to cry when subjected to deprivation or pain (such as from spankings). Tears then were not indictable offenses; folks did believe one should try to be disciplined enough to harness emotions on such occasions. That's now considered repressive, I realize, but that's Texas.

Displaying emotions about God, country, or family was not subject to such controls. A true Texan, never mind the transplanted kind, was permitted to show red rims around his eyes in case of hostilities against Mama, the flag, or God in Heaven.

Not that Texans claim, in addition to our many other monopolies, an exclusive right to adult emotion, especially when it comes to wars and patriotism. Anyone who watched that giant from New Jersey, General H. Norman Schwarzkopf, closely on TV during the hardest days of the Gulf campaign will have noticed how his eyes clouded up when he spoke of his feelings about battle deaths, even one casualty, among his charges. In an interview with my friend Barbara Walters, the general came out and said, "Any man that doesn't cry scares me a little bit."

I found it encouraging to see emotion legitimized by Big Daddy himself, the kind of leader we at home call "The Biggest Man in the Valley." Incidentally, this heart-on-the-sleeve display of feelings came just as naturally to Marine General Walter Boomer and our other post-Vietnam military leaders. And even to the President of the United States.

I was moved to see President Bush choke up when he recalled a televised scene from the Gulf campaign during his victory address to the joint session of Congress after it was all over. He was speaking of four terrified Iraqui soldiers surrendering with tears in their eyes, fearing the worst, facing the American G.I. who told them, "It's OK. You're all right now. You're all right now."

These are the role models of our more enlightened, nonrobotized folkways, and I'm glad. It's been a long time since I've heard anybody dictate, "Boys don't cry!" And it never did bother me to be real.

8

The Making of a Reporter—I

I HAD TO fight for my point of entry into the news business: my corner at Eighteenth and North Shepherd Drive, where I wanted to hawk the Sunday *Houston Chronicle* on Saturday night. I wasn't very good at this street fighting, I didn't always win, but I glowered, pushed, and when necessary scrapped with my fists to get and hold a toehold. I was nine years old, the Great Depression was barely beginning to recede, and I knew nobody with cash just to spend. This was the best way to make some.

Young kids, those under, say, twelve, seldom used weapons in the 1930s and forties. But every boy had to do battle for his corner. It was a rule of the times: If you wanted to work, the job wouldn't just be handed to you. I was skinny but tall, agile, and fairly sturdy, and even though this was before I took boxing lessons I did not get beaten up too badly too often.

To capture that corner at Eighteenth and North Shepherd I had to wage something of a campaign. On the first

Saturday, a bigger boy tried to scare me. He shoved me so that I fell over my papers.

"I gotta right to be here," I yelled as I tumbled back. Quickly, I raised my fists so he knew I'd fight. He gave me a dirty look and left.

The next Saturday a boy of my size arrived with papers and I told him to butt off. He hit me. I hit back. There was a quick flurry, and when I didn't get the worst of it he ran off and returned with two bigger boys just as I was finished selling and ready to leave.

"Don't come back next week," they yelled after me.

The third Saturday, another boy had already started selling papers when I reached "my" corner. I told him to scram and he wouldn't. We had a quick round. He left, but every second or third Saturday the struggle for turf started up all over again.

I never advanced to one of the rich intersections, like Nineteenth and Yale Boulevard. Those prize stations were monopolized by the strongest boys. Never mind. I netted as much as three dollars from my second-rate turf on a good Saturday evening. That was important money. As with all my income through my college days, half went into the family cash pool, the other half into a globe that was a piggy bank.

I had already gotten the word from Father about the importance of bosses. Nothing happened unless the boss made it happen. One of the first things I ever heard Father recite—and he repeated it often—was his guidance for all hired hands for all time: "I get off the truck in the morning and I ask two questions: Who is the boss and what is it that he wants?"

I don't go to work by truck these days, but I've never stopped asking myself Father's two questions.

The boss for whom I sold the Sunday *Chronicle* liked to see his boys show up on time. The papers arrived at the icehouse distribution point around 8:00 P.M., sometimes not until 8:30. I was never there later than 7:30. I wasn't going to give the boss any trouble, and I don't recall that I ever did.

World War II was roaring full blast across Europe. The headlines were exciting and often scary and I shouted them out to hype my sales, as was customary for newsboys. I cared more about the fun of yelling than about its content. I do remember shouting occasional victories like the sinking of the Nazi battleship *Graf Spee*. Early in the war, however, I mostly shouted defeats like the chaotic retreat of the entire beaten British Army from Dunkerque, one of the great military disasters of all time.

No independent news judgment was required of me. The news desks downtown had picked the night's top hard-sell headline. I followed their lead. I'd not yet heard of news desks or about the duties of reporters with press cards.

My start was on the business side of news, "throwin' papers," at the age of seven. I didn't have my own route yet, only a subroute for another boy who had too many front porches to bombard (and hopefully hit) with papers. That meant I got up around 3:30 A.M. to start for the icehouse loading dock. Before papers could be thrown they had to be rolled, and the rolls were kept tight by a piece of string that had to be firmly put in place.

The job was fine with me, including the once-a-month collection of the subscription money. I always collected enough to pay for my papers and had some change left over as profit. What I hated was having to circulate in the neighborhood to solicit new subscriptions. Not only were the times too tough for much success. I think I lacked the bravado of an unabashed salesman. I wasn't dumb, but I also wasn't slick.

So I procrastinated on that part of the job. Sometimes I faked stories about sales calls I never made, and I remain troubled to this day that I stooped so low. The fear of selling—if that's what it was—also led to my first conflict with a boss.

The fellow who was in charge of us boys was a reasonably competent sort of manager in what was even then a murderously competitive business. I soon realized that the sales quotas assigned for new subscriptions were set too high, because I asked around and nobody achieved them, ever. That irked me. It hurt still more when I learned that the boss got a bonus for every new customer. We boys didn't.

It's conceivable that this boss placed a bit of a chip on my shoulder about all bosses for all time. I'm not proud of that and I don't recommend it, but it may be so. He had a huge, scowling German police dog threatening everyone from the back of his car, a bit like today's pit bulls. And he didn't *share*. I didn't care for that way of operating.

(These days, when I feel shoved, especially about money, I'm likely to go along the first time, maybe even the second time. On the third round, I'm likely to think, "Don't push me!" By the time I got to my anchorman negotiations of 1979 and 1980, I said to myself, "This time, for once in my life, I'm not going to leave any money on the table!")

Nevertheless, I remembered Father's loaded questions: Who's boss and what does he want? So I yessirred and nosirred my leader at the icehouse. At least that was my stance on the outside. I was an independent contractor and nobody had to send me a rule book to let me know that I served at the whim of the man on the loading dock.

Within myself, these collisions with the rough edges of the entrepreneurial system performed a priceless service: they sharpened my determination to improve my lot and to overcome obstacles. I started shaping my own rules, and one of my first self-instructions was, "Don't tell me I can't do this!"

It's a great way for making lemonade out of lemons, as the saying goes. I particularly remember how my Rule Number One popped into my ears decades later when a rather smallish TV network executive tossed a put-down at me that I interpreted as a crucial challenge.

"You're not anchor material," the fellow said.

When I heard that, I bristled, I made nasty cracks to myself, and I became mega-determined to show 'em. My motto became, "I'm as good as anybody. Or if I'm not, I can be. And on my best days, if God smiles and I'm a little lucky, I just might earn the right to be called the best." Time, events, and scar tissue have softened that some.

In grammar school (we called it "elementary" school), Mother and one of my teachers noticed that my interest in newspapers seemed to be more than fleeting. Moving to create outlets for it, they helped me to become an editor and writer. Sort of.

In school, Mrs. Spencer and I collaborated on a one-page news sheet. It was more a newsletter, but we called it the school newspaper. Later, at home on Prince Street, Mother and I worked up a rudimentary neighborhood bulletin. Horace Greeley I was not, and we uncovered no skullduggery. Mother and I concentrated on the comings and goings of Prince Street, of which there weren't many. Mrs. Spencer and I worked up a story about the school celebration of Arbor Day. We planted trees at school to create more shade, so I had picked up the message about the desirability of encouraging their cultivation.

Neither of these enterprises prospered, unfortunately. Was their collapse due to lack of audience interest? Inadequate editorial zest? Possibly. More likely, mechanical limitations were responsible. My partners and I had no typewriters, so all of our news had to be hand-lettered. I'm not certain that we had so much as a hand-cranked, smudgy mimeograph machine available to us at school (this was aeons before Xeroxing) and can't recall how we produced any multiple copies.

It was fun and satisfying, though, especially when I

began to realize that as a reporter I got to know some happenings ahead of other people. Beyond gaining this privilege, I sensed a link between the act of reporting and achieving access to faraway places as well as to events that made a difference in people's lives. News mattered.

This insight could only have come to me from my father, who was perhaps the world's most passionate newspaper reader, and I'm not using the word "passionate" lightly. Critics who today worry about the passivity of audiences would never have needed to concern themselves with my father. He was the most active recipient of news I ever knew.

Among my earliest memories is Father surrounded—nearly engulfed—by newspapers. They were piled high around his favorite after-supper chair, like ammunition stacked around a soldier's foxhole. Only small portions of his inventory could be removed by Mother from time to time and only at her peril.

These newspapers had visible power over Father. They caused his usually well-controlled temper to ferment and explode. A single news item could do it. The rest of the family reacted with a meaningful rolling of eyes and an unspoken "Here we go again!"

It often didn't satisfy Father simply to let off steam against an offending purveyor of information. He felt compelled to act, to punish the transgressor, which meant that he was forever shouting at Mother to cancel this newspaper or that. His feuds never seemed to cease. Mother kept canceling and subscribing. She resubscribed whenever Father's ire had receded sufficiently and an old offender was considered rehabilitated after the passage of Dad's personal statute of limitations.

Eventually, he canceled himself into a corner. All three of the local papers had become permanent outcasts at my house and we were left, for considerable periods, with distant couriers: the *Christian Science Monitor* and the St. Louis

Post-Dispatch. Father didn't mind getting his news a week late. He wanted it right. Ultimately, even the stately *Monitor* committed some sin against his sensibilities. Perhaps the Pulitzer publishing family in St. Louis will be pleased to learn that they ran the only sheet that somehow failed to ruffle him.

Father's definition of properly presented news did not match that concept as taught in journalism schools. His crotchets are, however, worth noting because they are more than individual idiosyncrasies. Judging by my mail, quite a few TV viewers today react to the day's news much as my father did half a century ago.

A lot of them want to kill the messenger because they blame him for a depressing message. My, is that an ever-popular urge! I remember Father canceling one of the Houston papers over its perfectly accurate report of a battle victory by Hitler during the war. It seemed to father that the *Houston Chronicle*—or maybe it was the *Post* or the *Press*—was guilty of glamorizing the *Führer* by giving the devil his legitimate due.

Also, countless consumers of news still can't tolerate a negative word, no matter how accurate, applied to one of their inviolate sacred cows. In Father's case, as in many others still, such criticisms constituted an attack on him quite personally and also on his self-perception.

Since Father worked with his back and hands, he was surely entitled to consider himself a member of the working class, and he did. Since he was also an intensely prideful and independent Texan, this status did not reduce him to a faceless cog in some proletariat. He was a realist who recognized which side his hard-earned bread was buttered on.

I remember his anger when I was little and efforts were afoot in Congress to roll back Social Security. Everybody knows that similar attempts still surface fifty years later and still make tempers boil. In the thirties, the issue hit home even more deeply. Nobody we knew had any sort of financial cushion. Moreover, Social Security was an entirely novel New Deal idea. It was hope. It revolutionized care of the elderly, always a fearful problem, frequently discussed in households such as ours and with our neighbors. It was a lifesaver.

I can't exaggerate what Social Security meant to people like the Pages (my mother's family) and the Rathers and tens of millions of other Americans above and below roughly our economic situations. It was revolutionary in the most positive sense of the word. It is one of the most lasting positive legacies of the Depression. Before Social Security, Americans such as those in the Heights and in Bloomington frequently were terror stricken about what was going to happen to them when they grew old and unable to work. Fears about how they were going to get the necessities of life, especially health care, in their late years ran justifiably deep.

When the Depression came, forcing so many from their land and from their homes, causing younger family members to leave even the regions of their parents and grandparents to seek work, and crushing the ability of many children and grandchildren to help their older relatives, many of the older peers and what had been lower middle class became destitute. Their plight and the forced realization that it could happen to almost anyone except the very wealthy gave birth to the Social Security revolution.

Many people, including many farmers and other working people, weren't sure it would solve the problems. Even some of the people who created the legislation and voted for it had their doubts. But the Depression had caused such suffering and disgrace among the old and such fear among the soon-to-be old that enough people believed it to be worth a try. My grandfather Page and my father considered it a shining example of representative government at the federal level—and a miracle.

So when one of Father's newspapers seemed to him to allot legitimacy to the critics of this godsend, his tolerance for First Amendment rights faded in an instant. There went another paper for Mother to cancel.

My parents didn't see themselves as party people. They cared deeply about the bread-and-butter issues and felt strongly about leaders who seemed to them to care about making politics move for the benefit of working folks. Former President Herbert Hoover, our arch-devil, was not one of these personalities. My parents were convinced that this austere figure failed to understand why ordinary people were so wedded to New Deal reforms such as Social Security and rural electrification.

Franklin Delano Roosevelt was their man and the man of that time. I knew homes where he and Jesus literally faced one another on opposite walls and were accorded nearly the same respect. We didn't go that far, but FDR was at the top of the list of living people we admired at the time. We would assemble with some reverence in front of the radio to hear his well-modulated salutation, "My friends!," the theme song that always introduced his "fireside chats." I didn't realize that he was our first media president, but I could tell that he mastered radio brilliantly, displaying showmanship that made politics interesting, sometimes even for kids.

I recall how he twitted his opponents for allegedly attacking his little Scottish terrier, Fala. Such folksy oratory was designed to hit people like Father, and it did the job.

Given the attractions of the President's personality and his populist policies, it's understandable that my opinionated father canceled newspapers when they printed attacks on "that man in the White House"; or when they devoted space to attacks upon FDR by "economic royalists" or alleged Republican propagandists like "Martin, Barton—and Fish," names of reactionary enemies that Roosevelt managed to spit out with the air of an aristocrat dirtying his vocal cords.

Father was not a one-party man; neither am I. I'm a registered Independent, for many years now have refused to register as anything else, and am proud of it. Father, Mother, and I weighed issues and personalities of many persuasions and parties, often in lively debates. I remember that we had searching discussions about Dwight David Eisenhower. He was a Republican, which reminded Father of that terrible Herbert Hoover. He was also a decisive leader with good common sense who had helped mightily to win the big war. We all liked that, which made us like Ike, and we all voted for him—Father and Mother twice, I once.

I can't imagine I was aware that reporters covered news of politics and politicians, that newsmen penetrated places as legendary as the White House itself and got to meet the President in person, not just as a voice on the radio. Finally, though, one morning when I was eleven, I learned what most reporters actually do and got my first look at a species of the breed to which I aspired.

It happened on my turf, Buffalo Bayou. Unbelievably, a boy had drowned. It was unbelievable because I had never taken my mother seriously when she warned me of such accidents. We didn't know the victim, but Georgie Hoyt and I rushed excitedly downstream, where, we heard, a search mission was operating.

It had been raining hard. The water was up and running as swiftly as we had ever seen it. We watched men raking the Bayou with terrible long grappling hooks. They made us recognize what we had not considered before: We were looking for a body, not a boy.

In our boyhood conceit we decided that the adults were exploring the wrong place. Some hours after we launched our own "search" and found nothing, we gave up and joined the clusters of grim-looking searchers and spectators who lined the water around the site where we saw the body pulled out after two days of investigation. It was a horrible sight and I turned away from it after the briefest possible peek. That's about when it happened.

"There's a reporter here," someone said.

It was my eleven-year-old equivalent of glimpsing FDR at the White House.

There he stood, a thin man in his early thirties, looking ordinary in ordinary shirtsleeves, quietly writing notes into an ordinary notebook. He hardly moved. Once he approached some of the rescue workers and spoke with them quietly, briefly. I couldn't hear what was being said, yet here, obviously, was a professional person of competence with access to all that was transpiring, recording an event of significance, which, thanks to his powers, would become known to a great many people.

An ordinary person, yes, but I was thrilled to be absorbing the scene of watching him work. Here was my chance—an opportunity that wouldn't recur until many years later—to make contact with a person who knew how to handle this kind of job. I wanted so badly to talk with him.

I inched up in his direction with no idea of what I was going to say. Perhaps it was just as well that I never had the opportunity to open my mouth. My nerve left me and I never approached him. It was hardly my proudest moment of growing up. I was so close to my goal—and I turned chicken; I was never sure why. I guess I was too awed by rank, a handicap that wouldn't trouble me later in life. There would always be some risk to my hide, which is a subject I'll return to.

9

Terrorized at Summer Camp

THE STRANGE LADY made her way down dusty, unpaved Prince Street, holding up adequately under her hat and stockings despite the usual blistering heat that midsummer when I was about twelve years old. Georgie Hoyt and I were off to the Bayou and tried not to stare at this exotic intruder. She came up to us and smiled.

"I'm looking for George Hoyt," she said.

I was taken aback. Strangers never came to look for us unless we'd busted something, and this time we hadn't. The lady was obviously respectable, but since she wasn't from the neighborhood she was automatically suspect. She must have been a social worker. She didn't identify herself, though; and it wouldn't have helped if she had. We didn't know what a social worker was.

Still, since we were taught always to be very polite to ladies, Georgie reluctantly admitted who he was.

"How'd you like to go to camp?" the overdressed lady asked, still smiling.

Camp? Now we were truly confused. We'd heard of a soldiers' camp not far away, but that dated back to World War I, a generation earlier, and what would kids be doing in such a place?

The lady explained that camp was for games and swimming and that sometimes football players came to visit from their colleges. It might have been a script beamed at us from Uranus.

Georgie was suspicious and clammed up. I was electrified by the mention of real live football players and surely looked disappointed at being left out. In my dirty khaki shorts and no top, I must have come across like a ragamuffin out of a Charles Dickens novel. I was clearly entitled to a vacation in a place organized for what used to be called underprivileged children. So when the lady said she couldn't find Georgie's mother, I identified myself and volunteered how to find her at work: "We have a telephone. It's the only one on the block." I didn't feel I needed to explain that Father's company paid for it so he could be called out for emergencies in the middle of the night.

That's how Georgie and I fell into the worst ten days, by far, of our lives to date. The ordeal was called the Police Boys Camp. It was at Belton, three and a half hours into the unknown of central Texas via Yellow Dog. That's what we called a school bus. A Grey Dog was a Greyhound.

Looking back, the camp couldn't have been as gruesome a torture as I remember, yet even Georgie was terrified, and, as I've said, he was a big, beefy bruiser of a kid, not normally afraid of anything. In the past, I'd always felt protected around Georgie.

It's still a mystery why we were consigned to such a dungeon, because our mothers checked it out as best they could. My father was against my going at first. In fact, he was incensed at the idea. No damn way! It smelled like charity to him, a handout for poor folks. I've mentioned this before, but it bears reemphasis because Father felt so vehemently about the subject: "Poverty" was a fighting word to him. The Rathers *gave* to charity, they didn't take it.

Gradually, my mother won him over, as only she sometimes could. She argued that the police department was hardly an unreliable do-good outfit. She further cited the judgment she had elicited from our Joan of Arc, Mrs. Simmons, the principal of the Love Elementary School. Maybe Mrs. Simmons was fooled by the police sponsorship. Anyway, she approved of the camp, so it had to be OK. Besides, Danny deserved a breather in Belton, where the weather was cooler.

Georgie and I were enormously excited when we took off in our Yellow Dog with some dozen other kids whom we didn't know. We had been instructed to bring nothing, not even a toothbrush, and felt we were in suspended animation, like little hovercraft. What an adventure this was going to be! We'd heard of swimming pools but had never seen one. We'd be learning such Indian skills as braiding belts. And we'd meet up with those college football players; live, real football players!

Heaven turned into hell quickly. We didn't know the word "squalor," but if it had been part of our vocabulary we would have applied it to our shabby little cabins, even though we were hardly accustomed to Beverly Hills housing. We were handed a kit containing two underwear bottoms, a pair of sneakers, and a toothbrush, but momentarily it became evident that the concept of property was not well developed in this police camp.

A redhead from near Dallas arrived, placed himself in front of one of our bunkmates, and said:

"Gimme your [expletive deleted] toothbrush!"

Georgie and I couldn't believe our ears. In our home neighborhood, the "F"-word, while known and occasionally used, was not bandied about like a routine adjective. And why kidnap a toothbrush? Was this the redhead's idea of a gag?

It wasn't. The bunkmate who had been asked for his

brush refused to surrender it, more in bewilderment than defiance. The redhead thereupon sent the resister sprawling with one blow. Next he beat up my protector, Georgie. Then he made off with everyone's toothbrush. What for? I have no idea. Maybe he had found a fence for toothbrushes in Belton. It didn't look like much of a town.

Nor did the natives seem friendly, although this could have been too hasty a judgment because we were kept from contact with the locals. Camp was like living under quarantine. Twice we were taken to the town pool, which had been cleared for us as if we were fifty or sixty little lepers. That's how we must have looked to the townsfolk because we were transported to the pool in the back of a flatbed truck with chicken wire around it.

I remember being gawked at by the citizens along our route and feeling embarrassed to be a spear-carrier in this sideshow display of the needy. Swimming wasn't much fun after that.

Inside our prison, as Georgie and I thought of our camp, vigilance seemed essential to survival. The redheaded kid from around Dallas was not the only marauder, and toothbrushes weren't the only desired loot. The place lacked enough supervision, so Georgie and I decided that one of us had to stand guard over the rest of us all night, every night. We didn't always stay awake long enough to live up to that security goal. We did try.

We also seriously considered escape. It was hopeless. Belton might have been as far from home as Afghanistan, and it didn't occur to us to make a long-distance S.O.S. call from a phone booth. We'd never heard about long-distance or collect calls. Besides, the nightmare would soon be mercifully over.

As I look back upon this scary fiasco, it occurs to me that the practicalities didn't have all that much to do with our withdrawal into more or less stoic resignation. We were governed by The Rules, the values taught at home. Two commandments applied to the Police Boys Camp of Belton. You didn't whine and you didn't quit.

And I've never forgotten another lesson, the rule that says things aren't always what they seem. Just because a place is run by the police doesn't mean that law and order prevail within.

I picked up one further truth in Belton: Almost no life experience is all black, totally negative, not even the demeaning camp that hurt my pride so hard. The place had one counselor who took an interest in Georgie and me. He was a congenial, open fellow and I'm sad that I can no longer recall his name. He played center on the football team at Sunset High in Dallas and came from a background much like mine. This counselor imparted news that made me feel I'd just discovered electricity.

In the fall, so said this fellow who wasn't so different from me, he was going off to the University of Texas on a football scholarship. College! I was barely acquainted with the concept and now he made it real in my mind. College was the route out of the Heights Annex and football was the ticket into college. I didn't know about role models except that I'd just met one.

On the Yellow Dog back to home I made up my mind that I wasn't going to yelp at my parents about the stolen toothbrush and the other injustices committed against me in camp. No whining! I was going to tell them that I was going to go to college like that counselor.

He was the first to make college real for me. Perhaps because he was only seventeen years old, his word carried a strong degree of credibility. More: He fully realized, and he made clear to me, that he thought of college as the train pulling him away from *his* ditch. He had a vision of a career as a policeman, maybe even a lawyer. He encouraged me to stay in school and try for college. His encouragement and example were water and fertilizer on the seed already planted by my mother.

10

The Illness

THE FIRST great test of my soul started when I was ten, almost unnoticeably, without the slightest hint that it would last, off and on, for about five years and would come close to making me an invalid for life, unable to do many kinds of work.

My feet hurt, that was all. Even that is probably overstating the case. There was no pain; I merely felt an occasional ache. If I hadn't run around barefoot most of the year, I probably wouldn't have noticed it for the longest time yet. Barefoot, though, you're like the Indians, "you touch the earth," keenly aware of what connects you with the crust of the world.

For many months I said nothing. Remember? You don't whine, you don't complain. Not in the Heights Annex.

Eventually the trouble settled in the balls of my feet. Next, stiffness developed in both big toes. The ache occasionally turned into sharp pain. I don't remember how long this phase lasted; ultimately both feet really hurt a lot and then the pain spread to the insides of both ankles.

By now I was walking with a sort of half limp that I couldn't hide. Mother questioned me. I was happy to spill my story and was relieved because she was not alarmed. Mother, the resourceful house doctor, prescribed aspirin. It helped, though never for long. She made me soak my feet in Epsom salt, that ancient nostrum. The relief was small and never lasted. Then came the hot-water bottle in bed. Again, no real relief. Mother was running out of treatments.

Whatever was ailing me was especially frustrating because it kept changing its mind. Often it went away and our hopes would rise. Always it came back and got worse. I was still able to limp to school. To have stayed home would have been an admission of major infirmity, which didn't seem to fit my condition. Around our house my problem was casually referred to as "Danny's sore feet." Nothing alarming about that.

In time I wasn't just suffering from sore feet anymore. The illness, whatever it was, was creeping up my shins and seemed to be reaching for my knees. Mother began to worry and so did I. It wasn't only because I hurt. I don't recall how long I'd been in pain by then, but it seemed forever and showed no sign of going away. In fact, it was obviously getting worse; that wasn't the pattern of the ailments with which we were acquainted in our generally extremely fit tribe.

We were in uncharted territory.

Still no doctor was consulted, and this was neither neglectful nor strange. People in our circumstances very rarely went to see doctors in those times. They figured that most medical problems would go away without professional attention—as true then as it remains today.

And doctors weren't nearly so effective then. Often

they didn't know enough to do a whole lot of good. They've learned enormously, phenomenally, in the last half century, with the help from new machines, laboratory tests, drugs (antibiotics, to mention one vital category), all manner of treatments, and insights that nobody dreamed about when I was a boy. The difference is so enormous that it can hardly be described.

Doctors then had little more than a single characteristic in common with their colleagues fifty years later. They were frightfully expensive—yet another decisive reason why we shunned them.

Mother did realize she needed outside assistance and sought out her own consultants. The first was her sister, my aunt June, then down in Bloomington, Texas. She seemed a logical choice because she had been born almost deaf and had consequently seen more doctors than any of us. Fortunately for her and unfortunately for me, Aunt June's legs and feet had always been in pretty good repair, so she could suggest little. By then I was having a severe attack of whatever it was. I was consigned to the living-room couch, then to bed. No way could I get myself to school.

Mr. Sikes from down and across the street was thought to be a more promising authority because he had a problem with his legs. He carefully inspected my toes, my ankles, and my shins but could only agree with Mother that my affliction was mysterious because it was invisible.

In the end, Mr. Sikes diagnosed "growing pains." Everybody knew this condition, which was caused by the—at times rapid—sprouting of young bones. What, in particular, could you expect of boys who were forever dashing through the woods and not getting enough rest?

From somewhere my mother was hit by the notion that I might be suffering from some nutritional deficiency. What was lacking in my system? Who could tell? Mother reasoned that since I seemed beset by cramps and she knew that cream of tartar sometimes helped with menstrual cramps, I was to be given gobs of the white powder to wash down. It tasted awful and did nothing.

More than two years of guesswork had gone by while I was up and down, and it finally became obvious that my condition required more help than we could muster at home. A violent shooting pain pounded up my legs. I hurt so badly that I couldn't sleep. My parents considered giving me a shot of whiskey in lieu of one of the soporifics, all of which were unknown to us, but they abandoned the liquor idea as too drastic considering my age.

When I began to encounter serious difficulty walking at all, Mother became truly alarmed and insisted that I be seen by a doctor.

We had heard of Dr. Herbert Poynter, a surgeon at Hermann Hospital way downtown, because he was a consultant to the Houston Pipeline Company, Father's employer. Although this doctor rated as an almost mythical learned authority and was endowed with godly status by the pipeliners whose bones he had mended, he agreed to see Mother and me.

I'll never forget the trip. The more than three hours on the various buses and streetcars were never much fun in the usual heat. That day I was upset when I looked at Mother slumped in her seat on the steamy South Main Street bus. Normally, she accentuated the positive in any situation. That morning, having taken off from work, she looked as glum as I could ever remember seeing her.

And for good reason. The revered Dr. Poynter looked me over briefly and said, "Hm, hm, hm." Then he referred us to an internist.

Mother and I took little solace from thus learning indirectly that I was not a candidate for the scalpel. What in the world was wrong with me? It was not encouraging that even the great Dr. Poynter evidently hadn't a clue.

Neither did the next doctor, the internist. He tapped my knees with a rubberized hammer, told me to drink at

least twelve glasses of water daily—and sent us home without
a diagnosis. I'd witnessed once again that people, like events,
needn't be what they're cracked up to be.

Father had not been too interested in my travail thus
far. He opposed the coddling of children, and much of the
time I didn't look all that sick to him. The fruitless trips to
the doctors made him impatient. What could be so bad if
two downtown doctors found nothing amiss?

"He'll outgrow it," Father announced.

Increasingly, this sounded like wishful thinking. More
and more signs showed that the illness was outgrowing me,
not the other way around. I'd always tended to be skinny and
had to be pushed to finish my supper. Now I kept losing
weight, which alarmed me greatly because every upstanding
Texas boy was supposed to become a football hero—that's
right, not a player but a hero!—and I was dwindling way
below the needed heft.

I had no appetite. I was pale as a bed sheet. Sometimes
I ran a low-grade fever and passed discolored urine. The
pain was spreading to my wrists. The district school nurse
examined me to no avail and my teachers had become
alarmed. Having always been a good student, I still tried to
drag myself to classes as often as possible, hurting, limping,
but making lower and lower grades.

Enter Dr. Cope. R. Louis Cope. He was another downtown internist; otherwise he had little in common with the
doctors we had seen. I can't recall how we got to Dr. Cope,
but the aura of a super-doctor clung to his presence, or so I
remember. A mob of patients filled his waiting room. We
had to wait hours before he saw us.

Dr. Cope was a younger man, in his early thirties, a
Tulane Medical School graduate from Tennessee, slow in his
speech, languid in his movements, much friendlier and
more interested in me than the other doctors. He was softer,
cautious in everything he said. Seemingly lost in thought, he
spent a great deal more time with me.

I walked for him. He manipulated my limbs. He checked my throat and ears and made gently clear for the first time that I was suffering from something serious, he didn't yet know what. I had to come again.

The next time he zeroed in on a specific area of my anatomy that appeared to have nothing to do with my limbs. I was mystified. Had I had frequent sore throats? Yes. Fevers? Yes. Had I had my tonsils removed? Yes. Dr. Cope grew even slower and quieter. He couldn't be sure, he finally said, but there might be a connection. If so, I might be having rheumatic fever. He had never seen a case outside of a textbook. Until he committed himself to a firm diagnosis, which was to take nearly a year, he would handle me as if rheumatic fever was what I had. There was no alternative because this disease could not be taken lightly. Unless I was given complete rest, I might find myself with heart trouble.

Rheumatic fever? Well, what was the treatment?

That was one of the problems, Dr. Cope said. There wasn't any medication, only rest. A few years later, penicillin would become the standard treatment, but we were talking in another age, you might say B.A., before antibiotics. So my mother, ready to deal with the realities, asked how she was to understand the term "rest."

There was no longer anything slow or tentative about the doctor's response. The words will remain with me forever.

"I want him in bed and I don't want him to move," said Dr. Cope.

My world caved in. Not move? I couldn't do it, I wouldn't. I wasn't thinking of the threatened heart trouble down the line, only of lying there like some mummy. No! Everything within me went into automatic revolt. No school? No football? Who was the paralytic around here? Was I having polio? I was not. I could still move.

My father handled the news in much the same spirit of disbelief and denial.

"What kind of deal is this?" he burst out. Danny in bed, immovable like a log, lying there for nobody knew how long? What kind of doctoring were we getting?

The correct kind, said my mother firmly. If Danny was to walk again, if he was going to stay out of heart trouble, she would see to it that the boy did precisely what Dr. Cope had ordered. That man knew what he was talking about. This was not the time for male tough-guy emotion. We just had to adjust to a new life for me. She would arrange it and she did.

First off, she decided, I couldn't be totally cut off from the world while everybody else was out of the house. A view onto Prince Street and live people would be less depressing than looking forever out on the litter of the backyard and some chinaberry trees. I was moved to my parents' double bed in our front room. They moved into our little bedroom with my brother and sister, which was a mighty tight fit.

That accommodation to my infirmity was a sure sign that my father had come around to accepting what had to be done. I figured I'd better do the same.

Somehow I kept myself occupied at least a good part of the time. I read a little. I listened to the radio a lot. I watched for every sign of action on our street. And I kept up, barely, with the schoolwork brought in by my friends.

The boys were really good about coming by to keep me company. Georgie Hoyt came over a lot, naturally. So did Homer Bredehoeft. Charlie Stramler showed up. Still, kids are kids and kids get fidgety fast, and so I was alone for many hours every day, bored and brooding, especially brooding. The sense of being all alone, a crippled outcast, different from other kids, sometimes almost overwhelmed me. I felt like a nonperson.

What about the heart trouble the doctor had talked about? I didn't really understand that, although I knew that this was why my mother checked my pulse and counted my heartbeat every day in the way she'd been instructed by the doctor. Later on she checked one, two, or three times a week.

Never mind. The question stayed with me: Was I ever going to walk again? I wasn't at all certain.

I was, however, determined most of the time that I absolutely had to get better, and so I resolved to become the world's model patient. It probably helped considerably that I was too scared to do anything else. I tried so hard really to lie perfectly still, thinking carefully before I so much as shifted an arm. Would it be dangerous to do that? I couldn't be sure and I'd freeze like a rabbit. I rationed every tiny self-indulgence: moving that arm, shuffling shakily into the bathroom. What a treat it was to move as far as the bathroom! I scheduled each trip in advance; every outing was like a vacation.

Each day seemed to take a week to crawl by, and my pain didn't let up, not for a month, not for two, not for three. After that, in imperceptible steps, it did begin to subside. Mother had kept in contact with Dr. Cope, and eventually he pronounced that he hoped my siege was over. He also warned us not to be surprised if the symptoms came back. It was OK for me to get up, he said, but, as I interpreted Mother's report of her conversation with him, I wasn't supposed to *do* anything, just about nothing at all.

I felt like a caged animal, a prisoner. My sense of having changed from a free-running athlete into an invalid increased, really took hold, especially when I could watch how quickly my muscles and my body skills had atrophied. I couldn't have defied the doctor's instructions if I'd wanted to.

I was pitifully unsteady the first time I got out of bed, even with Mother and Father holding me up. The first time I was allowed outside, Father had to carry me in his arms like a baby. We went no farther than the front yard so I could sit awhile near the street. I didn't know what was worse: the humiliation of having to be carried at my age—carried!—or that I was feeling as weak and looking as pasty-faced as I did. And how my weight loss had shrunk me! If I stood sideways, you could hardly see me. Not the stuff of football heroes.

No doubt I would have carried away some sort of permanent psychological aftereffects if it hadn't been for the way Mother and Father got behind me. It goes without saying that neither of them ever cracked a child-psychology book. If they had, they might not have understood much of it. Some of the teachings of Dr. Benjamin Spock, soon to become the grand marshal of American child raisers, would have struck them as weird and sissified—"inappropriate," as one says in psycho-speak these days. Anyway, Dr. Spock didn't come out with his masterwork on baby and child care until 1946.

Truth to tell, my parents, as so many of their generation, didn't need outside advice on how to bring up their kids. They required no lessons on how to love a child. That came naturally, thank you. They were marvelous practicing psychologists, Mother and Dad. They knew instinctively what I, their tender-winged bird, needed. They knew how to hold me down in bed if necessary, and, all told, it did turn out to be required for more than an entire year and then some, a near-unbelievable stretch of tedium and immobility for a once-supermobile boy. At the same time, they made me feel supported—safe.

Mother moved many meals into my room so I'd have company. We ate on trays and sometimes at a folding card table. Given Mother's belief in praise and prayer, she was just short of infuriatingly positive about my prognosis. I kept getting bombarded by bromides like, "Time goes faster than you think."

Mother encouraged me to open windows and observe the birds. We had a little book about the birds of Texas and I remember Mother and I keeping a strenuous lookout, eventually successful, for a tanager with orange on the wings.

Father urged me to listen to the play-by-play accounts of the Houston baseball Buffs (for Buffaloes) on the radio. I used to memorize the games to while away time. Sometimes when I woke up in the middle of the night because I'd been resting so much that I couldn't sleep properly, I'd put in more hours mumbling the games to myself.

In my business now, they call this ad-libbing. In those days it was just another way to get through lonely hours.

Once I could walk a little without the pain coming back, I knew it was time for Mother to ask the good Dr. Cope (what a meaningful name!) when I could return to school. I was eager to go and I wanted badly to be back with my friends. Yet my most anxious question was about something closer to my heart: Would it be OK for me to *run*, to play football? I had never been a powerhouse player. I was shifty, though. I could maneuver. In baseball, I was good at shagging fly balls. And, my, I wanted so badly just to be in *any* game!

The answer was no. A resounding no. Worse, Dr. Cope sentenced me to life in slow motion. He wanted to know how many steps I'd have to climb in school. How could I get there making the trip very slowly and with minimum exertion? I was bursting to be up, up, up. He wanted me down, down, down. I was to watch for signs of getting tired. When I did, I was to slow down, sit down, lie down, put my head down. What an existence!

I followed orders. Dr. Cope had been demonstrating for a long time that he knew his business. And I was desperately afraid that my pain would come back. The doctor had warned Mother that this might easily happen, which would have meant another interminable siege in bed. No!

So I inched part of the way to school, straggling like a duck, stopping constantly, and for the rest of the trip I climbed on the book rack of Georgie Hoyt's bicycle and was driven to school as if by private limo. Or ambulance.

The mental part of my comeback was much more distressing. I'd lost my sense of self. I'd been like everybody else; now I was different. I'd enjoyed a strong sense of belonging to the neighborhood, to Texas, and to my friends and their camaraderie. Now I didn't know whether I could fit in again.

I didn't merely *feel* different. I *was* different, and not only slower and weaker. I'd always been lively, quick, a talker. Now I'd turned quieter, more serious, actually pretty grim. It was a passage, a cloud that didn't last but took years to recede, and it dropped all kinds of fallout.

Some of it was inconsequential. When we swam in Buffalo Bayou, my friends and I used to thrash pell-mell through the water with what we called "cow strokes." Years later I had swimming lessons. I hated them. I wasn't as well coordinated as the other boys, and that wasn't the worst of it. I was scared, a legacy of my year in bed.

Other fallout hit me as well, but I'm getting ahead of myself. . . .

11

More Illness

SHORTLY AFTER I'd resumed school I had to make a trip to the hospital for the first time in my life. My good friend Charlie Stramler, a jovial, tubby lad, was ill. He had leukemia, although this either wasn't realized at that point or wasn't said out loud as yet.

Charlie was a short, irrepressible guy, always smiling. He could have been out of an *Our Gang* comedy. He was a lousy football player but probably the smartest one of us. His mother was a nurse, and I could have pictured Charlie becoming a doctor.

I was shocked into near panic. Charlie looked a long way from jovial or chubby. He lay there small and white. We hardly talked, Charlie being too sick and I being too frightened.

When Charlie died, which came quickly, I was devastated. A fine friend was gone, but worse yet: If he could be sick and die, why couldn't I? What was so different between

leukemia and the rheumatic fever that Dr. Cope had said
might come back and might yet mean heart trouble? Even I
knew that people died of heart trouble all the time.

There was no way to avoid brooding about Charlie's
fate—and my own, by extension—because I was appointed
a pallbearer at his funeral, which was set for a Monday
morning. Here it was Sunday and I owned nothing remotely
fit to wear at a funeral. By great good fortune, somebody on
our block knew Mr. Zindler of Zindler's department store
way downtown.

I guess it was my father who managed to reach Mr.
Zindler by phone at home and convinced him that the occasion was of sufficient gravity to warrant the owner coming to
the store. He opened up especially for me, an exceptional
gesture of respect for the deceased.

This was how I acquired my first suit, a dark navy wool
chalk stripe. It cost around ten dollars, too much to pay all at
once. I think Father put down two dollars and paid off the
remainder at a dollar or two per week.

I hated that suit passionately. I'd never worn wool pants
before. They scratched like crazy and made me walk stiffly,
like a toy soldier. Father looked stunned when he suddenly
faced his firstborn looking like a mini-adult.

The funeral was frightful. There was Charlie in an
open casket, decked out in Sunday best, wearing makeup
that made him look more alive than when I'd seen him in the
hospital.

His death confused me, although everybody talked
about death all the time (never, never about sex!). Our regular Sunday sermons dealt with nothing more insistently than
with death. It was presented as life's central question: What
would be one's fate—eternally!—in the afterlife?

The hellfire-and-brimstone preachers thundered to
make the hell-or-heaven decision sound plenty close. Still,
the issue had always felt distant and rather academic to me as
a boy. No more. This wasn't about doctrine, this was about

my Charlie and he was dead. This was personal. I saw him
being lowered into the ground in a box myself!

What would happen to Charlie? We were down to bed-
rock now. Would Charlie go to heaven or to hell?

I took the matter up with Mother, the ecclesiastical
authority at our house.

"It depends on what kind of person you've been," she
said softly. "Charlie was a good boy, and God makes special
dispensation for boys because they're young."

Good for him, and there was hope for me, too. I preferred to hear Mother rather than the preachers talk about
God. She knew more about boys.

The pain came back, this time for a full school year. I feared
it would go on forever and never felt so low. I was running a
low-grade fever from time to time and lost weight again. My
parents whispered about me deep into the night. Dr. Cope,
whom Mother called once a month, was sympathetic but had
no suggestions. Time would have to be the healer. Just thinking about that platitude made me feel even worse.

I was transferring into Hamilton Junior High School
and Mother kept bringing me my homework. You could have
measured my motivation with a thimble. Still, I didn't fail
school. I think it was simply that I couldn't let my parents
down.

This time they rallied the covered wagons around me
real tight. Aunt June came up from Victoria to help around
the house and slept on the back porch. She was a sunny soul
and tried to spread her cheer. My ultimate defense, though,
was the iron-fortress atmosphere drummed up by Mother
and Father.

I heard a lot of quiet talk from them with the refrain,
"You can do it." And, "Never give up. You just don't quit!"
That was our article of faith, the ethic that always kept us
going, maybe out of no more than plain necessity. We never
had many choices in those years.

Happily, Dr. Cope had been right, as usual. My disease wore itself out before I did, in time for a new round of hostilities to begin about my convalescence. "Absolutely no climbing stairs," said the doctor. That posed a problem. Hamilton Junior High was three stories high and its bureaucracy seemed mountainous.

Mother went to see the assistant principal. Could Danny's classes be confined to the first floor? The doctor had laid down the law. The boy was weak. He couldn't even walk to school yet. Georgie Hoyt would pedal him on his bicycle; that was one hurdle scaled. But how was Danny supposed to clear the stairs?

The assistant principal was full of regrets. In the manner of all bureaucrats, he explained the rules he had to live by. Exceptions would be too disruptive.

He underestimated my steel magnolia, my mother. She would not be moved. I don't remember how many trips she made to lobby that principal. There were several confrontations, and for the last one my father took time off from work—unheard of!—and went along to demonstrate that our family front was unmistakably solid and could not be dismissed. The Rathers would not go away.

It was another triumph of our family rule, "Don't quit!" That would become my rule as a reporter, too. The school bureaucrats took pity. An exception would be made. I could take all my classes on the first floor.

I was embarrassed and humiliated by all the fuss. It brought home again that even though I walked around and felt no pain, I was still a cripple. Then again, I felt so warmed by my parents' backing. I admired them for it. What a tremendous act of love they had mustered on my behalf!

So much for the battle of survival. The war of my reentry into the world of functioning people still lay ahead.

12

"I'm Comin' Out!"

THE VERY LAST thing I wanted on coming back to school was to be excused from gym. Excused from gym? There was no such thing! I'd have just about preferred to drop the book-learning part of school instead.

Still, gym was out of the question for me. Dr. Cope didn't even have to be asked about that. If I wasn't supposed to walk to school or climb one step of stairs, how was I supposed to run down a football field?

This made sense to everybody except Coach Charles Kivel. He was head of athletics and also coached football, having once been a high school football hero himself and being just then engaged in the great task of reinstating organized football in junior high. The other day I heard coaches like him described as "lords of the locker room." That surely did fit Charles Kivel.

Kivel thought I was faking and didn't keep this judgment to himself. He called me a "sissy," a "mama's boy," and peered at me with the disgust that people reserve for cockroaches or hitchhikers with pets.

Excuse that boy from gym? That ran against Coach Kivel's religion.

"The least you could do is chin-ups," he barked at me.

He wanted ten of them. Although I tried my utmost, I couldn't do one. I couldn't even hold on to the bar.

I must have been something of a public spectacle because I recall that Charlie Snapp, the swimming coach, was there and he told Kivel, "We can't do that." Snapp was a decent fellow and he had respect for my doctor's instructions. So I was assigned to a vacant classroom to study during second-period gym.

This caused Coach Kivel to ignore me. Briefly. I guess my room was considered something of a holding cell for outcasts, because one day I received company: a lively kid who was being quarantined for some less-than-mortal sin. During one morning of reverie, this Mr. Lively, bored, sneaked out the window and returned with jelly doughnuts from Weingarten's supermarket.

Our mouths and faces were launched into this feast to the point when credible denial was no longer feasible, and in walked Coach Charles Kivel, livid. He was particularly incensed at me because I'd said I couldn't run; yet clearly—as he saw it, presuming my guilt in the un-American style of the late Senator Joseph R. McCarthy—I'd dashed along to Weingarten's for the jelly doughnuts. Which proved to him that I was malingering, as he'd trumpeted all along.

I denied that I'd left the room.

"Liar!" barked Kivel and hauled me off to the principal's office, where I got a scolding.

I'd had enough of my nemesis. I disliked him so much. No, that's wrong. I shouldn't let charity overrule accuracy. I *detested* Kivel. Seen through my eyes, he was unfair, demeaning, and had no right to swat me when I was down. Perhaps I was learning to meet a challenge from my mother, she of the steel will, and my father, the pipeliner who wouldn't be kept down in his ditch. I had had enough.

I wasn't going to take it anymore. For the first time in my life that I could remember, I was acutely aware of determination with a capital "D" surging through me.

This was turn-around time. Things were going to change. My mother and father long had taught: "There'll be many times in your life when you must dig in, stop negative momentum against yourself and your goals, and then come slogging, fighting back, little by little, inch by inch, to turn things around, to build positive momentum." For the first time it was coming together, I was beginning to understand what they meant. And I was determined to do it.

I was in absolute ecstasy by then to be back going to school. I was making my comeback, catching up with the class work, feeling stronger every day, triumphant to have fought the villain Rheumatic Fever—and won! No mere Kivel was going to keep me down anymore.

My friend Bebe Hooks was going out for softball in the spring, and she was a girl! Since I still was in no shape for football, I decided baseball would be my return-to-life ticket for the time being, and I went to tell Kivel so.

We were squashed into his "office," a cubbyhole in the corner of the gym. He tried to tell me that I was too late. The message that I inferred was, "Don't bother!"

"I have a right to come out and I'm comin' out!" I flung out my challenge as defiantly as I dared.

It was a high point of my life up to then. To my way of thinking, I'd faced the coach down.

Maybe I had. Trouble was that the coach, like most authorities, knew killing ways to fight back against a lower form of animal life, me.

He didn't let me play a single game. I wanted to play shortstop; he claimed that I had the wrong glove, that it was illegal. In fact that glove was merely cheap.

I shagged balls in the outfield but wasn't allowed to take my turn at batting practice. Still, I made it to every home game, winning grudging respect from the team as a kicked-around underdog. Nothing from the coach.

Came the last game and the last inning of the season with two out, nobody on, two strikes on the batter.

Kivel calls time-out and sends me into right field.

He meant it as the final disgrace. I saw it as victory. Better to be sent out on the field than to sit on the bench to the end.

One pitch and the game and season were over. I couldn't have been prouder or more in need of recognition. Mother wasn't home for a while, so I ran over to Mrs. Stramler—Mary Stramler— a nurse who was home afternoons because she began work so early in the morning.

"You know, I played today!" I burst out in her kitchen. My chest must have popped out like a balloon. She recognized my need and seized the moment to stop, listen, and smile. "That's really good!" she said, making sure that her approval showed through.

Mother and Dr. Cope had not discovered right away that I was doing sports or that I had been climbing to a mechanical drawing class on the second floor. I had diagnosed my recovery myself and soon I had confirmation that I knew myself pretty well. It came when Mother was taking my pulse after a walk. In the past, I'd always held my breath before she announced the results. Now I relaxed, especially when Mother delivered the verdict.

"I think you're getting well," she said with a big smile.

This news drove my determination to new heights and turned me into a boy possessed. I wanted a varsity letter in sports, a letter in something, almost anything. With some reluctance I settled on volleyball, not so glamorous a sport, but I was desperate. Volleyball was available because the coach, Charlie Snapp, as usual, had a hard time getting anybody to come out for it.

It was my last chance before graduation to acquire a

letter. I did make the team. We never made headlines—so what? I'd made it.

I'd come out, and stuck it out. In some ways I could not have been more satisfied if I'd made the All-City football team at quarterback.

Coach Kivel later gave me trouble when I came out for football and basketball in senior high school.

Why, I never fully understood. I guess something about me just rubbed him the wrong way. The feeling was mutual. But I got over it. I hope he did.

13

"It Was the Making of Me"

IT DOESN'T take much imagination to picture what would happen these days if a boy in his early teens was setting out to score a comeback from a five-year siege of rheumatic fever, much of it spent listlessly limping or flat on his back.

His parents would rally a delegation of specialists. An internist, troubled by the boy's severe underweight and pallor, would put him on an extra-nutritious pep-up diet, to be reinforced by a regimen of vitamin and mineral supplements. Noting the young patient's weakened and poorly co-ordinated physique, the doctor would prescribe wholesome bodybuilding exercises. In school, a guidance counselor would lay out a program of intellectual enrichment and catch-up.

The most intensive attention of all would be focused on the boy's psyche, so vulnerable right at the time of puberty. A psychologist would be deputized to work, twice a week for fifty minutes each, on the boy's crushed self-esteem. A mild antidepressant medication would be considered for a time. Everybody would realize that the boy was a setup. He was all but guaranteed to grow into a withdrawn, fearful hypochondriac, permanently doomed by his anxieties to function at levels well below his capacity.

In today's setting of enlightenment, specialists know how to limit the fallout of a long, traumatic illness and prevent a crippling outcome. During my adolescence in Texas fifty years ago, we were not so advanced. All that happened was that my father spoke to Jeff Stramler.

I don't wish to poke fun at modern medicine and psychology, nor to trivialize my condition or its delicate timing. It's just that life was profoundly less sophisticated then.

I could have used any and all curatives, because when my illness was through with me I surely was a wreck. I was thoroughly emaciated. I was scared to death, literally fearful of dying, constantly expecting a relapse, alert to every tingle in my knee joints and ankles. I felt that my identity was almost destroyed. I hated my weakness, my differentness, the inability to keep up with other boys. My world had collapsed. I was a shadow propped up by my private team of lay psychologists: my mother, my father, my uncle John, and my aunt Marie, a relentless bunch . . . and shrewd.

I can't recall which one it was who first held up President Franklin D. Roosevelt to me as an example. FDR himself! Here was a powerful notion, yet not farfetched. The President, too, had a chronic, crippling disease affecting his legs. He could only move in a wheelchair; still, that hadn't kept him from becoming President. I didn't have to be in a wheelchair, so there was hope. My "therapists" never let me forget that.

For all its goodwill, my support system did not seem adequate to help me scale the hurdles I faced on returning from my illness to the real world. The transition from the snug shelter of my Love Elementary School to the bigger, harder, faster track of Alexander Hamilton Junior High was forbidding. The new place towered like my personal red-brick Alamo at the foot of the neighborhood's main drag: Heights Boulevard. It stood for a far more impersonal, urban schooling than I was used to. In the best of circumstances, it would have been an intimidating change. Given my inhibitions, I found it very frightening.

I had three months of that summer to go before the onset of the ordeal when my father turned to Jeff Stramler, the father of my friend Charlie, who had died of leukemia. Mr. Stramler was our neighborhood's most successful entrepreneur, having gone independent in his own surveying business. My father knew that the turnover in the survey crews tended to run high, so the chances of an opening for his sickly son were pretty good, especially in the appalling heat of midsummer.

The timing was also fortunate because of regional economics. The oil industry was still expanding lustily. New pipelines kept snaking through the countryside and Jeff Stramler had just bagged a hefty contract to survey the site for another projected extension of the system. The new line was to run more than three hundred miles northeast from Refugio, at the Gulf near Corpus Christi, and eventually north toward Nacogdoches, in the piney-woods country near the Louisiana border, a goodly stretch even as Texans measure mileage.

Before the surveyors could set up their instruments and start taking measurements, they needed a line of sight and markers through the thick forests and overgrown swamps. That's where I was to come in, me and others in a crew of brush cutters.

I didn't know what I was in for, which didn't change much with Mr. Stramler's briefing, though he didn't try to prettify conditions. He took only a few minutes and he wasn't a bossy-looking boss. He was smallish, a bit beefy, and not given to making speeches. He did once play football somewhere, which impressed me, and my father considered him a fairly wise bird, hardened in a rugged business.

Mr. Stramler sized up my situation quickly and proceeded to inject some oral booster shots into my wobbly self. Leading me to the draftsman's table in his cluttered little office, he said that he wanted me to understand that brush cutting was hard work. I'd be with people stronger and much older than myself. (I'd said I was sixteen, but everybody knew very well that I was fourteen.)

"You can go farther than you think and work through this," Mr. Stramler said. "Don't kill yourself. Just keep going."

The main thing, he lectured, was not to get discouraged.

"Yessir," I said, having learned that there were times when it was best not to ask a lot of questions.

I had been eyeing the masses of large maps littering my new boss's office and I was intrigued. These intricate maps were something new to me, and I'd always been a sucker for anything new.

I never had another opportunity to get near the draftsman's table.

I also had a liking for the familiarity of accustomed surroundings, but that summer it didn't help that I was at home around my crew's start-up locations. I knew that my parents had once lived in dignified old Refugio, where Franciscan monks had run a mission to convert the cannibalistic Karankawa Indians. I remembered that Mother and Father had met at Victoria, the railhead a short way up U.S. Route 59, a respectably sized town of 7,400, some of whom lived in stately old-world mansions and looked upon oil as a smelly nuisance.

Our family had traveled the area often on our way to nearby Bloomington, my grandma Page's home grounds, but never mind all those family associations. This was my summer of communing with the true working life and with nature in the raw. It was my first time away from home and it was the making of me. I knew that even then.

We started before sunup to take advantage of the cool coming off the dew still on the ground, and normally we whacked at the brush for ten hours, six days a week. During those first subtropical workdays I often thought I'd faint. I never did. I wasn't going to embarrass Mr. Stramler or my father, that vocal crusader against all quitters.

Texas-sized mosquitoes—the ones big enough to mate with turkeys—were always with us and we dressed accordingly. I must have been hard to recognize. The top of my khaki work shirt was always buttoned, the collar always up all the way around. A red bandanna covered my neck and ears under a railroad man's visor cap. The sheath of my machete, around three feet in length, dangled off my belt. I'm not sure why we had to drag it along because my machete was swinging all day. We also carried five axes and two long brush hooks with curved blades for the entire crew.

Ah, what a crew! There were around a dozen of us, led by a crew chief, known as "the transit man." Assisted by another pro, "the road man," the chief was the project's absolute dictator. His total powers were indispensable because the flotsam under his command did not easily bend to authority. The men were muscle-bound types in their twenties, thirties, and early forties, and turnover was so high because some of them drifted into this line of work, and out of it, about as easily as most people change socks.

The pay averaged under fifty cents an hour, plus a daily living allowance of $1.50, and for that kind of money Mr. Stramler pulled in mostly mavericks, misfits, drunks, and dodgers on the lam from their wives, the draft, the cops, or simply from the world being too much with them. Since I was graduating to this foreign legion from the humdrum milieu of the Heights Annex, I found my co-workers educational.

Liquids were everyone's primary concern. Each man

Above: Dan's father, Irvin ("Rags") Rather, with his employer's truck in front of the family's Wharton, Texas, "shotgun" house, 1931, the year Dan was born. *Left:* Dan's mother, Byrl, with baby Dan in front of Wharton "shotgun" house. *Below:* The Rather home, 1432 Prince Street, the Heights Annex, Houston. Car in garage is the infirm 1938 Oldsmobile, source of much family lore.

Oil pipeliner gang: home team for Dan's father and, for a couple of summers, to Danny. That's the boss with derby-style hat at left front.

Dan's maternal grandfather, Mark Page, of Bloomington, Texas: tenant farmer, part-time blacksmith, and lay veterinarian. Note outstanding Rather family ears.

Dan's mother, Veda Byrl Page Rather, at about fifteen.

Dan's mother. The fancy convertible is probably from a touring exhibit in Victoria, Texas.

Clockwise from bottom left: The surprisingly grand Heights branch library on Heights Boulevard: a crucial opening onto Dan's world beyond "the ditch." / The Heights Theater: on Saturday afternoon, two and a half hours of dreams for a nickel. / The neighborhood: Buffalo Bayou, site of Dan's Great Turtle Hunt and other Tom Sawyer–style adventures. / Aftermath of Dan's long bout with rheumatic fever: feeling low at thirteen, shortly after getting out of bed for second attempt at convalescence.

Right: Dan, the happy schoolboy.
Below: The third-grade gang at
William G. Love Elementary School.
That's Dan at rear center (striped
tie). Pal Homer Bredehoeft is at
front, center (no suspenders).
Charlie Stramler, who died tragically
of leukemia, is at extreme left front.

Combination birthday/Halloween party at Rather home, 1940. That's Homer Bredehoeft at left rear. Pal Georgie Hoyt is at right rear.

Dan, aged eleven, with sister, Pat, and brother, Don, in front of window that provided his only view of the world from sickbed during his months bedfast with rheumatic fever.

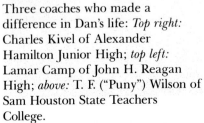

Three coaches who made a difference in Dan's life: *Top right:* Charles Kivel of Alexander Hamilton Junior High; *top left:* Lamar Camp of John H. Reagan High; *above:* T. F. ("Puny") Wilson of Sam Houston State Teachers College.

Dan moving up to the "A" team, Reagan High School, 1949. Note nickname "Rags" on helmet.

Dan at seventeen: off to Reagan
High School dance.

Dan at twenty-two: he managed to
serve briefly as a Marine Corps
private until it was discovered that
he had neglected to mention his
childhood rheumatic fever.

consumed an average of a quart of drinking water every hour. As the youngest, it was my job to lug four slabs of ice from the icehouse first thing in the morning. Three chunks would go into our portable tank, the fourth was wrapped in a burlap sack and tied to our truck.

I was proud of this assignment even though it didn't do much good. By 9:00 A.M. all remnants of ice had vanished, and it was close to the time of flameout for our heaviest drinkers of beer, bourbon, and other alcoholic beverages. One of these—I can't recall his name—became a special friend of mine and I watched his struggles with the demon rum closely. It was a terrible spectacle.

After drinking and then retching through much of the night, my friend reported for work equipped with his own antihangover rocket fuel: a supply of a headache powder called "Stanback." I tried it once; it was bitter, gritty stuff, simply dreadful.

My friend was magically transformed by it. He emptied a packet or two into a bottle of Coke and—whoosh!—he turned into packaged energy, like Popeye the Sailor after consuming a can of spinach. Now he was a cutting fool, thrashing his way through the brush like a combine.

It was an amazing performance that didn't last long. By nine-thirty or ten, having more or less appeased his hangover, my pal, in need of reinforcements, pulled out his popcorn box containing a pint or half-pint bottle of liquor.

"The trick is to reach a plateau and hold it," he told me, but I soon figured out that such a state of permanently pleasant wooziness was an impossible dream, as elusive as the unfulfilled visions of life that caused the pain that made him drink.

Nights were worst. I knew this because he had become my mentor and roommate. I did need protection. I had a tormentor, a Canadian of about twenty-five, one of the better-educated members of the gang, who has remained a familiar villain in the museum of my mind. In a random but inflammable moment, I annoyed this fellow at dinner in one of the dingy boardinghouses where we stayed along the route of our march because the weekly rates were cheap and included family-style meals.

My sole alleged offense was jabbing my fork straight down into my meat, as we did it in the Heights Annex, rather than applying it more daintily sideways. No doubt I was guilty of other crimes and misdemeanors in the Canadian's eyes, though these were never articulated before or after we clashed.

"Please pass the beans," I said, as was also customary in the Heights Annex.

Whereupon the Canadian poured a pot full of very hot beans on my crotch.

I yelled out, rose, and flared. My friend, the alcoholic, stepped in.

"Leave the kid alone," he snarled, which ended the incident and began our partnership.

I especially remember the pain I witnessed during the three weeks we roomed together in the squat, two-story, stone and wood Ott Hotel. It graced the railroad tracks at Liberty, and the whole place quivered like a pudding whenever a train chugged past. The rates were excellent, however, and the Ott was downright respectable, which I didn't find out until years later. Mr. Stramler felt protective about our morals and this was why he never let us stay in a place that stationed a "bellhop" out front under a shade tree after dark. During my summer of brush cutting I wasn't told that this was a code signal. It meant that the hotel offered "in-residence ladies."

How my poor partner suffered through the steamy nights at the Ott Hotel! The heaves, the sweats, the vomiting, and the cursing could hardly be borne even after I stuffed a pillow over my head.

That was the season I started smoking cigars to look more adult (I still smoke one as a special treat now and then).

On the credit side, this was also the summer I came away absolutely determined I'd never be a drunk.

In Liberty I met up with my "Liberty Belle," a wonderful, wonderful older woman. She was perhaps nineteen, a waitress, far more beautiful and personable than any of the "honky-tonk angels," the bar girls I'd been watching in hazy saloons with my colleagues, night after night, week after week. I wish I could report on a roaring romance with my lady from Liberty. I'd be lying. The most I did was order refills of iced tea just so I could watch her walk and see her smile as she poured. The truth is that I can't remember ever uttering a full sentence in her exciting presence, just "Yes, ma'am" and "No, ma'am." I didn't say much more to the bar girls either. My hormones were more than willing, but I didn't know what to say or do about that.

I was extremely curious, however, and was an insatiable mouse in the woodwork, lurking to eavesdrop on real men operating around real women, unrestrained by wives or preachers. It was interesting, all right, but the scene shouldn't be confused with the proceedings at a New York singles bar. We brush cutters were a weary, unbathed, unshaved, impecunious mob. Most of my colleagues didn't seem interested in more than a beer and a little heavy-handed joshing. Maybe I was naive and not as watchful as I thought, but I spotted few signs of what we nowadays call "action."

As I got geared up, beginning to pull my full weight as a member of the crew, the summer became a splendid time. My confidence and coordination were coming back. My fear of relapses receded. I was too busy or too exhausted to have much time for worrying. I was Paul Bunyan. I was on my own . . . I was free. When the brush cutting got monotonous, as it often did, my fantasies would take over in my mind, and I daydreamed a lot about, would you believe, Texas.

It was the romantic in me, a powerful pull since childhood. Grandma Page and my uncles had filled me with lore about those people-eating Karankawa Indians, and here I was taming the jungle where they had rampaged! Swinging my machete, I thought I heard the feet of their ghosts. My thoughts kept wandering. I knew the spot east of no place where, according to legend, the entire tribe was supposed to have been wiped out by the crush of one tidal wave.

The scene pounded through my head like a full-color movie sequence. I could *see* the Indians—allegedly, the Karankawa men were very tall, the women very short. They were spearfishing in the bay from long dugout canoes they had fashioned of crude tree trunks when the roar of the irresistible waters blew them up. To me, that didn't happen in 1780, as legend suggests. It was happening right now and I was there!

Turning our brush cutting north from Liberty toward Louisiana, the scene became less familiar but no less exciting. We were working through an area of about two million impenetrable acres aptly known as the Big Thicket. Although it was dotted with some bayous, this was mostly dry, rich soil, with only an occasional swamp. But talk about a thicket! Vines, creepers, ferns up to six feet, and palmettos up to ten feet tall had traditionally kept out everybody except Civil War service dodgers. We heard about bears and panthers and seven varieties of orchids and kept on extra alert for the snakes.

Here we faced more than the usual copperheads, cottonmouth (water moccasins), and ordinary rattlers. We had been used to those species all summer and killed around a dozen or so every day with our brush hooks. In the Big Thicket we had the company of the larger, more dangerous timber rattlers as well as the coral snakes, which we feared most because they made no noise whatever and their venom was the most toxic.

Some days along this stretch I waded chest deep in swamp water, spotting alligators and watching snakes make furrows nearby. Sometimes the cover shed by trees and brush grew so heavy that we worked in the dark at noon. A great sense of wonder, not fear, was my reaction.

I was the point man out in front one afternoon that did get scary. I was clearing small stuff for the others when I jumped back terrified. I'd come almost face-to-face with something about twelve feet long. I'd never come across anything like it. I first thought it was an animal, then it was clear that this was a snake, now wrapping itself around a tree.

I ran back, jabbering. The others came up and watched the giant in amazement. Circling its tree, we whacked the thing dead with our machetes. The attack gave me a thrill but then sadness set in. It struck me that we had wiped out something majestic. My romanticism was at work again.

We quit early that day, tied the snake to the hood of the truck, and drove to Nacogdoches to see the game warden, expecting to be hailed as heroes.

Instead, the man became abusive, calling us idiots and worse. He had gone to considerable trouble to import our catch, a black indigo snake and set it free so it would eat other snakes. The thing wasn't even poisonous.

So ended the summer when tigers turned into pussy-cats. I had passed through my puberty rites and felt steeled to meet anything that my Alamo, Alexander Hamilton Junior High, might hurl at me.

I didn't mind at all when my father reminded me after supper that it was time to march myself over to Jeff Stramler to thank him.

"Yessir," I said.

At the Stramlers I was offered milk and cookies and a lot of friendly silence on the back porch.

"Had a good summer?" asked Mr. Stramler as we listened to the tree frogs.

"Yessir," I said. "Thank you."

14

The World According to Uncle Dave, Uncle Corbin, and Other Role Models

IF SOMEONE had told me when I was a boy that my favorite uncles were failures in life, I would have hooted incredulously. The notion would have struck me as absurd and unjust. I thought they were a fabulous lot, and I still do. I learned a lot from all of them.

I mentioned Uncle John and his tenacious struggle against joblessness. He should have been called Uncle Job. The man was irrepressible and should have gotten a medal just for his courage in overcoming rejection. For someone with almost no education, he was also a stimulating intellect. He read up on matters and argued his views persuasively. Since he lived near us in the Heights Annex and was very close to his brother, my father, I spent a lot of evenings listening to him plead the case against America's early entry into World War II and a third term for President Roosevelt. I could see why it wasn't easy to disagree with Uncle John for long.

Down in Bloomington, my mother's brother, Dave,

flourished as a more elemental extrovert. Over six feet tall, handsome though never married, Uncle Dave possessed the shoulders of a boxcar, the waist of a wasp, and the brawn of a Paul Bunyan. He needed all his muscle because it was his job to wield a huge sledgehammer and pound cross ties into unending railroad beds outside of town. The job was semi-regular and Uncle Dave cherished it.

I remember bringing him his lunch in a paper bag and marveling at him and his fellow railroad men at work. They were huge figures who did their heavy labor stripped to the waist and loaded with enthusiasm, forever kibitzing and smiling. Or so I chose to remember. All this was the Bloomington version of a boy's excitement.

Although their work was repetitive, Uncle Dave and his pals never seemed bored. They sledgehammered away as they sang or hummed, with subgroups rhythmically picking up individual lines from answer songs:

> "T is for Texas," somebody started up,
> "And T for Tennessee," was the answer.
> "And T is for Thelma" came next,
> "That girl made a wreck out of me!"

Uncle Dave was one of the world's gifted storytellers. He specialized in Indian tales. I remember his version of the last Indian raid on Bloomington, how wives and kids were whisked away to safety, rescued from under the trapdoors of their cabin floors, all at the very last possible moment. He also told several versions of the story of little Jane Parker. In one of the accounts he told of how the unfortunate young woman's parents were scalped right in front of her, while my eyes grew to nearly the size of plates. The Parker girl was raised by the Indians but was ultimately retrieved under circumstances that varied according to how Uncle Dave chose to tell the story.

Uncle Dave walked with a slight limp. He said he had once been a bronco buster and had been thrown by a particularly vicious horse. That mishap had been a rare event. Usually, so Uncle Dave told it, he was able to bring a horse to reason by looking it straight in the eye. Staring it down, as it were. As the years rolled by doubts crept into my mind about just how extensive Uncle Dave's experience as a broncobuster actually had been. But to this I will attest: he had the soul and the spirit. And he had the limp.

For a couple of years during World War II Uncle Dave came to live with us in the Heights Annex. While we really had no room to spare, there was never the slightest question that my parents would take him in.

Uncle Dave had high ambition as an artist. He drew cartoons and had visions of himself as a social commentator, something of an early Garry Trudeau. It was not to be. The best job he could get was to run false teeth from the manufacturer's laboratory to its dentist clients. When the work became too boring, he retreated in dignity back home to Bloomington.

If Uncle Dave did not reach his aspired heights, could he be called a failure? Never. I know professional entertainers who are a whole lot less fun. And maybe he *had* really been a bronco buster. My brother, Don, and I liked to think so, and after Uncle Dave's death we conducted a wake for him at which we sang a song he'd taught us—

I am an old cowpuncher, tho' here I'm dressed in rags.
I used to be a good one and go on great long jags.
But I have a mother, boys, a good one know you all,
And I'm going home to see her when the work's all done this fall.

Go with God, Uncle Dave.

The star performer in my spirited cast of uncles was Uncle Corbin Bandy, married to my aunt June in Victoria (she was the aunt who came to stay with us on Prince Street to help out when I was down with rheumatic fever). Uncle Corbin would have ranked as a wild success by most standards anywhere. My family considered him plain wild. We all loved him a lot.

Uncle Corbin had a steady job working *on* trains, not on the tracks, and he had his conventional side. He was what is now called "upwardly mobile," starting his career on the Southern Pacific as a fireman's mate for the steam engines and winning promotion, over the years, to become a fireman and finally an engineer. This was highly coveted work, truly a big deal.

Uncle Corbin worked mostly on trains running through the rough country between San Antonio and El Paso, and each trip seemed a venture with Christopher Columbus overtones, especially to a kid full of romantic fantasies. Like me. Merely to look at Uncle Corbin could cast a spell. I remember that we were visiting in Victoria when he came home literally (and completely) blackfaced. Soot also covered his forearms. He'd been shoveling coal into the engine, but to me he was King Arthur returning victorious from a crusade with the Knights of the Round Table.

Some of Uncle Corbin's perilous contingencies might have befallen any engineer. Like the time he brought a long freight train to a screeching halt just inches from a school bus that had stalled on the tracks. It was loaded with Mexican-American kids. Other exploits were the product of his own enterprise.

Uncle Corbin loved to race his trains against cowboys on horseback and sometimes he needed no excuse whatever to "let 'er ride wide open, the whistle wide and the throttle back." Once or twice he got himself suspended for that, but never for long because the railroad appreciated him as a sound guardian of trains.

Coming from San Antonio, he once ran a heavy freight completely *through* a gasoline tank truck. It had stalled straddling a crossing and Uncle Corbin knew he couldn't stop in time. What a scene that must have been! The truck exploded and burst into flames as Uncle Corbin hit it at full speed. He never touched the brake, just kept going, never stopping until the last of his cars and caboose were clear of the fireball at the crossing.

It was the safest thing to do, so he told me as I took in his account, bug-eyed with excitement, practically able to hear the train, whistle wide and throttle back. He had done right: Damage was minimal, the driver of the gas truck leapt from his cab miraculously uninjured, and there was no doubt that Uncle Corbin could tell one whale of a story.

Considering his love affair with high speed, he led a charmed life. This couldn't have been easy to bring off because back then, when hardly anybody owned a motorcycle, Uncle Corbin was master of a huge, powerful one that rushed him noisily to and from work and most everywhere else.

It had a sidecar, and sometimes my aunt June, who was blessedly hard of hearing, would ride in it alongside him. She was ambivalent about the cycle, terrified yet also stirred by the excitement of the thing. Her response to her dilemma was constantly to admonish her husband for heaven's sakes to "go slow." Slow for Uncle Corbin was maybe around fifty.

He was riding the motorcycle alone one late afternoon, coming home from work through a residential section, when an elderly woman in a Buick opened her car door fully, only to have it sheared clean off by my uncle on his motorcycle. The stories that the woman and Uncle Corbin told the police would be at variance. The lady said he had "come out of nowhere, like a bat out of hell." He said he was going so slow that he feared his motorcycle would tip over.

There was agreement, however, that my uncle was thrown high into the air, like a circus clown shot from a cannon. Tumbling ankles over head, he landed on the roof of a house and was hospitalized for a very long time. I visited him, finding him immovable, wrapped up in white like a mummy, yet still in his usual good humor.

"Danny, I had 'er wide open," he confided. The openings in his bandages were sufficient to let me see that he was smiling and winking.

The accident became family legend, but otherwise it didn't change much. Uncle Corbin went back to his trains and bought another motorcycle. Only Aunt June had second thoughts. To my knowledge, she never rode a cycle again. My uncle's ardor for speed never waned. Possibly he became a mite more circumspect with the new motorcycle. I wouldn't bet on it.

This happy uncle also nursed an infectious enthusiasm for train *songs*. He could belt them out rather audibly, fairly on-key and he kept going pretty well forever. His repertoire was encyclopedic, as was his memory for lyrics, and he found in me an appreciative audience.

I learned "The Wabash Cannonball," "Casey Jones," "The Wreck of the Old '97," "All Around the Watertank," "The Runaway Train," "The Saga of Number Nine," and many more. Other impressionable boys of my time were drilled in the Italian arias of Enrico Caruso. I was bathed in train songs by Uncle Corbin, and I confess I still remember all the words:

"Twas in the year of '89, on that old Chicago line, when the whittle wind was blowing shrill. The rails were cold. . . ."

And: "All around the water tank, waiting for a train, a thousand miles away from home, sleeping in the rain. . . ."

And: "Oh, they gave him his orders at Monroe, Virginia, saying 'Pete, she's away behind the dime. . . .' "

Yes, I can produce this wordage and much, much more straight from memory, and so can my son and daughter, now in their thirties. There can't be many adults, within Texas or out, who've had to listen to more train songs than they have. Uncle Corbin is long gone. He passed over the last trestle years ago. But if there is a Heaven or a Hell, or even a Purgatory, you can bet that Uncle Corbin, somewhere, somehow, is still running wide open with the throttle back.

In some respects, one of my most influential early role models was Glenn Sikes, known as "Glide." He was only three or four years older than I, and he really functioned as the older brother I never had. I was in awe of him.

Glenn was worldly, he was suave, he was loyal like a real brother. When I lay in bed, bored out of my teeth with my rheumatic fever, Glenn was one of my most steadfast and entertaining visitors. Everything he did seemed so stylish, so effortless. It was his smooth running style in football that had given him his nickname. Glenn would glide across the field like a skater! Tacklers would lunge at him but grasp only air. Glenn was so elusive that he seemed untouchable.

As the star of our neighborhood football team, Glenn also impressed us with his timing. Typically, we might be three touchdowns behind when Glenn would glide onto the field and win the game for us, seemingly without strain.

The Sikes family lived catercorner across the street from us, and I spent so much time with them, playing, chattering, and raiding the "icebox" (it was never called a refrigerator), that Glenn's parents treated me like an extra son. They were real people, believers in hard work like us. Indeed, Mr. Sikes worked much of the time. He may have been the most-employed man on Prince Street next to my father. Sometimes he was a guard, minding stores and plant gates around Nineteenth Avenue, for which he sometimes carried a .38 revolver in a holster. Glenn's mother was an earth-mother type who, I believe, sometimes got jobs as a waitress.

Glenn was my principal purveyor of sensitive information. He knew about sex and poker and the latest in music, but especially about sex. In my time, kids were expected to learn about the birds and the bees by way of osmosis, and so our little heads were heavy with misinformation. Glenn could set a person straight. I remember lurking in front of a mannequin at the window of a Sears store with Glenn lecturing on basic female anatomy. Later, using Sears and Montgomery Ward catalogs, he explained the workings of bras, girdles, and garters.

And not all of Glenn's tips were frivolous. "Bluff the gun, flee the knife," was one of the ground rules of life in my set when I grew a little older. Glenn was the source where I first heard this wisdom, and it wasn't academic. Knives (though never guns) showed up in my junior high school.

Blessed with the touch of an artist, Glenn fashioned exquisite model airplanes out of balsa wood and tried to teach this hobby to me. My planes looked as if I'd built them with a hatchet and rarely moved off the ground. Glenn could coax his handiwork airborne with a rubber band. It was of a piece with his general finesse.

Music enthralled Glenn. He was the first in the neighborhood to own records of the brand new boogie-woogie, the early equivalent of rock and roll. This was different, breakthrough stuff, the buzz of the neighborhood. We played the records very loudly hour after hour, and Glenn had a girl, a beautiful girl, who knew how to dance to this sophisticated stuff, to jitterbug to music by the Glenn Miller Band. It was heaven, though not for long.

• I'm unclear about the details, but Glenn married his girl and also quit school when he was fifteen, and his golden touch deserted him. He never had a real job, never made a go of his marriage. It was another jarring exposure to personal tragedy, although it didn't hit me that way at first because my friendship with Glenn grew even closer. He was increasingly protective of me. Sometimes I wondered whether my mentor was now living vicariously through my own modest successes.

"Stay in school," Glenn preached many times. "Don't make the mistake I did."

He drilled me in football endlessly, teaching me the

moves until I knew how to shake loose and catch my passes. When I made the first team during my senior year in high school (I played end) Glenn was about as proud as I was. We were issued new-style maroon-and-white helmets just before our first game that season, and Glenn painted R-A-G-S, my nickname, vertically on my helmet.

This nearly caused trouble. To the great Coach Camp, our Jefferson Stadium was the ancient Colosseum and his rules had the power of Roman law. I didn't know that Coach Camp had a rule against special markings on team gear. My friend and teammate Jack Kurtzman warned me when he saw my helmet. Too late. We were already in the locker room in the last hour before the game. Kurtzman got busy. Even then Jack could talk a cat out of a dairy when he set his mind to it. He took our old B Team coach, Leroy Ashmore, aside and explained to him. He said something about a "good luck" sign, something else about "family pride," and still something else about no one from the Heights Annex having ever before made the varsity on any Reagan High School team, ever. Ashmore interceded with Coach Camp. The Great Coach glared at me but said not a word. He left me in the starting lineup. I played well. We won. Coach Camp never said anything about the nickname on my helmet. Why I have never known.

Glenn told me he thought it was because Coach Camp, beneath his hard hide, was wise and understanding, that he knew much about methods of subtle motivation, and besides, was probably, like many veteran athletes, more than a bit superstitious.

I suppose I lacked the nerve to investigate the fate of Glenn (Glide) Sikes, my unofficial older brother. We lost touch. I heard only that he died when he was about twenty. The circumstances were evidently mysterious. At least I knew nobody who would tell me what happened.

I see Glenn as an American tragedy of the Great Depression. He happened to be too much, too soon—too soon a football hero, too soon married—and then he couldn't buy himself a break. He was a man/boy, not a boy/man, and had no way to support himself, much less a family. He began to argue with his own family, frustrations showing through. He moved in with his wife's people, and since they lived quite a distance away from me, over time we lost touch.

Glenn's fate saddened but didn't devastate me. Partly, I was too young to understand it. Then, too, I lived with my marvelous memories of him and see him even now as a potential successful insurance man or perhaps an artist. This I will tell you: I think of Glenn often. He is in the museum of my mind forever as another child of the Depression, one who after a certain point in his life always seemed, like my uncle John, to draw deuces instead of face cards.

There were many young men such as Glenn Sikes in the Heights and all over during the 1930s. Some of them wound up like Clyde Barrow, of the bank robbers Bonnie and Clyde. Others went on to win the war. Still others, like Glenn, faded into oblivion. Whatever the medical records may say, I'll always believe that he died of a broken heart.

All these mentors had certain qualities in common. Foremost were their sheer ebullience and the dignity that came to them so naturally. The figure I remember most fondly is Uncle Corbin, probably because he most closely fits my model of breaking away from the predictable and the conventional, the tedium of grinding in a rut. Uncle Corbin was my Christopher Columbus, all right. I've observed some of his qualities in myself, and sometimes I still see Uncle Corbin at my side.

"Hey, let's have a good time," he is saying. "Let's take a chance. If life is without risk, what kind of life is that? It's good to feel the wind in your face."

The wind in my face. I thought of that while I was reporting from Afghanistan, from Tiananmen Square, and from the deserts of Saudi Arabia, Kuwait, and Iraq. And I thought of Uncle Corbin when I was out there. He would have loved it, the sense of élan, of doing something exclusive, of not running with the pack, of breaking away from the herd. He had no bridle on him. A great feeling!

No, I never thought of my uncles or Glenn as failures, far from it. They had spirit. They were not afraid to take their shots, to go it alone, against the odds. In my young eyes, they stood larger than life. And as I saw them, they never quit, they never gave up.

15

My Texas 'Tis of Thee

AT FIRST nobody could believe it. It was a lazy Sunday, December 7, 1941, and suddenly in early afternoon the kitchen radio came alive with bizarre-sounding bulletins. Without warning, swarms of Japanese planes were said to be bombing a place we'd never heard of: Pearl Harbor on the island of Oahu in Hawaii. Why, that was part of America! Damage upon the Pacific fleet, almost all of it moored there, was said to be horrible. The harbor was described as a smoking mass of dive-bombers, explosions, fires, and bodies.

Later it developed that we in the hinterlands were not alone in being incredulous. Right on Oahu, one of our admirals watched an enemy plane dropping its first bomb and thought it was an American aircraft releasing its weapons accidentally. In Washington, Navy Secretary Frank Knox, receiving the word in his office, exclaimed, "My God, this can't be true!" He was not being naive. A delegation of Japanese diplomats was in the capital blandly conducting "peace" negotiations.

I was in bed that day with bad pains in my feet and lower joints, the early symptoms of my incipient rheumatic fever, and I was following events in a state of great excitement. Within minutes, the radio reports became sufficiently detailed so we could tell this was an authentic attack, not a spoof like the fictional 1938 Mars broadcast from the prankster Orson Welles. This was real. This would be war.

I was trying to visualize the horror in Hawaii, wave after wave of attackers from Japanese carriers; dogfights with our brave pilots, the few not caught on the ground; sailors firing antiaircraft guns from sinking ships inexcusably bunched up at anchor. As it turned out, my fantasies failed to measure up to the facts of that bloody Sunday. Nineteen naval vessels would be sunk or severely damaged, including eight battleships; 2,280 men would be killed, 188 aircraft destroyed.

Grim-faced neighbors filled our house. Discussion was agitated. Should the men go downtown to volunteer their services at the recruiting station that very afternoon? By about 3:30 P.M., my father, my uncle John, and about half a dozen others decided to do just that. After all, the Japanese had not merely attacked the United States. They had taken action against Texas. The menfolk considered it entirely likely that we, too, would shortly be subjected, somehow, to air raids.

This was not a surprising reaction to the horror at Pearl Harbor because Texans had for some time been taking the war more to heart than most other Americans. According to one gag, Congress had voted for the draft in 1940 mostly to get somebody into the army who was not from Texas. So many Texans had flocked north to enlist in Canada that there was talk there of "the Royal Canadian Texas Air Force." We were itching to fight. Soon signs went up saying, "Buy Bonds and Help Texas Win the War."

And win we would. Nobody doubted that; so when President Roosevelt went before Congress shortly after noon on Monday, December 8—his White House was already being measured for blackout curtains—he faced a country perhaps more united than ever.

"Remember Pearl Harbor!" (like "Remember the Alamo!") was a slogan that would never turn sour. Ours would be called the "Good War."

In an uncommonly steely voice the President told us: "Yesterday, December 7, 1941—a date which will live in infamy—the United States was suddenly and deliberately attacked. . . . No matter how long it may take us to overcome this premeditated invasion, the American people in their righteous might will win through to an absolute victory. . . ."

The ensuing applause lasted for a full minute. Nobody who heard these proceedings could ever forget them.

As the weeks and months went on, however, our optimism was shaken, if not our resolve. The war news was ugly. In the Atlantic, U-boats were sinking ship after ship. In Africa, the "Desert Fox," Field Marshal Erwin Rommel, devastated the British armies. In the Philippines, the death march of American prisoners from Bataan infuriated us against the brutality of the Japanese.

Increasingly, we suspected that the war would move closer to home. People talked of likely U-boat attacks upon our nearby coastlines. New Orleans was said to be endangered. My father and his friends talked of taking their guns to defend the Gulf coast. A lot of people trekked to Galveston in the irrational belief that the coast artillery batteries left over from World War I would become important targets. Rumors circulated about spies using Morse code to flash signals to Hitler's vessels from the Texas coast at night.

Sick as I was, I wanted to help. Anything involving aircraft and flying was as thrilling to kids as the space race is today, and a lot of aviation lore was buzzing around in my head, starting with Charles ("Lucky Lindy") Lindbergh crossing the Atlantic in 1927, four years before I was born. I knew about ocean crossings by zeppelins and the aerial exploits of that quintessentially illustrious Houstonian,

Howard Hughes (see Chapter 19). Furthermore, I was aware of the sad downside of air traffic. Dirigibles were being touted as the future of air travel; then we heard the radio broadcast the heart-stopping eyewitness accounts of the *Hindenburg* breaking up in flames on landing at Lakehurst, New Jersey, and we knew that the age of zeppelins had died that day.

I also helped to mourn the death of much-loved personalities: Amelia Earhart being reported lost over the Pacific, the grand sage and wit Will Rogers killed in a crash in Alaska.

While I never made it all the way out to the Houston airport—it was much too far—the flying bug was kept alive in the neighborhood by the amazing Mr. Bredehoeft, Homer's father, whose hobby it was to zoom through the sky on Sundays in a Ryan open-cockpit craft with a single radial engine.

My age and disability notwithstanding, I wanted to become a combat pilot right after Pearl Harbor and dreamed—like Danny Kaye playing Walter Mitty—of my turn at the stick of a P-40 fighter. Meanwhile, I learned to identify various aircraft models, enemy and friendly, from little silhouettes of their configurations. This identification game was actually serious business, inspired by the nation's civil defense campaign, with its warning systems, air-raid wardens, and big-city shelters.

As with all technological advances, Father was very much up to date. Together we had shuddered at movie newsreels of Stuka dive-bombers unleashing an early vision of "carpet bombing" on Poland, and we'd been moved by the incredibly young faces of the boy/men of the hour, Royal Air Force pilots who saved England in the Battle of Britain. Winston Churchill—how we loved that bulldog of a fighter with his V-for-victory sign, his cigar and bowler hat—had seemed to include us in Houston when he delivered his famous line: "Never in the field of human conflict was so much owed by so many to so few."

Once again, Father got himself expertly briefed. I remember him coming home with a fat bestseller, *Victory Through Air Power* by Alexander de Seversky. I don't know whether he read through it all, but he sure could talk knowledgeably about the importance of the air in war, then a dramatic novelty.

He also grew extremely sensitive to the bad word from the front. Like everybody else, we sat transfixed nightly before the radio, eager to be instructed by the commentator-oracles of the airwaves who seemed so all-knowing. But there came times when we were not anxious to hear the facts. One night, one of our authorities, the excitable Gabriel Heatter (ah, who remembers him now?), started off his newscast with the latest triumph of Marshal Rommel's *Afrika Korps*, and father lost his cool.

"The Desert Fox is fifteen miles from Cairo," Heatter began, breathing hard. Dad reacted to this new reverse in our fortunes by taking out his anxiety on the messenger. He picked up our radio and threw it at the wall. Mother shooed us kids out of the room.

She was very worried. She made a point of not crying in front of the children, but every time she emerged from her room with red eyes we knew what was going on. She was heartsick over the possibility that Father might join up. He had been unable to back up his surge of patriotic feelings on Pearl Harbor Sunday because the army recruiting place was closed. He reported there again some days later but the recruiting people did not encourage him. They took nobody with three children and a job in an essential industry. In 1942 he went again, this time hoping the navy would take him. Again he was turned away. Still, Mother found it hard to live with uncertainty. Like most women in the Heights, she turned more frequently and more prayerfully to the church.

Every milestone of the war found its own resonance on Prince Street. When our navy won the four-day Battle of Midway and destroyed three Japanese aircraft carriers, we were relieved to see Pearl Harbor at least partially avenged. The marine invasion of Guadalcanal Island left us depressed because of the fearful casualties; we cheered all the more when the place was finally mopped up after six months of battle. Our commander in the Pacific, Admiral Chester W. Nimitz, was a Texan, which added to our caring.

I was personally engrossed in the war's vicissitudes because I kept hawking the corresponding headlines when I sold my papers: "The *Bismark* Sunk!" "Hitler Invades Russia!" (I knew only very vaguely where Russia was), "British Stop Rommel!" "Stalingrad Holds!" On June 6, 1944, we were up before 5:00 A.M. to cheer the tiny drops of censored information about the Allied landings in Normandy.

From then it wasn't long before I could shout at my corner, "V-E Day!" and then "V-J Day!"

Along the way, I was envious when some of the older boys quit school to join the service and their families put up pennants with a star for each family member in uniform. We went to a lot of propaganda-by-Hollywood movies, such as "Wake Island" and "God Is My Co-Pilot" (which I saw several times). And we tried not to complain about the pretty severe rationing of gasoline, sugar, and meat.

"Don'tcha know there's a war on?" was our morale-reinforcement, and not even in the Persian Gulf War did the country pull together quite as closely as we did then. America *had* to be defended, and I did my part. I was an also-ran in the citywide contest to collect wastepaper and twice won the neighborhood prize for gathering up aluminum in the form of old pots and pans.

Aluminum was in short supply and I was duly decorated with a small campaign-style ribbon that came with a medal bearing General Dwight D. Eisenhower's picture. It was a prized possession and I still have it.

If the pains and gains of the war seemed to us to impact more on Texas than on the United States, our state's legendary self-image was hardly blameless. The Germans have a marvelous word for such chauvinism. They call it *Lokalpatriotismus*, or local patriotism, and in Texas this brand of "place-centeredness" looms as mammoth as, well, the very outsize of our dimensions.

I feel no need to dwell here on the relevant superstatistics or on the jokes about them: Texas being so big that people in Brownsville call the Dallas people Yankees . . . or our bragging that we have the spinach capital, the tomato capital, the honey capital, the rose capital, and so on and on. What was contagious about all this pride for small boys was the driving spirit behind it.

We didn't simply harbor these phenomena of giantism. Like the Russians, we *invented* everything! I was sixteen years old before I heard the lyrics, "I've been working on the railroad." I'd been taught that the correct words were, "The eyes of Texas are upon you."

And from my first day in Love Elementary School, I learned that the pride and the bigness and specialness of Texas are rooted in historical fact. It is the only state to enter the United States more or less on its own terms and of its own free will after nine years and 301 days as an independent republic, a nation, no less. That's what we became in 1836, a year of hallowed heroism, filled with deeds that were more painstakingly drummed into every schoolboy than any others.

First, on March 6, we suffered defeat at the old fortress in the heart of San Antonio, the Alamo. Before dawn, with bugles sounding the *Dequello* ("Death to the Defenders"), troops commanded by General Antonio López de Santa Anna, the despised president and dictator of Mexico, known as "the Napoleon of the west," assaulted all four walls. Twice they were repulsed. The third time they penetrated the north wall. Davy Crockett and his Tennessee Boys dropped to their deaths in hand-to-hand fighting at the chapel doors. Colonel James Bowie emptied his pistols and wielded his famous Bowie knife before he was killed. There were no male survivors. So much for Epic Number One.

Next, on April 21, a force of 783 Texans under General Sam Houston drove the Mexican legions into final defeat at the junction of Buffalo Bayou and the San Jacinto River, twenty-two miles southeast of the settlement that would become the city of Houston. The Mexicans were enjoying a siesta when Sam Houston and his men rode to the attack, crying, "Remember the Alamo!" Santa Anna, disguised as a peon, was captured. General Houston became president of our Republic. Thus ended Epic Number Two.

Rousing boyhood games (and memories) are made of such exploits, of course. We constructed our own Alamo, my best cronies Georgie Hoyt, Homer Bredehoeft, and I, and replayed the siege over and over. I took my favorite role, Jim Bowie. Using my father's sharpshooter shovels, we dug an enormous hole in a vacant lot of the neighborhood. It was hot as hell. We labored for several days, going deep enough so our heads did not peek out. We piled dirt high all around as emplacements; excavated a system of tunnels and trenches; and thought that the resulting fortifications looked magnificent and adult. With our rubber guns we fought Santa Anna until hell wouldn't have it.

Mother came to inspect us when word spread in the neighborhood. She seemed amazed and praised us, but I could tell that she was also worried. She thought the tunnels might cave in and wanted Father to look our project over before it got dark. He was the ideal consultant, a practitioner who knew quality digging. So Father came. He likewise complimented us and advised Mother that our Alamo was "probably" safe. That wasn't good enough for Mother. She wanted the "Alamo" closed down. Father felt for us. He didn't want us to have to ruin all our work. Its fate hung in the balance. Finally a compromise: We agreed to fill in the tunnels and still had a pretty good time storming about in the rest of the fort.

The battle of San Jacinto required no work on our part. My school organized a bus trip to the site of what the teacher called one of the ten most decisive battles in the world. We were shown the tree under which the wounded Santa Anna was allegedly found, an assertion that I considered dubious even at the age of ten. The battleground monument of Texas limestone is undeniably stunning, however. Jesse Jones, our superrich "Mr. Houston," arranged to have it put up at a height of 570 feet, fifteen feet higher than the Washington Monument.

That was no coincidence. Jones, a Texas advocate with enough money to back up his loyalties, consciously wanted an edifice at least equal to anything offered by the federal government, and our schools encouraged such competition. We never thought much of the prewar "America First" isolationist movement. Our affections were devoted to "Texas First," and no formal organization was needed to boost this philosophy.

At Love Elementary School, the Texas flag fluttered next to Old Glory, but the state song, "Texas, Our Texas," with its hard-to-carry tune, was what we sang most frequently. On March 2, Texas Independence Day, there was no school and Father did not go to work. April 21, San Jacinto Day, was another major holiday. A year of Texas history was required to graduate from high school; world history was not mandatory.

I may have showed unusual enthusiasm for walking with the ghosts of my heroes. I admired Sam Houston, in particular, and studied lesser-known periods of his life that preceded his victory at San Jacinto as well as events that followed his glory days as president of our Texas Republic.

By the time Houston settled in Nacogdoches, Texas, at the age of thirty-nine, he had already lived a lifetime of patriotic accomplishment. He was a veteran of Andrew Jackson's Indian wars and had been governor of Tennessee and a congressman. In Washington he had commanded national attention for his brilliance and for the gaudy Indian blankets he wore, having been adopted by the Cherokees in his youth.

I was most strongly taken by the occasion in the cotton-controlled Texas legislature of 1860 when Sam Houston made the best speech of all his life. He was standing up for a lost cause and he knew it. He argued for the Union, against secession. The legislators rebuked him and kicked the father of Texas out of his own house. He got on his horse and rode away, never to return. The first night he slept within a few yards of where my wife, Jean, was born. Not much later he died.

Schoolchildren are not told about these great scenes of my hero, beaten because he spoke for what he considered right. I think they should be told; such occasions bespeak character and dignity. I've made it my business to remember the general at every opportunity and I'm proud that, according to my college yearbook, my school friends remembered me as "Mr. Sam Houston," although an element of sarcasm was probably involved. I bet I burbled on about my idol until everybody got bored.

Incidentally, I'm not the sole admirer of Sam Houston's failed Last Stand. John F. Kennedy wrote a long chapter about my hero and his gumption in that classic celebration of gumption, the 1956 book *Profiles in Courage*.

Character and dignity were not the stuff of another boyhood interest of mine, this one a contemporary public figure who became the greatest vote-getter in Texas history and perhaps our most notorious buffoon. While we did not love him in his later roles as governor and senator, W. (for Wilbert) Lee O'Daniel figured in our lives in the mid and late 1930s as "Please Pass the Biscuits, Pappy" O'Daniel, bringing us joy via the radio as the impresario of a country-and-western band, the Light Crust Doughboys.

Pappy sold flour. He sold it with pungent words and soft music for fifteen minutes daily, beginning at 12:30 P.M.

Not so incidentally, he also sold himself. It was the most popular entertainment in Texas.

And how Pappy huckstered Texas! His gig started up daily with a typical theme song of his own composition. It was the quintessential Pappy:

> Beautiful, beautiful Texas,
> Land where the bluebonnets grow.
> We're proud of our forefathers,
> Who died at the Alamo.

Next to flour and Texas, Pappy claimed to worship motherhood. Since mothers were his principal midday audience, much of his music was addressed to them: "Marvelous Mother of Mine," for example, and "The Boy Who Never Grew Too Old to Comb His Mother's Hair." Robert A. Caro, biographer of Lyndon Johnson,* became all but mesmerized by the Pappy phenomenon and recorded the opening of one program:

"Hello there, Mother, you little sweetheart. How in the world are you, anyway, you little bunch of sweetness? This is your big boy, W. Lee O'Daniel. . . ."

It's a sign of those gullible times, and of my beloved Texas then, that folks who listened to this phony mush did not spit up their meals. Their support encouraged Pappy to quit his job and establish his own Hillbilly Flour operation. It simply bought flour from other mills and packaged it in sacks marked in red, "Please Pass the Biscuits, Pappy."

The point of Pappy's efforts—and he was a carpetbagger from Kansas who had never paid his poll tax—emerged during his show on Palm Sunday of 1938. He asked his audience whether he should make a run for governor. He said that a blind man had asked him to do it. Listeners should tell him what to do. They did—54,446 telling him to

---

* Pappy appeared in Caro's history because in 1941 he beat Johnson for the Senate, by 1,311 votes out of nearly 350,000.

go ahead. As he reported the results, three said he shouldn't. They told him he was too good a man for politics.

Pappy was the twenty-ninth candidate to enter. No political observer took him seriously. If they had asked around in the Heights, they would have been able to predict the outpouring of affection when Pappy turned his attention from flour to votes.

To begin with, there was the golden appeal of Pappy's voice. In our kitchen, we just loved how he sounded: "It was a voice you could trust," Robert Caro would write. And we trusted it for a time because it wasn't merely Texas. Pappy talked "Fortworth" (we pronounced it as one word), not eastern-looking Dallas. He said, "hoss," not "horse." To me, he conveyed country-style body language even though we couldn't see his body over the radio.

Pappy left me with an echo of my family and its land, of the grandfathers whom my parents had also called "Pappy." We would never laugh at him because he was different. Eccentrics tend to be appreciated among the nonconformists of Texas, as they are in Britain. Perhaps Pappy's most valuable asset was that you could never have exposed him to New York. There, he would have made the locals just snicker.

Pappy's music was another seductive come-on for us. Whenever he ventured beyond his stickiest sentimentalism, he helped to pioneer a new art form we called western swing. That was the invention of yet another beau ideal of mine, the Mozart of western, Bob Wills. Wills started with the Light Crust Doughboys. O'Daniel fired him in 1933, but Pappy continued swinging.

It was an upbeat sound, a lot happier than the sadness of "The Yellow Rose of Texas" and other wails that we had become accustomed to. Cheeriness was a lot of what Pappy was about. He injected a precious commodity, optimism, into awful times. Even we knew that his humor was as corny as wit could get; still it was worth a chuckle when chuckles were scarce goods.

Pappy's cheeriness got to us and he brought us "togetherness"—a nonword not then yet invented by the advertising industry. Pappy's fifteen radio minutes were precious in our house, especially on weekends and on such weekdays as Father's work brought him close enough so he could get home for lunch. Pappy made Mother and Father smile and feel at home. They'd hum along and tap their feet. He carved a worry-free quarter hour out of their day, not a small talent.

Pappy was a shameful opportunist, no question, but perhaps I've made him sound out of touch with what we liked to call the "new Texas." He wasn't. He sensed that the Great Depression was ending, that the growth of the petrochemical and shipping industries would eventually cause our state to prosper, that the New Deal (and eventually the war) would propel us out of our relative backwardness and isolation.

My parents, in turn, picked up on Pappy's optimism and shared it to some degree, although initially theirs was mostly wishful thinking. If Pappy O'Daniel was the beseeching voice of the new Texas, his crystal ball was less murky than that of other leaders. The ancient cliché applies: Everything is relative, including foresight.

Even before Pappy moved into the governor's chair, however, his madcap finance schemes made him the Don Quixote of Texas politics, at least in our eyes. A little sadly, we figured that we'd lost an entertaining radio performer and gained another fool in Austin, the state capital, and later in the U.S. Senate.* My parents wrote him off their radar, and such banishment was irrevocable. They meted out the same treatment to Charles Lindbergh when, early in the war, the Texas legislature passed a resolution denouncing his isolationist views.

To me, these were demonstrations documenting the

---

* It was said that the Texas Establishment shoveled money into Pappy's Senate race just to get him out of the state.

brittleness of pedestals. By the time I had passed halfway through junior high school, I realized that some of my heroes were not flawless and that our teachers might have overrated the impact of the triumph at San Jacinto upon the course of history.

My liberation from the jingoism of the Lone Star state eventually extended all the way to my taste buds. I consider this a notable accomplishment because, like all boys I've ever heard of, I believed my mother was a great cook. On the other hand, her skills were limited to normal Texas kitchen practices, which is to say that they had their bounds.

I recognize that I'm venturing into controversial territory. Texas cooking, like Texas everything, never lacked strong-minded defenders. As far as I know they're all from within our state. Even a sturdy Texas loyalist like Stanley Walker attacked our cooking as a "gastronomic wasteland," and he knew both sides of the skillet. Walker hailed from Lampasas, Texas, and found good fortune in New York. Having made himself a legend as city editor of the old *New York Herald Tribune*, he came back to retire and wrote a delightful book, *Home to Texas*, containing his kitchen indictments.

Texans fry too much, Walker charged. "Their baked goods are heavy, doughy, and indigestible. . . . They are not venturesome and fear all deviations from the ordinary. . . . Their steaks . . . are cut thin and cooked to a crisp or 'chicken fried' in a white batter. . . ."

Walker was venting his spleen way back in 1956, and I've been back to Texas often enough to know that our cooking has grown up quite a bit since that time, like the rest of us. I must admit, though, that thin-cut chicken-fried steak, *very* well done, seared in the skillet, with cream gravy, was my parents' favorite dish, as it was mine when I was small, and I still relish it.

I still drown many of my main dishes in A-1 or barbecue sauce or, best of all, Tabasco. Tabasco sauce ranks with me as a near-magical potion, and so I carry both the red and the green varieties with me when I travel. Just in case. In many ways Tabasco spells home to me. It functions almost like a talisman; I carried a supply with me to Vietnam, when I served as a reporter there, and to the Persian Gulf.

While Mother was probably guilty of all the sins cited by Walker, and then some, I categorically deny that she shunned variety. She fixed wonderfully digestible buttermilk biscuits and served them often for breakfast. She used several delicious techniques for cooking venison, and she made deer-meat sausage, which is more than one can get in New York these days. Her catfish deep-fried in cornmeal batter was a delight, and so was my favorite dessert, "Poor Man's Pie"—bread pudding in pie crust.*

Chili, naturally, was our mainstay, our staff of life, as multifarious as Texas itself. I loved it and still do, especially the way my wife, Jean, fixes it poured over salad. Father liked it with venison, which was in a class by itself. Another gourmet version featured barbecued cabrito, or goat meat. The proportion of pinto beans or tomatoes would regulate the optimal taste for some people, but I preferred my chili hyped to the last measure of hotness by Mexican "jalapeño beans" (the peppers mixed with pinto beans). I guess you could call that "five-alarm-plus," one to four being the spiciness index for wimps.

Mother could fix chili in maybe twenty ways, some of which might even have impressed Stanley Walker. We tended to have it more frequently toward the end of the month,

---

* Here is how she made it:

4 eggs	2½ cups milk
½ cup sugar	1 teaspoon vanilla
½ teaspoon salt	1 to 2 slices of bread (the staler the better)

Beat the eggs slightly. Stir in sugar and salt. Add milk and vanilla. Stir it all up. Break the bread into pieces and add it to the mixture. Stir it slightly and add lots of cinnamon on top. Bake in a pie crust at 375–400° F for 30 to 35 minutes or until set.

when the money dried up. If Mother was away or not feeling well, we'd heat up chili for a mighty long time.

Considering her budget, Mother deserved field marshal's rank for her economy skirmishes at the stove. Baked potato filled with butter and cheese and accompanied by snap (or green) beans was one of her low-cost vegetarian dinners, and we all liked her homemade vegetable soup (with no ingredients from cans!), which she served as a complete meal with lots of corn bread to help fill us up. I wish she'd had a chance to show Stanley Walker a slice or two of her kitchen art!

Having done my best to protect the Rather family honor, I concede that I no longer live on Texas recipes alone. Indeed, I've come to consider myself an adventurous eater. In the course of my duties as a correspondent abroad, I've feasted on goat eyes in Laos and pickled webbed duck feet in China. In the Gulf War I learned to respect bedouin coffee, strong enough to float horseshoes in; and Saudi "champagne," which is sparkling water and fruit juice, period.

I've learned that it's practical and survivable to eat and drink off the land; that is: anything that everybody around you happens to be consuming. I'm not a gourmet, certainly, and I do consider myself easy to please.

And yet, and yet . . . Texas is never far from my palate. Perhaps two or three times a month, like an addict, I crave down-home cuisine. Jean and I will enjoy chicken-fried steak or chili at Juanita's, our favorite Tex-Mex restaurant in New York, or Jean fixes that "Mexican Salad" for which she is famous among our friends: lettuce and tomato covered with crushed Fritos and chili poured over the whole thing. Did I say Fritos? Yes. So sue me! I happen to take a strong position on Fritos. They are one of the most civilized inventions Texas has produced.

Perspective matters. I've not forgotten that I haven't lived in Texas full-time since 1962. Almost thirty years; it seems unbelievable. Where have they all gone? Why so quickly? Why do we all have to run faster and faster only to stay pretty much in the same place?

The answers are quite beyond me. I do know that in my craft I couldn't possibly be further away from Grandma Page and Saturday afternoons at the Heights Theater. The recollections remind me of where I come from, and that makes me feel good, even though they also tell me that I'm no straight arrow. Nothing personal, but I doubt that even the noble Gene Autry himself ever was one. Still, better to have a cowboy creed on the wall than to survive on West Fifty-seventh Street with no creed at all.

16

Digging Out of the Ditch— Father's Story

MY FATHER spent much of his life in the ditch, but he spent the rest of the time in an unending struggle to climb out. Memories of my childhood and adolescence are crowded with images of Father bent over his books and papers, studying, filling the nights straining to improve himself and to get the rest of us out of that ditch with him. Some pipeliners drank and gambled. After work, worn out as he was, Father kept working. I've never admired anything more.

Hitting his correspondence course books was hardly easy for him. He had finished ninth grade and made it through only about one third of the tenth when he had to quit formal learning to go to work full-time in the oil fields. That was pretty much routine for boys then.

Father was bright, however, and, what was probably more important, he was always intensely curious. Most everything fascinated him. Curiosity was at the root of his affinity for newspapers, no doubt about it; but his hunger for information did not stop at the level of journalism. He searched out authoritative background to understand significant phenomena and sometimes reached all the way through to the basic sources.

I recall his absorption in his effort of trying to understand Hitler. Today the mystery is long solved. Everybody knows that the *Führer* was a raving madman, one of the overwhelming evils of history. In the 1930s this was not so plainly evident, not even to college professors, let alone oil pipeliners. Hitler built Volkswagens and *Autobahnen*, for instance, and created millions of jobs. The price that had to be paid by the Germans and the rest of the world for these achievements did not become clear for years. Our tight finances notwithstanding, Father dispatched Mother to get a copy of *Mein Kampf*, the well of Hitler's megalomania. This was a major order for our isolated neighborhood, and I'm not sure where she got the book. She did get it finally, perhaps at the library, where she and I were steady patrons.

When she had rounded up Hitler's opus, Father and Uncle John took to arguing about it long into the night. How serious was this fellow?

It dawned on me quite early that Father's preoccupations were not limited to everyday concerns, and when he decided to focus on a major world phenomenon he was able to discern how it might affect our personal fate on Prince Street.

Take Adolf Hitler again. The fellow would never win the war, but until around 1943 some experts believed he might yet find a way to attack the United States, perhaps even with rudimentary nuclear devices. Fortunately, the *Führer* turned out to be a transitional influence. Another of Father's interests affected him (and the rest of the family) much longer and more directly, and that was electricity.

These days that sounds quaint. What's more commonplace, more taken for granted than electric current? Not so when I was growing up. My grandmother Page in Bloomington, Texas, read to me from her Bible by the light of a coal oil lamp. Bloomington, like most of our state, was yet to come under the sway of another of President Roosevelt's alphabet-soup New Deal agencies: the REA, or Rural Electrification Administration.

Father decided that electricity was going to be around a lot longer than Hitler and he determined to learn all about it. As with so many working Americans bent on self-improvement, Dad's enrollment in the International Correspondence School was an almost holy mission. He referred to the ICS as the "poor man's university." To him, it resembled a second religion. I knew innumerable people who started courses in the ICS; Father is the only such student of my acquaintance who ever finished one.

He started studying electricity in 1933 and I remember he was still at it in 1940. Most nights around nine or nine-fifteen, Mother would shush us kids and Father would say, "I'm going to do my correspondence school work." Sometimes he would sit up with it until well past midnight.

His teachers, the permanently anonymous invisible authorities whom he respectfully called the "institute boys," were his idols. They were electrical engineers and their badges were the slide rules that they wore on their belts the way cops display their service revolvers. The slide rule, precursor of the computer, was Father's long impossible dream, his whale, his Moby Dick. It took him about eight years to pull in this prize trophy, and I remember the time when he finished at last.

He beamed with the pride of great accomplishment. He had been unable to make the slide rule work for some time. Now he understood it. Mother beamed back at him when the great day arrived. They could have posed for a Norman Rockwell cover on the *Saturday Evening Post*. It would have been called, "The Conquest of the Slide Rule." It was Father's Ph.D. He couldn't have been happier wearing a mortarboard and a long academic gown. Ever after, he sported his slide rule in a leather sheath on his belt, like a real engineer.

Father's marathon struggle with the slide rule was another of the many examples in our lives that hammered his most heartfelt motto home to me. He often joked that he'd like the words carved in granite on his tombstone. They were simple: "Don't quit." He hated nothing more fiercely than a quitter.

The concept came up as frequently at my house as it does in this book. One time when I was around twelve I was selling ice cream from a three-wheel bicycle. It was a hateful job. I had to waste hours traveling to my route and back, and somehow the income melted down to pennies. So I quit in disgust and announced my move at supper.

Father was taken aback.

"You will not quit!" he stated emphatically.

Mother, as so often, intervened successfully as mediator.

"Danny has already arranged another job," she said, which was reasonably accurate. I had applied for a job to load cans in the dairy, although the deal was not yet firm.

The fact that Father relented didn't mean he was retreating from his initial position, and I realized that. He didn't mind that I was using my good sense to get rid of an unprofitable job. He just couldn't abide the word, the concept of quitting. That was not done in the Rather family.

Father would have been amused or possibly scornful if someone had told him he was striving all his life to be "upwardly mobile," yet that was demonstrably true. He thought that his electrical studies were his route out of the ditch, as indeed they turned out to be when he managed to get himself promoted to work as an apprentice lineman for his pipeline company.

This still was backbreaking work, but all of it was done at ground level, or, at the time, farther above the ground than was ideal, as I soon learned. It meant that he was setting telephone poles as well as stringing and repairing wire for the company's rudimentary private telephone system. Father's bosses needed to communicate about oil deliveries, pipeline leaks, and other emergencies. The conventional phone system did not suffice for their needs.

While Father's correspondence classes had taught him to have plenty of respect for the dangers of electricity, they could do nothing to keep him from occasionally getting knocked off a pole by electric shocks when he was working on power lines during a rain. Nevertheless, he was in time promoted again and now he "ran trouble," meaning that he reestablished communications when lines came down.

Sometimes he was assisted by two helpers. Most important was the "grunt." This would be a pipeline gang man who was learning to become a lineman. He handled the troubleshooter's climbing rope and the bucket with his tools. The other assistant was the "swamper." He did easy work around the truck, a job that was usually handed to a relative or friend of the foreman.

One night during a huge storm when I was nine years old Father was called on our company-paid telephone and told to fix a break in the line at some still-undetermined point around El Campo, Texas, about seventy-five miles away. That wasn't much of a distance as car miles are measured in Texas, and Father was used to these crisis missions. He was, however, tired, having already put in a heavy day's work, and the wind-driven rain was bombarding the road in noisy sheets that made the driving strenuous. That night I worked as Father's grunt. Humphrey Bogart and Katharine Hepburn didn't have a wilder adventure aboard the *African Queen.*

I'm pretty sure that Father wanted me along, at least in part, to keep him company, because it was obviously going to be a long night. I also had three other chores. I was to keep him awake. I was to warn him when he came too close to running off the side of the narrow road (multilane highways were unknown). And I was to help him run his tools.

First off, though, we had to find the wire break, which took us forever because of the poor visibility. We drove back and forth in the company's 1939 Ford coupe until Father miraculously stopped at the place where the wire was down. Whereupon he launched on a well-practiced routine with the professional precision that a surgeon brings to bear when performing an operation. The sequence is etched into my memory.

First we had to make the car safe. It had to be far enough off the road not to get hit, yet not so far as to get stuck in the muddy ooze. I helped with the maneuvering.

I had watched Father on Saturdays when he cleaned and oiled the tools of his trade in the backyard. I had never seen them in use until that night. We had, of course, already put on our long two-part slickers, black bottoms, and yellow tops, and I had tied his rope in a knot to his tool bucket. Father strapped climbing hooks on the inside of each leg and clambered slowly up and up, as if by magic, through the continuing heavy rain, up about forty feet until I could barely hear him or see him through the darkness. It seemed to me an amazing performance to watch. I was awed to see such skill in motion, however awkward an operation it clearly was.

"Gimme the big pliers," Father shouted down as he lowered his bucket to me for the required item.

Eventually he climbed back to the ground, fastened the insulated part of the broken wire over his shoulder, and headed up the rain-slick pole a second time. The power must have been shut off; anyway it was safe. Nevertheless, I held my breath.

This time the magic didn't work. The pole was too slippery. From about twenty-five feet up, my father came plummeting to earth, not making a sound until I heard him hit a length of barbed wire. The fence wire made a stretching and screeching sound. Then he hit the ground with a big thump.

I was as close to panic as I have ever been before or since. I couldn't tell in the darkness how badly hurt he might be. The barbed wire had broken his fall. It had also slashed his clothes, and I could see that he was bleeding in his midback region. He had taken his long White Mule work gloves up the pole but had to take the right one off to get his work done. So now the hand was covered with large splinters from the pole, and I wasn't at all sure that he could get on his feet.

"Don't do anything," Father said very quietly, and I followed orders.

He moved a little, very little. It seemed to me that his back was wrenched. I tried to think of how we might get out of there. It was past 2:00 A.M., still storming, and there were no cars on the road.

"I gotta get up," Father said, talking to himself, not to me.

And so he did. It was hard to believe. I could see his determination physically, his centering of will, his plain refusal to quit, to do anything other than to rise. I watched him as he sat up unaided, then as he got to his feet, still without help, stiff, looking a mess, his right hand largely useless because of the splinters.

After some rest, he picked up the broken wire, climbed up the pole one more time, very slowly, managed somehow to splice the break, came down, and drove home with me. He was awesome. He was obviously in considerable pain. Consistent with his own inner law, he hardly showed it and never mentioned it. Stoic like the Spartans, for sure. It was a moment never to be forgotten by a nine-year-old son and admirer.

We got home long after sunup and Mother went to work on her husband. "There, there," she said, calmly like a real nurse. "Everything'll be all right. We'll take care of this." And then, less professionally, "Thank God you weren't killed!"

She picked out the splinters with her tweezers, one by one. She let Father soak a long time in a hot bath, her favorite remedy of all. Then she touched up every one of his wounds with Mercurochrome and he dragged himself into bed, slightly bent over. Nobody mentioned going to see a doctor. The next day Father was back on the job.

It was a defining event. Awesome or not, it determined in my mind that I was going to seek other work.

No glutton for punishment, Father plodded on stubbornly, still trying to upgrade his lot in life. He decided to open up his own business and to put Mother in charge while he kept his work at the pipeline company.

He admired a businessman who had operated a nursery at Shepherd Drive and Eleventh Street and then had moved on to another location. Father decided to fill the gap in the market. The nursery man had done well. I knew this because he dressed in dark trousers, not khakis or denims. He also wore a white short-sleeved shirt; dark lace-up shoes, not boots; and he drove a car, which he may have bought new. Quite possibly, Father measured this man's success by little more than the same criteria.

With small monthly payments over many years Dad bought a tiny lot on Shepherd Drive; that street was paved by then and saw more traffic than any road in the area. Pavement was still a novelty to us.

The whole family pitched in. Mother staffed the business full-time. Father worked there every evening and weekend. We children helped out as best we could, planting, replanting, and watering our merchandise, which seemed to rot and die at an alarming rate. The Houston weather was murderous, as always, and it didn't matter how many times we all tumbled out for three to four hours in the middle of the night to perform rescue watering missions.

The enterprise disintegrated into a losing race against disaster. Could we make it for another couple of weeks? For another week? We couldn't. Our inventory was too puny, we didn't know anything about running a business, and the damned plants refused to cooperate. We were forced to shut down in less than five months. No amount of Father's pluck helped, and this was another lesson I had to learn. Although determination goes a very long way, it cannot always surmount reality.

Father did not give up. Toward the end of World War II, money being relatively abundant thanks to the war boom, he took the big gamble of his life. He left the Houston Pipeline Company after twenty years of employment and went into business with a good friend. They would refurbish junk electric motors. Finally, his years of indenture to the wisdoms of the International Correspondence School were to pay off. The American dream of independence beckoned.

Basically, sick motors made a more likely business prospect than sick plants. Motors were in strong demand and in short supply. Technically, Father and his friend did excellent work. Alas, they did too well; each project took them too long. Also, they didn't have enough start-up capital, like most small new enterprises; they had no business plan; and both partners were detail men lacking in a managerial overview.

The business lasted only a year and this time the failure was traumatic. Father was downhearted for a while. I think he sensed that he was never going to get another chance at the American dream, and, though he was only in his thirties, he didn't.

From the heights of entrepreneurship it was back into the bear trap and down into the ditch for him. At that, he couldn't reconnect with Houston Pipeline, and it took months until one of his pipeliner friends got him on with Humble Pipeline (which we Texans pronounce "Umble," by the way). Still, Father hitched up his belt—I mean this literally, for that was his way of showing that he was girding his loins to face the lions—and within only a year he had made a comeback of sorts.

He had sprung the bear trap once again and was back working as a lineman. A long time later he earned a top of twelve thousand dollars a year.

17

Digging Out of the Ditch—My Story

WHEN I MET her at the age of eight, I didn't have a clue of the explosive influence she'd have on my life. I'll call her Miss Rose, although I'm embarrassed to say I'm not positive that I remember her name correctly. She picked me up in the Heights Park on Nineteenth Street. She was young-ish, shy, wore her hair in a bun, and looked a bit lonely, the type then known by the awful label "spinster." She surely was a social worker, which wouldn't have meant a thing to me then. I didn't know what she was. I thought of her as the lady in the park.

The city ran a summer recreation program in that park and Mother enrolled me. It was for "underprivileged kids." If Father had known that, his pride probably wouldn't have let me enter. I suspect Mother didn't inform him fully. The facilities were sparse—a few swings, a seesaw, and a baseball diamond—and one day, when I was idling on a bench, Miss Rose joined me and we began to chat.

She had some books along. She read to me, which I

always liked a lot, and over a time she started to talk to me about the place of books in the world.

"You know, your only way out is to read," she told me. "Sooner or later you're going to think about getting out of where you are. And whether you think of it in vicarious terms or literally, that's the best way out. To read."

That was startling. The way out? What for? Where to? It hadn't yet occurred to me that anything was missing from my universe right there in the Heights. Nevertheless, it sounded vaguely interesting, and I remembered what she said about some day leaving the neighborhood. I also looked up the word "vicarious." Its meaning, too, was intriguing. It sounded venturesome. It was also the most educated word I knew for years.

Miss Rose kept trying to get me interested in visiting the local public library. It sounded dull. Finally I gave in, though, and the place turned out to be unexpectedly grand and exciting. I was really surprised. To this day I can't imagine what possessed the Houston city fathers to put up such a splendid edifice on Thirteenth Street and Heights Boulevard. It was incongruous, palatial by any standards, a temple, built in the Italian Renaissance style of hollow tile and stucco (so I've since read). A garden surrounded it. The outside of the building was a soft shade of rose, inside the ceilings were two stories high in some places. The library seemed not to be in the same country as the Heights Annex, my turf, about a mile away. I'm still not quite over my bedazzlement.

Miss Rose helped me get a yellow library card and tried to explain the system for finding and borrowing books. That felt unreal, as if she'd commanded, "Open sesame!" I took books home, especially the adventures of my hero Paul Bunyan, and began to grapple with the first glimmer of Miss Rose's suggestion that the world didn't stop at Heights Boulevard.

Her next campaign was to get me interested in visiting

the main library downtown. By then I didn't require per-
suading to find out more about books, but Mother was
against such an expedition. I can't remember whether she
said why. Maybe she was protective because downtown was
such a long trip away. Maybe she thought that the social
worker's offer was too much like charity for the "underprivileged." And come to think of it, I'm not certain that I'd *ever*
been as far away from home as downtown in my life.

I lobbied, she gave in. Equipped with a brown paper
bag in which Miss Rose had brought lunch for both of us,
she and I boarded the Eighth Street shuttle bus for what
became a defining adventure of my life. When we got to
McKinney Street I might as well have landed in Rome. The
three-story library took up an entire city block and contained (so I later learned) 165,000 books. I gawked like the
country bumpkin that I was.

"Look how many Paul Bunyans they have," said my
companion. There was an entire shelf full of them!

And there weren't only books and books. We took all
day to wander through places like the genealogical collec-
tions, where you could research your family, and the Texas
room, with an awesome collection of knives. And the special
treasures! Sheltered in its own glass case was a Latin Vulgate
edition of the Bible. I was glad to see that it was open, the
way we were taught to keep our Bibles at home.

I owe Miss Rose a lot for showing me the way out of the
ditch and on to books, to reading, to college and white-collar
work. I've thought quite a lot about her and how she came to
pick me for so much individual attention. It seems strange
that I can't recall another child from the playground in the
Heights Park who was taken to the main library downtown.
Could I have been the only one to take her offer to go out
and meet the world?

Meanwhile, my parents and I embarked on betterment
schemes right at home. Among the umpteen enterprises

hatched by Mother or Father to scratch together a little extra cash was Mother's brainstorm to manufacture and sell kites. It was necessary to be inventive in the Great Depression and kites looked to be a road less traveled.

I laid the groundwork inadvertently when I heard about a kite-flying contest coming up in the neighborhood. Since I was bewitched by anything that could fly, I wanted to participate and asked Mother how one made a kite. It did not occur to me to buy one. We never bought anything that we might possibly be able to make ourselves at home.

Mother was intrigued. She liked for me to have fun and wanted to encourage my curiosity. She also scented a business opportunity. Somehow she always found time for her many new businesses. She consulted Father, who came up with a relevant article from one of his how-to magazines. Mother and I went to work on a diamond-shaped kite consisting mostly of newspapers. While it wasn't too substantial, it seemed airworthy enough for an experimental model. Later, when Mother hoped to have a kite assembly line going, there would be time for a more advanced design.

The making of the bridle eluded Mother, so Father was again brought in and figured it out. He also told us what to do about another problem: gauging the optimal length of the tail. We were to make it extra long, experimentally, to be cut down as flying conditions dictated. The tail consisted of rags tied together in knots.

I was very excited when I got to the site of the contest on Saturday morning. More than a dozen kids assembled on the large vacant field between the Heights Annex and Buffalo Bayou. Parents stayed in the background. My kite took off with almost no trouble, and I was swept away by the thrill of the new world of winds and vistas to which I'd never paid attention before.

Success was measured by the amount of string unspooled, and the feeling of the pull from the kite, as it rose up and up and up, was wonderful. When I could barely see my flying object, the sense of power and accomplishment was yet another new sensation.

The sweet-sour moment at the end spoiled nothing for me. The kite broke free and zoomed into the sky. I hated to lose it, but everyone was craning necks, watching it disappear into the unknown of space. This was a lot headier than another fate I'd been warned against: a power dive to destruction in a crash.

Still on the track of commercial opportunity, Mother enlisted me to help manufacture kites for sale. She showed me how to remove slats from wooden vegetable crates, and these became the skeletons for eight-sided kites that we laid out on the kitchen floor. We tied the joints with string. Instead of newspaper, we pasted in tissue paper saved up from Christmas wrappings.

To attract customers, we placed a sample kite in our front window and eventually sold around a dozen or so for twenty or twenty-five cents each. By April our business was gone with the wind. Literally. That's the time when the Houston air turns to molasses, and kites were grounded. I kept making my own kites in future seasons, but Mother and I were in silent agreement that kites were not the way for us to become another General Motors.

Father and I decided to take a flier in watermelons, of all things. Early one Saturday morning we went to the farmer's market downtown and bought half a dozen melons for twenty cents each. We still owned "the lot," the vacant patch on Shepherd Drive where my parents had once failed in the nursery business. It was a financial strain to carry, but they had not gotten over the dream of beginning another business someday when the lot might be handy. Meanwhile, starting smaller than ever, Dad and I hammered together a little stand there and managed to sell out our melon inventory at fifty to seventy-five cents each, the price depending on whether the melon was warm or cold.

The second Saturday my father left me in sole charge and an amazing opportunity happened my way. An ingratiating farmer type drove up in a truck loaded with Mexia melons. I never did find out what had brought him to the Heights. Maybe it was a vision of a sucker like me. If so, it was a mighty distant vision because Mexia was a prosperous little cotton-and-oil town way north of Houston near Waco. It was a nice enough place but its watermelons were smaller and yellower than those from our region and did not enjoy the best reputation. Indeed, even the inside of Mexia melons tended to be yellow instead of red, although I didn't know that.

The man from Mexia got off the truck, looked my micro-operation over, and ventured that I'd do better with a bigger inventory. When I agreed he made me an offer I couldn't refuse. If I gave him a down payment of two dollars, he'd unload his entire truck and stop by the following week to collect twenty cents for each melon. I should pile up the melons so they'd form a pyramid, he suggested. That would make melon-hungry buyers stop.

I was giddy with delight, savoring success as a melon king, and thus became the mentor of four hundred Mexia watermelons. Big was beautiful! This was business for real, though not for long.

My few sales didn't make much of a dent in my pyramid, and before the day was half gone I had a visitor who made me realize what a giant task I'd taken on. He was the owner of a dilapidated little drugstore farther up Shepherd, and he came over to inspect my inventory, nibbling on his pipe.

"You gotta *lot* of watermelons there," he muttered, shaking his head sadly and turning away. "You sure do have a lot of them."

Advertising! I said to myself. You've got to advertise!

Anyone old enough to have taken to the highway in the 1930s and 1940s remembers the road signs for a shaving soap called Burma Shave. Shaving soap was big stuff, nobody having heard of electric shavers. Each Burma Shave ad consisted of a series of four lines that added up to a doggerel. Each line took up one small sign. The signs were spaced at short intervals along the roadside and made the best entertainment while driving. They went like this:

> If your peach
> Keeps out of reach,
> Better practice what we preach.
> Burma Shave.

Or:

> Within this vale
> Of toil and sin
> Your head grows bald
> But not your chin.
> Burma Shave.

While I couldn't compete with the wit of Mr. Burma Shave's ad agency, I wanted to apply the concept, and so I put up three signs at the appropriate intervals: "Big Water Melon Stand, 2 Blocks," "Big Water Melon Stand, 1 Block," "Big Water Melon Stand, ½ Block."

Advertising being an arcane art, it did little for my sales. Still, when Father showed up after work that evening I anticipated praise. I thought he'd be pleased by my entrepreneurship. He wasn't. Instead, he called me fairly rude names, which he rarely did, and asked some uncomfortable questions. Who was going to watch those dumb melons at night? How was I going to keep them from rotting in the intense heat if they didn't sell right away? And more.

Crushed, I helped him rig a tarpaulin so the melons would rot more slowly and, hopefully, not be pilfered by every passerby. All that week I ran a desperate rear-guard battle to minimize the spoilage of my rapidly decaying stock.

We bought ice. My friends helped me transport the most-decayed fruit by handcart for dumping in the Bayou. An awful lot of melons wound up there, so I had a busy several days, and I kept wondering what to tell my supplier when he showed up from Mexia on the weekend.

"I want to talk to him," said Father, frowning.

And he did, chastising the trucker for having taken advantage of a kid.

The man from Mexia said he wanted twenty cents for each melon.

"You owe *us!*" said Father, explaining about the ice we had to buy.

In the end, no money changed hands, my father calmed down, and I consoled myself with the thought that Mexia melons never were very popular.

I failed at more jobs than I can remember, and one of my worst embarrassments was selling Bibles. I hated it. Selling door-to-door was widespread all during the 1930s and forties and on into the fifties. Everything from life insurance to household products and cosmetics to magazines and books was sold this way. It was big business. There were jobs to be had and money to be made for people who mastered the techniques of cold-calling in person at houses and apartments.

Unfortunately, I was not one of them. My previously unsuccessful efforts at selling newspaper subscriptions were an early indication. Trying to con people into buying Bibles was another, much worse. One reason the work was so depressing was that if my bosses ever had heard of the commandment that says, "Thou shalt not steal," this was not apparent. Their deal was basically a bait-and-switch proposition. I knocked on doors pretending to be hawking a Bible at two dollars while I really only sold one that was overpriced at four dollars.

Given the price and the large supply of Bibles already

in use in most homes, I sold very few. The only lesson the job taught me was that chow dogs are the most stubborn breed for nipping at the heels of undesired callers.

I also let down Benjamin Franklin, the lineal founder of the *Saturday Evening Post*, then the largest and most prosperous magazine in the country. Its price was right, five cents, and its cozy cover illustrations by Norman Rockwell were pure hinterland America, populated by rosy ragamuffins and furrow-faced codgers in mackinaws.

It's hard now to convey the huge popularity of the *Post*'s legendary fictional characters: Tugboat Annie, Alexander Botts, Mr. Moto, and the others. They were the stuff of everyday conversation and hardly sophisticated. Alas, I sold practically no copies of the *Post*, and I'm pretty sure I can pinpoint the reason why: The magazine was too highbrow for the Heights. Luckily, I doubt that anybody in my neighborhood penetrated to the *Post*'s editorial page to discover that it was the enemy of the working person. It loved Herbert Hoover. If that had gotten out, I'd have been yapped at by even more chows.

Not all my jobs were dreary. One summer I answered the telephone on Sundays for a one-room travel agency downtown in the nine-story Commerce Building, one of the taller structures in town. I was thirteen and had wandered into the place because I hoped to take a fifty-mile excursion flight to Galveston, my itch to fly having turned nearly unbearable. I'd seen the trip advertised.

The ticket turned out to cost nine dollars, which was out of the question. Still, my call on the agency wasn't a total loss. I guess I was polite and presentable enough, and so the lady who owned the place offered me the weekend job. Sometimes I also worked as a gofer on Saturdays, which presented a tactical problem. The office was so small that I had to occupy a folding chair on the landing outside. This was great fun because there was a window and I could

look out and make believe that I was seeing the city from a
plane.

One Saturday at lunchtime the boss sent me to James
Coney Island for a chili hot dog and gave me some of the
chili.

The devil possessed me that day. Way down on the
street below I spotted a man most splendidly turned out in
an all-white planter's suit and hat and two-tone, black-and-
white shoes. With the world at war I'd been reading a lot
about bombers and air raids. Of a sudden, I was seized by
the notion of bombing this juicy target with chili, and I
did so.

My timing was flawless. The chili container splattered
on the sidewalk right in front of the man in white as if I'd
aimed it with a Norden bomb sight. Bullseye! He got soaked.
I felt like an early version of Snoopy, swashbuckling as the
Red Baron, the hero in the much-later *Peanuts*.

Pretty soon the man in the chili-dyed white suit walked
into the building superintendent's office. Eventually I was
called in and questioned and denied my way out of my
predicament. My boss knew I was lying, as it turned out later,
but she was a good soul and covered for me.

I still carry around a guilty conscience over this bit of
rascality. I'm ashamed of what I did and I ought to be. I
suppose the man in the white suit could have become the
first American casualty of World War II to be severely in-
jured by chili. If I could find him, I'd buy him the best white
suit that gets hand-tailored in London. It's nice to be out of
the ditch and able to splurge for a good cause.

Until the summer of my fifteenth year there was always a
chance that I might wind up working at least many of my
early adult years in the ditch like my father. But that was the
season when I spent two and a half months living the
pipeliner's life and my determination ripened some more:
This was not for me. I absolutely *had* to do better than this.

The work had its merits. It was available; it paid well by teenager standards, about twenty-five dollars a week; it lasted dependably all summer, regardless of the weather; it was in the family tradition; and I learned what Father meant when he preached, as he had all my life: "Lift with your legs."

The rest was downhill.

Sometimes it took only fifteen minutes by bear trap to get to where I worked, other times it took up to two and a half hours one way. I didn't mind a long commute because when you were riding you didn't have to be digging, not a small difference.

Much of the time that summer I had to leave the house at 5:15 A.M. to make it to the bear trap's home base, across town, from where we traveled on to the work site to dig up lengths of leaky pipe in various places near and far. It took one and a half hours each way getting to and from work; that is, to and from home and the base-camp work headquarters near Sam Houston's San Jacinto battlefield. The proximity of this hallowed ground did not move me as it once did. Sometimes I slept on the floor of the bear trap, although often it was too noisy. My colleagues were playing poker, and I spent some time and money learning to play.

Luckily, the games went off in surprisingly gentle style. There was no playing "off the hip"; you played with whatever money was on the table. No reinforcements were allowed so that nobody could raise you out of the game.

I had learned about physical labor during my summer of brush cutting, but pipelining was worse. Not just that it required even more sweat. I disliked it because I found it more impersonal and much less varied and therefore less interesting. It was pretty stupefying to spend all of one's day in a ditch. I felt like the most primitive of robots.

My second summer season in the oil fields was less relaxed. I was roughnecking on an oil derrick: four hours on, four hours off, twenty-four hours a day, seven days a week. I'm not sure at what age I read about Dante's inferno, but the unceasing grind turned that summer into one of the more hellish of his circles.

I stood on the floor of the rig, periodically connecting and disconnecting the long pipes holding the drill that kept boring ever deeper into the ground. Each time we strained over wrenches that measured three and a half feet and sometimes could only be made effective by the concerted effort of two or three men. Just as we did with the giant tongs pipeliners used to screw the larger-diameter pipes together in ditches, the final tightening turns with these giant wrenches usually were accompanied by grunts and groans. These we called "Songs of the Derrick Floor."

It was all of a piece with life in the ditch, and I had to get out. I had to get out!

I can't recall when or how I first became aware that I grew up speaking with an accent or when it dawned on me that an accent stamps a person and that I had to work on mine. My Texas twang was part of drudging in the ditch, rusticating as a provincial bumpkin. Getting rid of it was part of getting out, graduating from the shovel.

Geographical accident helped. Texans living along the Gulf coast tend to have relatively light accents, and my parents luckily fell within that pattern. The language isn't hidden like in, say East Texas, where a New Yorker can hardly make out the words in the slur, "Y'all-hurry-on-back-now-ya-hear?" We did all drop the g's at the end of words as if the letter weren't there. We substituted *i* for *e* so that "ten" came out as "tin." And we said "far" instead of "fire" and "tar" instead of "tire."

Mother, being more sensitive to our environment than Dad and more active in efforts to get me out of the ditch and off to college, was the engine of my first efforts to launder my speech.

The Texas twang has still not completely released its hold on me. I regret to say that those who listen closely may be able to hear it sometimes, mostly when I'm involved in constant on-air coverage over many hours and I'm extremely tired. As in "tared."

One high school teacher, Mrs. Ruth Wilkison, and one teacher in college, Oscar Schmidt, helped some with this. But I never took special speech lessons or did exercises. When I went into radio in Houston, my friend Bill Zak and my boss, the late Bill Bryan, pointed my Texas inflections out to me. I muted them without trouble by listening carefully and then listening some more. A young colleague and fellow Texan, Al Anderson, practiced with me from time to time. So much for my Texas speech. My Texas way of thinking was another story. It required more work.

As I was leaving for New York, some of my colleagues counseled that I should show up with the dress and mentality of Tex Rather: faded jeans, silver-tipped cowboy boots, and aw-shucks innocence. "Tell 'em that you got your horse parked outside," said one friend.

I decided instead to *listen* closely again, and, sure enough, authoritative advice came to me very quickly. Its source was Blair Clark, a senior executive of CBS News. I suppose one would describe Blair as a low-key, button-down Ivy League type, so I was startled into speechlessness when he issued the dictum, "Dress British and think Yiddish!"

I could deal with the part of getting into English attire, long readily available in New York, but what in the name of Sam Houston did Clark mean by "thinking Yiddish"? When I arrived in New York, I hadn't even heard that there was a Yiddish language.

Fortunately, I latched on to a new colleague who became a great friend, a CBS producer named David Buksbaum, a Brooklyn boy with an abiding curiosity about Texas. So I talked to him about things Texas and he taught me about things Yiddish. Blair Clark hadn't been talking about language. To *think* Yiddish, as David explained to me, was to be wisely skeptical, shrewd, worldly, clear-eyed, realistic about the risks of wishful thinking.

I had spent six years covering the police beat, city hall, the courts, and the Texas state legislature before coming to New York. So it was not as if I had just fallen off a turnip truck and that Buksbaum's instructions were entirely new. His was more of a quick refresher course, with added context and reminders that what I had already been through might seem tame in this new place and with these new people.

"Part of growing up," he reminded me, "is realizing that no matter what you do, not everybody is going to love you." And, he said, "If you think Texas sidewinders and back-shooters are bad, just wait until you've competed in the big time and traveled the world." This put "think Yiddish" in clearer perspective. It also was shining valuable light onto the dark alleys of Manhattan and, let's be candid, network television.

I acclimated. I took on more baggage; I didn't drop any. Did I change my identity in the process to edit out my Texas core? Nope. My talk is still not purged of Texanisms. I'll say of a faker or fraud, "He's all hat and no cattle." Or, "If you believe that, you'll believe that rocks grow." Or, "If you believe that, you'll believe that you can find a stick with one end." Sometimes strangers mistake this habit as an affectation. It's not.

If something strikes me as super-rough, I may call it "hellacious," which is not in the dictionary. As in: "U.S. Marines along the Persian Gulf highway are in a hellacious fight tonight." If it's merely audacious, I may label it "bodacious." As in, "The Army's 101st Air Assault force made a bodacious move into the Euphrates Valley."

I remember that when my pals and I went to see *The Outlaw* with Jane Russell, whose bosoms had been called "hypermammiferous" by *Time* magazine, one of us, it could have been me, talked admiringly of her "bodacious ta-tas."

It was a phrase popular among boy/men in our part of the country at that time. I was amused to hear it used years later in the film *An Officer and a Gentleman*. The film writer used it in the dialogue of a character from Oklahoma. He was marveling at the feminine attributes of a young woman similar to Jane.

Bodacious echo from the past.

Every time I return to Texas, especially to the stretch along the Gulf from Beaumont to Victoria, it feels like home. I've never lost my affinity for the vastness of the sky, the smell of pine, the stickiness of the humidity as long as it doesn't get too bad.

Texas *is* a magnet, and not just for me. "While thousands of Texans sojourned around the world, and Texas millionaires found pleasanter havens in which to live, few completely broke their ties with home," wrote the historian T. R. Fehrenbach. "A frequent phenomenon was the return of the Texan prodigal from Los Angeles or New York." Like Stanley Walker, the Sage of Lampasas. And me.

I can go home again. I often do. In many important ways I never left.

18

Father, Mother, Bonnie, and Clyde

IT MUST have been in the boiling heat of mid-August 1932 when my mother and father, driving northeast from my birthplace, Wharton, were stopped by lawmen at the outskirts of town and questioned closely at gunpoint. The officers were jittery. It seemed to them that my parents roughly fit the description that had been circulated of Clyde Barrow and Bonnie Parker, the storied bank robbers of their age. It was some little while before young Mr. and Mrs. Rather were permitted to proceed toward Houston.

My parents felt far from humiliated or libeled. Quite to the contrary, they were proud and pleased and talked for many years about this swashbuckling high point in their lives. They felt they had been identified with greatness. Bonnie and Clyde ranked high among their heroes, and they were far from alone in supporting a glorification that sounds somewhat misplaced today. Something about Bonnie and Clyde stirred the American soul. Six movies were made commemorating their lives; the last film, by Arthur Penn in

1967, with Warren Beatty and Faye Dunaway, is remembered as a classic and a box-office smash.

Since I was one year old in 1932, one may question the eyewitness authenticity of my parents' encounter with the law in Wharton. OK, I wasn't in the car with them, not even as a baby, but my account comes firsthand from prime sources. Many was the time when I was around nine and ten or eleven years old and we were on the way by train or car to Grandma Page's at Bloomington and passing through Wharton. We would have finished singing "The Yellow Rose of Texas," repeatedly and always at the top of our lungs. This songfest took a while because the tune was my mother's favorite and she knew the words to every verse.

Then it was storytelling time. This meant that Father launched once again into the true saga of the quasi-meeting with Bonnie and Clyde during the vintage days of this mobile young couple when they roamed the Midwest and Southwest in relays of stolen cars. Knocking off banks like bowling pins, they left behind the corpses of officers whom they had cut down with their sawed-off shotguns, and a trail of headlines normally reserved for visiting notables.

It was easy for me years later to pinpoint the timing of my parents' "getaway" in Wharton because mid-August of 1932 was when my birthplace was historically linked with one of Bonnie and Clyde's greatest bravura performances, a breathtaking (and thoroughly documented) escape from almost certain capture.

Accompanied by an irritable accomplice named Raymond Hamilton, the couple drove through all of one Sunday night from San Antonio to Victoria near the Gulf coast, the same town where my father had dated my mother not long before. In Victoria the robbers replaced their stolen vehicle by stealing two more, a Ford V-8 sedan, which they assigned to Hamilton, and a Ford coupe driven by Clyde. A swaggering, jug-eared professional car thief, Clyde had acquired a sizable fan club of macho drivers all across the country. They were awed by his madcap skills at extracting impossible feats from ordinary cars, and that Monday morning Clyde solidified his reputation as the wildest getaway driver of them all, the champion of wheelmen.

Having been alerted to the car thefts in Victoria, the police there notified the cops in Wharton, who guessed correctly that the gang had to be on its way to Houston. A seemingly foolproof ambush was laid at the bridge across the Colorado River on the western outskirts of Wharton. The eastern end of the bridge was blocked. The western end would be closed as soon as the robbers had driven well across.

It didn't work. The operational skills and communications capabilities of the rural police didn't run high, and radio was lacking altogether. The Wharton cops didn't pick up (or weren't told) that they were looking for two cars, not one, and so they hesitated in momentary confusion when Clyde approached, followed by Hamilton.

Clyde never hesitated. He spotted the cops, swung his coupe around in a brutally tight U-turn, and screeched off, Hamilton trailing, the proverbial hail of bullets coming too little and too late.

Father relished every turn in this showpiece of Texas enterprise. He conveyed his admiration to the rest of us, and we were always cheered by his belief that Bonnie and Clyde lived in or near the Heights. I checked on this report and found no evidence that it was true. Our heroes were residents of West Dallas and evidently never made so much as a sleepover in Houston. No matter. To Mother and Father, Bonnie and Clyde weren't exactly family but they came close, and the reason was the enormous spell cast upon us by that overwhelming presence in our midst, the Great Depression.

I don't feel qualified to join the critics, philosophers, and ethicists who have driven the supposed sources of Bonnie and Clyde's mass appeal pretty much into the ground, although some of the arguments strike me as interesting and probably valid. Bonnie's presence as a full partner, for instance, was novel and engaging. She was no Faye Dunaway; she looked and talked like the scrawny hoodlum that she was. In her real-life role as an early liberated working woman, adept at shifting a cigar from one side of her mouth to the other, Bonnie was bound to stir the sympathies of early feminists and their allies and perhaps intrigue some so-called he-men as well.

But these are speculations. In my family, Bonnie and Clyde's appeal was based on nothing vague. We liked them because we chose to view them, at least for a while, as fellow victims.

I want to make clear that my parents never came out to defend crime. They realized perfectly well what and who these criminals became—killers. Mother and Father were not so naive as to believe the stories that Bonnie and Clyde gave of their loot to the poor, like Robin Hood. Nonsense! They knew this couple would wind up on "the pea farm," the state prison at Huntsville, Texas, a piece north of us, or more likely dead—and deservedly so.

Yet it was easy for Mother and Father to identify with some of Bonnie and Clyde's travail because in the Heights they, too, were victims of the terrible times, the economic malaise that would last a seemingly interminable decade, all through the 1930s. Many of the people around our family were worse off, worse victims. They, too, like Mother, Father, and most everyone around us, wanted to break out, to make a getaway to greener places and less-punishing times. That's why my parents and everybody they knew could despise much of what the pair did but at the same time feel empathy for the desperation of Bonnie and Clyde. Mother and Dad, too, wished to rebel, break free, hit the open road and live lives of boldness, risk, and adventure. Even more, they wished it for their children.

This was by no means unique to our neighborhood or even to Texas. Oklahoma, for example, had its own version of Bonnie and Clyde, an outlaw named Pretty Boy Floyd. He did bank stickups and shoot-outs with police and would then hide out near the Red River. Throughout the Dust Bowl many farmers and working people cheered for him, just as Mother and Father did for Bonnie and Clyde, for the same reasons and with the same ambivalence.

Tennessee Williams, among others, said "Desperate people do desperate things." So it was with the desperadoes of the Depression.

The bad ones, and in some cases just unlucky ones, turned to crime. The good ones rededicated themselves to determination, to self-improvement, "bettering oneself," and to a belief in progress. Or, as my father liked to put it, in a phrase his sons and his daughter never forgot, "We can be beaten but we will never be defeated."

He said that a lot during the Great Depression and even more later during the war. He always said it with a slight smile and a wink.

In the 1990s it's all but impossible to do justice to the impact of the Great Depression, especially for Americans under the age of forty-five or fifty. It's too big a story. It persisted too long, especially in the memories of the afflicted. I know people who shudder at their extravagance every time they fork over today's fare of more than one dollar for a ride in the New York subway. Everybody of their generation knows that the subway is a nickel, which was plenty, and the *New York Times* is three cents.

The statistics that measured the extent of the Depression are too huge to convey meaning. How is one to visualize the failure of 5,000 banks and 90,000 other businesses? Total wages and salaries nearly cut in half? Unemployment up from 3 percent to 25, the highest ever? Some 18 million people asking for public relief in order to subsist?

If we were obsessed with work and carried our preoccupation to such extremes that they seem silly now, it was dead serious business then. I remember that when *Snow White and the Seven Dwarfs* came out in 1937 we went to see it as a family more than once, the unusual expenditure notwithstanding. The charms of the film's story and music were obvious to us. Still, I'm convinced that its strongest appeal, especially for my father, was the uplift of seeing those doughty dwarves march off to work, hi-ho. Full employment in Disney animation was better than no employment at all.

Our unemployment statistic was my uncle John. Nobody tried harder over more years to land a job, most any job. Nobody stood in vain for more hours in front of more plant gates. How I admired that man's doggedness! Even the unions didn't want him as a member, although he was strongly on their side long before organized labor had much voice in Texas. He won over my father to the recognition that pickets were our people. Which was why the Rathers respected picket lines.

Later, after World War II, after Korea and Vietnam, unions and strikes and picket lines operated in a much different context. By the 1970s and eighties it was not uncommon for one's own union to advise, even demand, crossing the picket lines of other unions. In such situations people of my generation and background were routinely torn by conflicting emotions, beliefs, and loyalties.

In the 1930s and forties it was easier to know which side you were on. In these times, Uncle John became understandably embittered. He would hear of real jobs and find that they had evaporated by the time he got in line for them. "Where do these jobs go?" he kept asking. He suspected nepotism and other forms of favoritism, and so did my father. Nothing made their necks swell in fury more readily. They were as good as anybody! I inherited a measure of this chip off their shoulder, probably more than is good for me.

I was stung by the evidence of the stigma, the searing humiliation of not working and having to go "on the dole," accepting fifteen or twenty dollars a month from the government. Everybody knew the helplessness, the inner rage, of welfare clients. Nobody said, "They ought to get a job." Everybody believed they'd welcome most any job warmly if they could find one.

I can think of three welfare families in our immediate environment, and I remember the corrosive effect that unemployment had on their self-respect. For our kind of neighborhood, that's very, very few people. All three families, incidentally, were white, with the nuclear family intact. I happened to be in the house when the mother in one of these families came home with the family relief money. The father couldn't go to pick it up because he was disabled. The mother's face was relaxed and smiling as I hadn't seen it in a long time. She took the money out of its envelope and started to count it. When she saw that I was watching, she stopped and tucked it away in slight embarrassment. She didn't want to be revealed as a victim. It was almost as if she blamed herself for her predicament or even for the Great Depression itself.

Perhaps we blamed Herbert Hoover unfairly, but in our neighborhood everybody did blame him.

Of course, the causes of the great tragedy were complex and remain in controversy to this day. Forget it. We knew a villain when we saw one. President Herbert Clark Hoover in his stiffly starched Hoover collar fit our vision, and his statements matched.

"Conditions are fundamentally sound," said Hoover in December 1929, right after the historic crash on Wall Street. "The Depression is over," he announced in June 1930. Perhaps no President was ever more fiercely hated. The shack cities of the homeless that sprung up in the cities were instantly dubbed "Hoovervilles." "Hang Hoover! Hang Hoover!" chanted crowds during his 1932 reelection campaign.

From my earliest childhood I listened to accounts of

the horror that Hoover visited upon the Bonus Marchers that summer. These were the more than twenty thousand veterans, most of them unemployed, who roused themselves from everywhere and marched on Washington to demand payment of their World War I bonus for military service. Representative Wright Patman, one of the great Populists and chairman of the House Banking Committee, had introduced a bill to that effect. Patman was from Texarkana, Texas. He was one of my family's shining knights, so our interest was personal.

The Bonus Marchers built temporary camps from boxes and wastepaper in the Anacostia flats adjoining downtown Washington while Congress wrangled over Patman's bill. The House passed it. The Senate rejected it. When the marchers still refused to give up, President Hoover ordered the army to evict them. General Douglas MacArthur, the chief of staff, strutting down Pennsylvania Avenue, ordered the marchers' camps set on fire and drove them out of the city. Some were killed. It was one of the most disgusting episodes in American history. My father and my uncle John just about burned up in wrath each time they told about it.

Ours were not ideological stands, however. We had no difficulty admiring a conservative like Jesse Jones, known as "Mr. Houston." Jones owned the *Houston Chronicle* and its radio station, the three leading hotels, and most of downtown. He was the chief stockholder of the biggest bank and his personality was ice and steel.

"He carried a stronger note of the implacable than anybody else I have ever talked to in American public life," wrote John Gunther, one of the most knowledgeable reporters of the time. Still, Jesse Jones could do no wrong in our eyes. He was one of us because he had enough money and clout to make sure that not one Houston bank failed when banks everywhere went into meltdown like ice cream.

A more likely of father's heroes was Congressman Maury Maverick, the populist from San Antonio. This wasn't the original maverick whose name is still synonymous with untrammeled independence. *That* was his daddy, Samuel A. Maverick, a rancher who was too free-spirited to have his cattle branded. The Maverick of Father's generation came from the same mold. He was Dad's man because he was a "take-'em-on-and-throw-'em-out" kind of guy, Father's kind. I never actually heard my dad call himself a maverick, but he could have.

One innovation that helped to make Franklin D. Roosevelt such a hero with us was his regular visits in our home as the first radio President. We absorbed his "fireside chats" like informal messages directed at our family.

When he said, "I see one third of a nation ill-housed, ill-clad, ill-nourished," my parents could feel proud that he was not talking about them. They surely knew what he was talking about, however. The evidence was all around us and FDR was doing something about it. He was good to us.

His New Deal brought electricity into Grandma Page's home, and when FDR philosophized in his first inaugural address that "The only thing we have to fear is fear itself" my father knew that this wasn't high-flown rhetoric.

Father had no fear of fear, he had fear—dreaded, abject fear—of poverty, meaning destitution, not only for himself but for the older members of our family, of whom we had quite a few for whom Father felt responsible. Nursing homes were not yet known. Families kept their infirm and demented senior citizens locked in the attic. In the Great Depression, many companies simply would not pay out their retirement-benefit obligations; they needed the money elsewhere.

If Roosevelt had accomplished nothing else, my father would still have revered him merely for jamming the Social Security Act of 1935 through a reluctant Congress. That was real relief from fear of dependency and charity. "Charity" was an awful word. To be a charity patient at the huge new (and free) Jefferson Davis Hospital on Buffalo Drive was a disgrace, and the worst fate that could befall a sick person was to be taken there to die. There was no greater shame.

In the Annex, we made it our business to protect the pride of the destitute. We knew people too ashamed to join the procession of families who came to our back porch to ask for "extra" food, and their pride prompted Mother to organize a face-saving arrangement with one hungry man. She used to notice that he came around on garbage day to rummage through our refuse. The practice troubled her, not just the indignity of it but the health danger. So every Tuesday she double-wrapped some leftovers and placed the securely tied package under the lid of our can. The man picked up the food and never had to beg.

Ingenuity made up for other deficiencies. In my first-grade class, our very special principal, Mrs. Simmons, discovered not only that the teeth of many youngsters were deplorably neglected but that quite a few of my classmates could not afford a toothbrush. So she arranged to have us bused to the local dental school for checkups and showed us how to make a toothbrush by tying a chunk of clean rag around a stick from an Eskimo Pie ice cream bar.

Next to the mosquitoes, bill collectors were among the most detested scourges swarming across our neighborhood. The reaction to bill collectors in the current generation may be more along the lines of, "Well, if people don't pay their bills, someone should hold them accountable." I admit this may be fair and proper and a reasonable societal attitude. In the 1930s, no one I knew could afford to think that way. The times and circumstances were such that almost everyone in our community either owed money, had owed money, or was about to owe some. We had respect for most authority—the boss, schoolteachers, parents, schoolteachers, the boss—but we hated bill collectors.

I used to think of them as hunchbacked, greedy parasites out of Charles Dickens novels. While this was a wildly exaggerated fantasy, it was true that even little kids could spot the feared emissaries. There was something about the way they dressed. We could tell that they didn't fit in the neighborhood; they didn't belong.

Kids would run and warn householders when bill collectors were about to descend. Targeted families would hush all children and try to make believe that no one was home. That rarely worked. The collector would threaten to have the sheriff come and seize the furniture. Voices would rise. Guns would be waved to shouts of, "Get your damn ass off this property!" And sometimes the sheriff would indeed arrive and furniture would be moved out.

We knew that ever so many people were worse off than we were in the Annex. We went out of our way to save by buying day-old bread, but we read of bread lines and former businessmen reduced to selling apples on street corners. Our hearts went out to the "Okies," the tenant-farmer families evicted from the Dust Bowl—twenty-five thousand square miles of Oklahoma and surrounding country that had been turned to dust by greedy soil management, just in time for the Depression. We saw news photos of farms made almost invisible by dust clouds, and of jalopies on the move, most of them with mattresses piled on top. Often bumper to bumper, they clogged U.S. 66 en route to the vegetable fields of California.

While we didn't know Oklahoma, we thought we knew the Joad family, who suffered through the Okie migration in John Steinbeck's *Grapes of Wrath*. We saw the movie, and since we knew Steinbeck had spent months living and moving with migrant families the film looked more like a documentary than fiction to us.

We had families like the Joads among us right in the Heights. They cruised our streets in their rattletrap vehicles with the mattresses stacked high, stopping to ask for vacant garages where they might set up temporary shelter. Often they used our bridges as roofs over their heads. We had two overpasses, one over our creek and one over the Bayou, and underneath was a bit of sleeping room if one didn't spread out too much.

Our family's very own Okies were the people in "the tin house" across the way on Prince Street. This structure, perched on unsteady concrete blocks, really was built of tin sheets and was an eyesore even on our street. I don't know how Father came to be responsible for it. It may have been abandoned property that he picked up by paying a few dollars in taxes now and again.

One extra cold afternoon a family showed up and asked to stay in the tin house. They looked as downtrodden as the migrants in *The Grapes of Wrath*. There was no Pa Joad, however—just a bone-weary mother and six children, including a baby in arms. My mother asked whether they had a little money to make a deposit. They did not. Mother let them move in anyway. It was too cold for them to stay in the open.

When Father came home from work he was not happy to see them. He told Mother wearily that we would never see any money from these people, and he was almost right. They stayed with us for four or five years and only very rarely forked over a few dollars.

A father did exist in that family, but he appeared only once or twice a year. I think he rode the rails the rest of the time, like many of the thousands and thousands of hoboes who lived more or less permanently on roving freight cars. It was hard to be a hobo, but it was not considered disreputable.

One night a boy from the tin house showed up at our supper table. He was perhaps twelve years old.

"I can't wake Mama," he said.

We all ran over to the tin house and there was the woman flat and motionless on the floor, covered with crawling ants, her children screaming all around her. We thought that perhaps she was dead, but Mother found a pulse in her throat and told me to get a cup of water. We concluded that the woman had collapsed because of malnourishment.

Someone from down the street brought soup and a little food. The patient was lifted onto a board, carried outside, and told to breathe deeply. It was one of our central beliefs that fresh air could alleviate practically any acute symptom. Certainly we saw no reason to call a doctor.

The neighborhood's women having thus discharged their duties, the men, six or seven of them, convened in one of the backyards. Four or five dollars were collected for the immediate relief of the people in the tin house. Full responsibility was fixed on the absentee father. Neighborhood justice ordained that an effort was going to be mounted to find him and persuade him to send some money home. Nobody talked of enlisting outsiders like cops or lawyers.

I don't remember whether the sanctions of the neighborhood's fathers ever bore fruit, but I know that our attitudes changed toward the family in the tin house.

The people in that house had struck many of us as an eccentric bunch. Sometimes we kids ridiculed them, even picked on them. That never happened once we had faced the woman who was starving but too proud or too weak or too defeated to beg for food.

Crime decreased in America during World War II, after exploding all across the country in the years before the war began.

Although the connection is not often noted as a by-product of the Great Depression, the chasm between the country's haves and the have-nots encouraged a boom in criminal activity. (Repeal of Prohibition also helped; bootleggers looked for new sources of income.) More people simply yelled "Stick 'em up!" and grabbed what they couldn't attain legitimately. In 1933, an astounding 3,000 kidnappings for ransom took place in the United States, along with

12,000 murders and 50,000 robberies of banks and other places worth looting.

Murders were a specialty product of our ubiquitous Texas gun culture, and even the kidnappings were considered a personal threat. The twenty-month-old baby of the wealthy aviator hero Charles Lindbergh had been kidnapped from his New Jersey home four months after I was born, and $50,000 ransom was paid. It was pretty farfetched to imagine that such a fate might befall a Rather baby, yet my mother worried about this possibility, as did mothers throughout the nation. The alleged Lindbergh kidnapper, Bruno Richard Hauptmann, became the incarnation of villainy. During the height of his trial the Lindbergh family received an almost unbelievable 100,000 letters a day!

Aided by their mass-produced fast cars, their machine guns, and police incompetence, petty types like Clyde Barrow, born in Telico, Texas, and Bonnie Parker, from Rowena, Texas, operated with relative impunity until 1934, when they were ambushed. It happened on a deserted country lane on the Louisiana side of the Texas border. They were shot in the back by a large posse that trapped them and cut them down in a rain of bullets that rocked their car. Father was still upset years later. He felt they shouldn't have been shot in the back. Clyde was twenty-five. Bonnie was twenty-four.

"God, didn't they have guts!" he would say. "They didn't take anything off anybody!"

By this he meant that they were out-and-out Texas, one might say *Ur-* (better: "our") Texas. We didn't use the word "style" then, but that's what Father would have said if he'd known the term. Mother didn't care for the way Bonnie smoked cigars. Nor did she applaud Bonnie because she made Clyde treat her as an equal. Mother did see qualities for commending Clyde's companion, a former waitress like Mother herself. Mother approved of the gumption Bonnie displayed, as when she once broke Clyde out of a prison chain gang. Bonnie took care of her man and stuck by him. In those days before women's liberation, those were values that perhaps meant more to more people than is the case now.

As for the couple's crimes, well, those were bad, especially the cop killings. Yet as long as Bonnie and Clyde were still running about free, Mother and Father considered that bank robbing was not an unreasonable technique for raising money in the Great Depression.

As the country grew out of its worst times and law enforcement grew more efficient, I grew out of knee pants and slowly our respect for police authority increased. The gangbusting triumphs of the FBI (combined with the publicity skills of J. Edgar Hoover) helped. We kids played "Gangbusters," inspired by a hit radio program of that name. When the good guys went against the bad guys in this show, the good guys won, and we played out crimes in the same way when we shot each other with "guns" made of rubber bands and clothespins.

"Gangbusters" was emceed by H. Norman Schwarzkopf, the retired director of the New Jersey State Police, a former general and the father of the commander in the Gulf War of 1991. The show was among the first to move to television and, come to think of it, this was the first time I ever heard about TV. Somebody in the neighborhood was saying, "In New York, they've got a new system: radio with pictures!" It bordered on the inconceivable: In New York you could actually *see* "Gangbusters"!

Everybody and everything was growing up.

Somebody soon was speculating that one day, maybe, we might even be able to see wars on the radio. Not just hear them, as my hero, the broadcaster Edward R. Murrow, had done with World War II on the air, but actually see them. And not in a movie theater as part of a newsreel with dated pictures but at home, in a little box; actually see happenings such as wars just as Murrow had helped us to hear them—as they happened. Nobody believed it.

19

Values

NOWADAYS schools teach something called "values inculcation." Specialized handbooks instruct teachers on how to impart the esoteric new art of injecting values into the heads of kids. New textbooks exist to help students to divine the standards they're supposed to live by, heaven help us all.

To do one exercise prescribed in one widely used text, students sit in a circle and are asked to pretend they're on a life raft. One of them must be thrown overboard so the rest of the group can survive. Each student must justify why he or she shouldn't be killed. Whereupon they all vote to decide who gets heaved out. Then they sit around and chat about the values that went into the decision.

I was relieved to read that some thoughtful kids rebelled against this abhorrent drill. It's almost beyond belief: Schools are making students worry about the value of life instead of reassuring them about it! It's hard to dream up a straighter route to youthful drug use and suicide.

This is not the place to weigh the pros and cons of "values inculcation," in the home or at school, and its role, if any, in the curriculum in these days of murky rules. That's a complicated business and subject to legitimate debate. I brought up the sea-going murder exercise because it made me shudder at the turmoil it must trigger in the minds of teachers who are asked to teach this nonsense. That, in turn, reminded me of Ms. Alberta Taylor, Mrs. Ethel Simmons, Mrs. Spencer in my Love Elementary School, and Miss Bresky at Hamilton Junior High and how they "inculcated" values.

To give a fair perspective, we children, in the vast majority of cases, including myself, arrived on the first day of classes with values firmly implanted by our parents. So the teachers had a more solid base to build upon than they often have today, no question. It also helped that they themselves seemed to have no doubts about what was right or wrong and that they knew what they were doing.

The robust Mrs. Simmons, our principal, was, to begin with, a brilliant administrator, which meant that she knew what was going on; I mean she was aware of what was *really* happening in her kingdom. These days experts tout what they call "managing by walking around." That sounds silly. In truth, it's the next best thing to clairvoyance, and Mrs. Simmons (we called her "Missus," naturally) knew the skill well. I sometimes suspect she invented it.

She seemed to have eyes in the back and on the sides of her head in addition to the usual places, and her little feet seemed to carry her everywhere all at once. She knew which of her 120 charges wasn't getting enough breakfast at home and needed an extra helping of school lunch. She seemed to grow out of the ground whenever there was a fight, judging when to break it up and when to leave combatants alone so they could learn to stand up for themselves. She made sure that the boys opened the doors for girls at least some of the time. We were supposed to do that then. She sent notes home when someone looked peaked, and I've written elsewhere how she arranged dental checkups for everybody.

There couldn't be much doubt about her values and the values she wanted us to take along into our teen years.

Miss Bresky, whom I admired at Hamilton Junior High, flourished in remarkable style within a considerably less quiescent environment. Let's face it: Some of the older boys carried hidden knives, and at the age of twenty or twenty-one this teacher was herself barely out of her teens and not too experienced in the workaday world.

I don't know whether it helped or hindered Miss Bresky that she was beautiful, at least in my eyes—a dark-haired, dark-eyed woman with an excellent figure. I noticed that the seams in her stockings were as straight as a ruler. Some of the boys occasionally marked her for mild passes, which she fended off with quiet good nature, usually a humorous, low-key remark.

Once I saw a boy of maybe fourteen slap her lightly on the posterior. I was braced for trouble. Miss Bresky kept going, smiled, and said nothing, indicating that no big deal had transpired. She radiated the feeling that she was comfortable with men, which was all-important. To have over-reacted to the slap might have encouraged more rowdyism, or so I believe in retrospect. Of course this was in a vastly less violent era.

I do recall a breath-stopping scene in the school parking lot. Miss Bresky was headed for her car. A group of our toughest guys were waiting for her and encircled her, blocking the car door. I was certain she would bolt or that there would be some kind of bad trouble.

Miss Bresky, relaxed, smiled and talked to them. I was out of earshot and couldn't hear what she said. I could only see that the circle opened, soft as melted butter, and Miss Bresky drove off, still smiling. I wish I knew exactly what she told those ruffians.

She was also effective at helping girl students when

they were molested. She formed a mutual security alliance with them and instituted "networking" long before the word existed. Simply by being unfrightened herself and letting rowdies understand when they were out of their class, she gave the girls a handy model. And some of the boys, too.

My exposure to life beyond Prince Street had begun with Ms. Taylor, my second-grade teacher. I had yet to discover the books in the library and other exits to break out of my Heights Annex ghetto when Ms. Taylor announced that she wished to invite me to visit her at her house. She said she wanted to get to know me better.

Mother was against it. I don't remember why, but for some reason she didn't think it was appropriate. Maybe it was simply that, as she said, she'd never heard of a teacher doing such a thing. She soon relented, probably because I could report that the teacher was also inviting everyone else in class, one per afternoon.

I considered it a golden moment to enter Ms. Taylor's home. It was my first breakout from my home setting, a little strange but very exciting, down to the odor of her books. They smelled not so much dusty as, well, book-y and promising, and there sure were a whole lot of them. I was there for an hour, perhaps an hour and a half. Ms. Taylor served me cookies and milk, and I chattered away. Then she read aloud to me and put her arm around me while she did so, more like an aunt than a teacher.

Another seed toward my system of values was planted by Mrs. Spencer, my fourth-grade teacher. It happened the day my class made our thrilling visit to the San Jacinto Monument—the memorial that celebrates the battle where Sam Houston's fighters shouted, "Remember the Alamo!"

Reverberations of that day's outing are still very much a daily part of me, even though the incident has little to do with Texas, for once.

On our tour of the monument, I discovered the mysterious sentence, "Thermopylae had its messenger of death, the Alamo had none." I inferred that Thermopylae had to be the name of another battle, which made it important because Mrs. Spencer had lectured us that societies tend to be defined by their battles—another manifestation of the tempestuous Texas outlook on the outside world.

We were still gawking at the writing on the monument when I tugged at Mrs. Spencer's sleeve and asked what Thermopylae was.

"It was in Greece," she said, herding the class along. "I'll tell you about it later."

Mrs. Spencer never forgot a promise. Back in class she got out an atlas.

"Let me show you Greece," she said and she proceeded to point out Thermopylae as well. From there she launched into a mini-introduction to the culture and glory of the ancient Greeks and explained how Leonidas and his Spartans were totally wiped out at Thermopylae in a heroic battle against Xerxes and his Persians in 480 B.C.

The strange foreign names and places became relevant to my experience when Mrs. Spencer linked the meaning of the battle in ancient Greece to an event I knew backward and forward: the history of the Alamo. In that Texas massacre, Jim Bowie and his men had fought their valiant but losing battle to buy time for the bigger confrontation at San Jacinto later. The Spartans had allowed themselves to be martyred for the same reason.

This history lesson stirred me and stayed with me so that I looked into Thermopylae further when I got to junior high school. It was then that I encountered the text of the never forgotten message that the Spartans had left behind for the fellow soldiers who came to relieve them but arrived too late:

> Go tell the Spartans,
> Thou who passest by,
> That here, obedient to their laws,
> We lie.

That hit me hard. Perhaps it would be a shade too strong to say that these lines became my talisman for life. Certainly they were the touchstone of my thinking during my earliest thinking days. They pointed to something larger than oneself, something to die for. They reminded me to be in touch with my core; that ideals did exist that transcend one's baser instincts, standards beyond the normal grubbing of daily existence. Besides, the words were intrinsically valuable for their beauty. They accompany me as a permanent reminder of great men, heroes who have done more than I ever will.

I don't talk about my Spartans much, but the message they left behind at Thermopylae is printed in small gold letters on my office door. It's a little hard to see there—gold on blond wood. That's just as well. I've had the words affixed as a reminder to me, not anybody else. They're not an invitation to chat.

Visitors rarely notice my nonstop confrontation with the Spartans and their battles, conflicts that sometimes seem to have vague similarities with my own. When people ask about the words from so far away and long ago, I usually say no more than, "It's from the ancient Greeks." If they persist, I'll say, "It's something for me."

And so it is and has been since I started working in an office. On each new door, the message goes up. It's been on a lot of doors, and when I move on from my present door it'll follow me some more.

Values. I wonder what they would have said, Mrs. Simmons, Ms. Taylor, Miss Bresky, and Mrs. Spencer, if somebody had told them they were engaged in "values inculcation."

Our family attitudes toward blacks were untypical of those prevailing in Texas. I want to be careful not to appear self-congratulating. It would be ridiculous to suggest that we were civil rights activists or even that racial injustices were much in our minds. They surely should have been. They weren't. In everyday living, the Rathers seemed pretty much to ignore color.

This is curious because blacks—they were mostly called "niggers," sometimes "coloreds," and occasionally "Negroes"—were all around us. The black district, "Niggertown," was only a block and a half away from us on Prince Street. Individual black boys regularly drifted into our neighborhood and played casually in our pickup baseball games. I did not rate blacks as second-class people in any way.

In retrospect, I wonder why I didn't. There were nearly a million blacks in our Jim Crow state (around 14 percent of the population) and their segregation was nearly total. The society of my boyhood is unrecognizable now. Buses, public toilets, and schools were segregated as a matter of course. No blacks were admitted to the University of Texas, not even to correspondence courses. Bureaucratic shenanigans kept most blacks from voting. There had been no lynching for a while, but in 1947 John Gunther, that master reporter, spotted a road sign outside a west Texas town that said, "Nigger! Don't Let the Sun Set on You Here!"

I can think of two reasons why I didn't grow up racist. One is the bread-and-butter equality between the Heights Annex and "Niggertown." From our end of the telescope, our black neighbors seemed no worse off than we were. That was a powerful equalizer. The other reason had to do with my parents' values. They simply did not denigrate people, and I picked up on this basic tenet early. To Father and Mother, decent people were like all other decent people. That wasn't open to debate.

The colorlessness of people came into my view when, during the rise of Joe Louis to the heavyweight championship of the world, I watched the effect of his triumphs on my father. Boxing was one of Father's specialities (which was perhaps another reason why I later took it up myself, sort of). He knew the sport well and was extremely partial to Louis. Together we listened to all the fights of the "Brown Bomber," and there were quite a few of them.

The most emotional of these experiences hit us on June 22, 1938, when I was seven. Louis battered Germany's Max Schmeling to a bloody pulp in two and a half minutes. Our very radio set seemed to be rocking under the pounding. Nobody listening that day has ever forgotten the excitement. Father could forever after recite every blow of the event, and Joe Louis could do no wrong in his eyes.

Why? I learned a lot about straight thinking when I figured that out as I grew older.

I never heard Father say a word about this champion in terms of race. Nor did he view Louis's fights as contests between black and white or German against American. To him, Louis was, first off, a professional, a model fighter. He was economical and didn't waste a lot of punches. He was fair, careful not to hit on the breaks when the referee stepped in.

Next, Father appraised Louis as a man and found his demeanor low-key, plain, with an appealing sense of humor.

Finally, Louis, a kid out of the Detroit slums, son of a southern sharecropper, deserved respect because he had fought his way out of his ditch. Why should anyone give a damn whether such a person was brown or green? The man was colorless. He met my father's idealized view of what an American hero should be.

Did I really grow up oblivious to prejudice, ignorant of schisms that divide Americans? Yes and no.

By way of example, if you'd asked me in my early teens what anti-Semitism was, I would not have been able to give an intelligent response. I had a Jewish friend but didn't know it. His name was Paul Rosenthal. He was a little guy who didn't live in the Heights Annex but several miles away from me, in the Heights. We went through junior high and high school together and threw the football a bit. When I was down with rheumatic fever, Paul rode his bicycle to Prince Street to bring me a textbook that I needed from school and to visit awhile. Mother was impressed by his loyalty, Paul having troubled to come such a long way.

My friend became a pediatrician in Houston, but until well after we got out of high school I had no idea he was Jewish. I didn't really know what the word "Jew" meant. I had heard my father speak of "what happened to the Jews in Germany" and, of course, had heard and seen references to "the Jews" in the Bible. But out of sheer dumbness, I guess, and a lack of firsthand knowledge or experience, I couldn't have defined the word if my life depended on it.

"Catholics," as in what Protestants call "Roman Catholics," I knew and had heard a bit more about. But only a little. If anyone with whom I was personally acquainted was Catholic, it was lost on me. Certainly at the time it didn't matter. "Catholics" and "Jews" were not the subject of conversations nor of controversy insofar as I knew and was taught.

Color was a different matter. The color of people's skin was the subject of conversation, controversy, and, yes, hate with some people in my early times and place. While I have long considered myself relatively blind to color, my own experience and education with (and about) this is no flat-footed proposition. It's complicated and requires probing in the interest of candor. It's possible that my memory is playing tricks on me. I may be repressing certain events because they're unpleasant. That wouldn't be unusual.

It could be meaningful that I do not distinctly recall two incidents remembered by my sister, Patricia, while we were combing through our memories not long ago, preparing for this book. Pat, a teacher in Houston, eight years younger than myself, dates the first incident to the time when she was around four and I was perhaps eleven or twelve. The vignette is vivid in her mind.

It was wartime, the Great Depression was finally and

definitely over, and the war economy had improved Father's earnings so that my mother could occasionally hire the help of a good-natured black baby-sitter named Daisy. Daisy went about her duties unobtrusively. Mostly she just kept an eye out while a group of us played in the backyard.

Pat remembers that one afternoon, unaccountably, we formed a circle and danced around shouting, "Daisy is a nigger."

As I've said, the word "nigger" was not then rare and appalling, not among many whites and some blacks. It was, however, clearly pejorative, a definite no-no among decent Texans. When word got out a little later about the scene with Daisy, so Pat remembers, my mother did something most extraordinary. She took me from the backyard to the front yard, beat me up as publicly as was feasible on Prince Street, and admonished me, "You don't use that word ever again!" It was evident that she wanted to set straight not only her own kids but youngsters throughout the neighborhood.

Pat is a reliable reporter and I have every reason to believe that all this happened as she recalls it—even if I don't.

What did I know and when did I know it?

I must have known *something* about the existence of discrimination early in life because the other incident in Pat's memory took place quite a while before the awful embarrassment involving Daisy.

It was a Sunday afternoon and two black kids had wandered into our turf from their end of Sixteenth Street to join a ball game as so often before. This time the peaceful scene was shattered by parental interference: a shouted command from a white woman who was watching her son.

"Johnny, you come home," she ordered. "You don't play with that nigger!"

The game thereupon broke up, and Pat recalls that I ran home angry and crying.

"Why do they have to be like that?" I evidently asked.

Good question. Furious, Father tried to explain the injustices of inequality. While I don't recall what kind of case he made on that occasion, I have a graphic mental picture of another time when I was present to see my father literally rise in defense of men fighting for their civil rights. I was fourteen or fifteen years old, World War II had either ended or was very near its end. I have written of Father's gutsy stand before, but since it shook me up quite a bit it deserves another look in present context.

The scene was the dilapidated Civic Club on North Shepherd Drive, the one and only hotbed of politics in the Heights. A Democratic precinct meeting had been called. As yet, there was, in effect, no Republican party in Texas, so the Democrats ran affairs much as they pleased. The precinct leadership was "lily white," as the saying went. So were the candidates in Democratic primaries. Nomination amounted to election. The process was almost invariably neat and un-eventful.

Mother, her private radar alert as ever, had sensed that the upcoming gathering might be different. Veterans were starting to come home, including black veterans. Some might show up at the meeting. Knowing how Father felt about the rights of blacks, she didn't want him to go. There might be trouble. Perhaps she had picked up static to that effect from the wives' grapevine.

Although wives in my environment were remarkably well informed and often influential, they stayed behind the scenes. That was good form. Not many women tried to penetrate the smoke of a precinct meeting, not in our community, until well after World War II. So when Father insisted on attending, Mother sent me along as a kind of security guard. I suspect that she figured he was unlikely to become involved in a scrap in front of a son.

Several black veterans did show up, which was unprecedented, and these were of a new breed: They had fought for their country and knew their rights. The key vote was on whether those assembled would approve, en masse as a slate, a list of delegates from our precinct to go to the Democratic party's county convention. The names had been worked out before the public meeting. The slate, as it had been for well over half a century, was all white.

"Those not in favor of the nominations as read, stand," said the chairman. The few black veterans rose. So did my father. He had grown up in the neighborhood, he knew these men, and he had made up his mind that what they were doing was right, what others were doing was wrong. It was time for change. The war had changed things.

"Rags, you don't understand," said the chairman. "It's not your time to vote. You're standing up at the wrong time."

"I understand all right," he countered. "These people have a right to be here. From now on whenever they stand up, you'll find me standing up with them."

I thought there'd be a fistfight and got scared. There was only a quick flash of anger, however, and when we left we were targets of some rough words and a little shoving.

I was immensely proud of my father's independence, and I'd learned in that precinct meeting that one could stand up for one's principles, regardless of the odds, and survive, perhaps even win.

The Rathers made many mistakes. No doubt we made many regarding people of other races, nationalities, and religions. But my mother and father tried hard to be, and to have their children be, tolerant and understanding about differences among people.

In this, as in so many other ways, what I didn't know then but do know now, is how lucky my sister and brother and I were.

At my right elbow, on the side table next to the corner of the dark green leather couch where I conduct a lot of my business when I'm in my CBS office, there is room for only two articles: a telephone and a Bible. The Bible is open. Some visitors have wondered, occasionally in print, whether the open book is some quaint affectation. It's not. It's me. I have strayed from the Bible's teachings many times, too many. I have never stopped reading it.

Religion, especially prayer, has been an intimate personal companion at my side in my everyday routine ever since the earliest mists of my childhood. After saying grace with breakfast at home, as we normally did each morning, I stood in class, head bowed, in silent (and then noncontroversial) prayer at the start of the public school day. On weekends, Sunday school started at 9:15 A.M. and church didn't let out until 12:30. A booster shot—consisting of another service lasting one and a half hours—was administered on Sunday night, again on rock-hard seats. Bible study was held Wednesday night. And the preacher dropped in at home most anytime to check on our spiritual status.

Not that we were a particularly religious family. We were not. Father occasionally said "damn" and worse (Mother pretended not to hear him), and he'd have a cold beer on weekends, sometimes even a shot of whiskey after coming home from hunting on an icy night. Our religious observances were nothing unusual; this was how things were done. The truly religious folks were believers like the members of the Texas Baptist Convention who in 1945 denied an honorary degree from Baylor University to President Harry Truman because he had been known to take a drink and play poker.

We, too, were Baptists. Indeed, we were "hard-shell, hymn-singing, foot-washing, total-immersion Baptists." I doubt that even everyone in our church considered us to be that. It's what we called ourselves. This meant that we belonged to the predominant of Texas's 45 "major" and 87 "minor" denominations. Exactly 759,860 of our kind were counted in the early 1940s. The next-ranking power were the Methodists, with 488,584 Texas members. They were supposed to be a higher caste of people; as an old joke had it, a Methodist is a Baptist who learned to read and write. Happily, we were unaware of our lowly status. Somewhere near Washington Avenue there was rumored to be a Presbyterian church, but I knew nobody who claimed to have seen it. We thought we had something of a monopoly on all of Christianity.

Paradoxically, what others called organized religion didn't interest us. We had nothing against the religion of others. We just didn't know much about other religions and they didn't interest us. Our denomination knew no bishop, no hierarchy, no central authority. That was Baptist tradition. Our preachers were hired (and not infrequently fired) by the congregation. The minister spoke from a lectern and wore an ordinary suit. At that, he held too much authority to please my father, a God-fearing man who loved the Bible. When the preacher came calling, however, Father usually stayed only briefly. By his departure he wished to assert his almost fanatical belief in his own beloved independence and his preference for what he called "the church within." "Peacock preachers"—show-offs—were among his pet peeves.

Mother was more forgiving of the church's trespasses, and I followed her lead. Doing everything reasonable, and even some things unreasonable, to get right with God seemed the right thing to do.

Our God had two faces. He could send you to hell for sinning, as promised in the hellfire-and-brimstone sermons common in Baptist pulpits. Or He could redeem you and guarantee your future if you got right with Him. And only God Himself could do it. No middlemen. That was your first order of business, to get right with the Lord, and for Baptists it was a simple, personal process requiring no complicated qualifications or rituals. It was an imperative, not a choice, but it was benign.

"God is love" was the theme I took away from Grandmas Page and Rather, from my own mother, and from Sunday school. He was in our home and in us. We believed in the power of prayer. The Lord's Prayer ("Our Father, who art in Heaven . . .") was the mantra for working people when I grew up. No one believed anybody could live up to the Ten Commandments and the Sermon on the Mount all or even much of the time. But everybody I knew well believed in them as goals, as distant stars to be traveling ever towards.

When I came to live in New York in 1975 I passed a synagogue on Fifth Avenue on which was carved in stone, "Do justice, love mercy, walk humbly." I still pass that spot regularly and always it makes me glow with memories of Grandma Page and Sunday school. I'm happy with the transplant of this biblical wisdom from Bloomington and Prince Street, Texas, to the east side of the big place where I now live. It makes a comforting connection. Even when I can't live up to it, it is comforting to hear a murmur of the distant past and what I was taught.

It was with great conviction that I also recited, from early on, "The Lord Is My Shepherd, I Shall Not Want." At Hamilton Junior High School or at CBS, I might pass through the valley of the shadow of death. No matter. "I will fear no evil: for thou art with me; thy rod and thy staff they comfort me." *Comfort*, there it is again. That was what I most needed and what I drew from my schooling in the faith perhaps best of all. And always the Bible was the link, the lifeline.

Mother and Father gave me my first Bible when I was seven. It was an edition with Jesus' words printed in red. Mother taught me to treat it as a precious possession, but not to hold it aside like a Sunday suit to wear only on institutionalized occasions.

The Bible was part of life's fabric. "Wither thou goest, I will go," from the Book of Ruth, was a promise as close to me as the pledge of allegiance to the flag. Joshua, the commander at the Battle of Jericho, where the sun and the moon stood still, might as well have lived in the Heights Annex.

At times, my piety caused me concern. I remember Mr.

Stramler, my friend Charlie's father, trying to brief us about the Trinity—the Father, the Son, and the Holy Ghost—when he was teaching Sunday school at our West Fourteenth Avenue Baptist Church. He did not do a great job explaining the Holy Ghost. He did mention that this ghost lurked "everywhere." I became alarmed. Was the ghost in the room right now? It sounded like that and that was scary. As soon as I got home I consulted Mother, the ecclesiastical authority.

She caught on at once that Mr. Stramler had unleashed an unfortunate image. The Holy Ghost, she said, was not literally a ghost. It was really a holy spirit, nothing spooky or threatening. At bedtime that night I no longer felt troubled when I recited, as I'd been taught before the age of two, "Now I lay me down to sleep . . ."

The total immersion required in my baptism was a more palpable worry. I was seven, possibly eight years old and realized that this would be my debut, so to speak, as a real person, a member of my church. I vaguely knew that other churches performed christenings at a baby age and merely sprinkled a few drops of water at a little newcomer to the congregation. We Baptists didn't believe in such wimpy, premature proceedings. The new member had to be a thinking person; and to be purified of all sin he had to be dunked all the way. After that he'd be born again. This was the central tenet of the church, the principal difference that made us Baptists.

I hadn't grasped the symbolism of the ceremony, probably because I was preoccupied with its safety aspects. I discussed these with my friend Georgie Hoyt, who was equally mystified. Total immersion sounded risky. How does it work? Does it hurt? How do you keep from getting water up your nose? I'm not sure whether we went ahead because of our faith in God or mostly because we knew that all the other kids were doing it and all had survived.

It actually wasn't so bad. Behind the choir I hopped into an oversized tub of very cold water, filled chin-high. The preacher, in shirt and jeans, was with me, praying. His hand was firmly behind my head. "This is going to be easy," he said quietly. Holding his hand over my nose and mouth, he dunked me for several seconds as he intoned, "In the name of the Father, the Son and the Holy Ghost." Afterward, I must confess, I didn't feel like a better person, merely proud that I'd withstood the procedure without incident and relieved that it was over.

The significance of the Baptist feet-washing ceremony did not escape me. It meant that I'd be "walking humbly with thy God," a demonstration of humility. Jesus had not minded washing the feet of tribesmen and neither should we. I participated in this ritual two or three times when I was around twelve years old and the ceremony was beginning to go out of style. I washed another boy's feet and he washed mine. We thought it was fun, especially when we could watch adults do it.

Abuse of prayer got me in trouble a time or two. When I told Mother that I had prayed for better grades in school and for a certain Christmas present, I forget what, she explained that this was improper. I was embarrassed. We had several discussions about this dilemma until I understood that prayer would cause "thine" to be done, not necessarily mine. It was OK to pray for His favor, but not for a B in algebra.

These and other stumbles were not too distressing to me because we Baptists are not traumatized by one troublesome force: guilt. We know that nobody can accomplish the feat of living by the Ten Commandments every moment of every day. When lapses occur, redemption is always near and available—if you're repentant and get right with God.

All members of the Rather family still try to work at that each day, each in his or her own way.

My wife, Jean, is a Lutheran, as both sides of her family have been for centuries. Her mother, Hilda, is a consensus saint. Mostly because of that, when the children were young we agreed to begin them in the Lutheran church. While at least part of me may always be Baptist, the truth is that, like a lot of people, members of our little family have tried a number of different churches of various Protestant denominations over the years. Partly that may be because we've moved a fair amount all over the world. Also, our children were educated for a long while by the Society of Friends (Quakers). Then, too, we got to know a remarkable Episcopalian pastor, Keith Rockwell.

Frankly, our faith is not as rock solid, not as well founded as that of our fathers and mothers, and their fathers and mothers. We must face the unpleasant fact that because we have had an easier life and more of life's riches we're inclined to become soft and flabby spiritually, and especially in the religious sense. The trials of the Great Depression are long gone. So is our great war, World War II, which we could have lost to demons who were real threats to conquer our homeland. A lack of fear in day-to-day living can lead to malaise of the soul; maybe that has happened to us. Also, since Jean and I are children of the Depression, we tend to be forever restless, seeking and moving on.

Father had his own way of measuring men, and on his radar set Howard Hughes was no big deal, even though this local boy was a nationally celebrated wonder whose seemingly inexhaustible fortune had been made in Texas oil.

Oil being Father's turf, he naturally knew all about the Hughes "rock bit" (or "roller bit"), a drill with 166 cutting edges that could crunch at underground oil with an efficiency not previously possible. The drill, developed by Howard's father and his associates in a dingy workshop on Crawford Street downtown and instantly successful, dated back to 1908, when Howard was three years old. It was a money machine, and when I grew up in the thirties it was still rated as one of the wonders of the world.

Father showed it to me in operation when he took me to

the one oil field we had working close to home, at Eleventh Street and North Shepherd Drive. My pals and I had passed by it on rafting trips, and it was nothing like the brawling world of derricks that would later enthrall moviegoers in Edna Ferber's story *Giant*. The Heights oil field was a laughable dwarf: three or four derricks in the pine trees. Still, it encompassed all the essential elements of drilling. Father pointed them out and explained everything patiently and understandably. Remarkably, what he didn't comment on was the Howard Hughes phenomenon. The name came up only tangentially.

At the time, Hughes wasn't yet the eccentric and reclusive hypochondriac of his later years when his whereabouts weren't known, he didn't wash, and his fingernails grew into fangs. When I was a boy he was admired as a formidable achiever. He was constantly big in the headlines because he designed aircraft, raced them across the country and around the world, and began to create TWA airlines and numerous other enterprises. More noticeably yet, he made movies in Hollywood, very, very sexy and wildly notorious movies that he directed and produced personally.

Years before he discovered the expanses of Jane Russell's bosom and immortalized her in *The Outlaw*, a version of Billy the Kid's life, he introduced the world to Jean Harlow, a sex goddess with startling, almost albino blond hair whose breasts were likewise famous. They were so firm that she never wore a bra. Hughes starred her in a sensational aviation battle picture, *Hell's Angels*, in which she seduced daring young pilots and uttered the immortal line, "Do you mind if I slip into something more comfortable?" The picture cost 3.8 million Depression dollars to make, an unheard of budget.

Throughout his capers, the tall, lanky Hughes remained shy, boyish, almost bashful, and he was by no means sleazy. He dated women by the bushel basket, his taste being generally fastidious. Among his ballyhooed longer romances was one with the classy Katharine Hepburn (who eventually dropped him as boring).

Although there surely was no other Houstonian who could, by conventional standards, remotely compare with Howard Hughes, my father, characteristically, was awed by another local Hughes who impressed him more. The day we went out to the Heights oil field, Father spoke glowingly and at length about Joe D. Hughes, a Hughes of an earthier stripe and no relation to Howard. Joe Hughes was one of my father's heroes because he was the greatest oil field truck hauler ever.

His fleet of trucks moved drilling equipment down most any corduroy (log) road, no matter how deep in mud. Father had witnessed such feats many times. When a piece of equipment absolutely, positively had to be in an appointed place at an appointed hour, Joe D. Hughes would get it there. That deserved respect. This man moved mountains.

"We're going to have to get Joe D. Hughes to haul all this stuff," Father joked when once we tried to clean out our cluttered garage. He meant that his hero could perform the impossible.

The causes of this extravagant admiration were clear to me as a boy. Joe D. Hughes was a Texan and he had stayed at home. He had achieved his success on his own without family money. He was a man's man who still worked in khakis, like Father. And utter dependability, Joe's hallmark, was a value prized by my dad.

Why was Joe deemed better than Howard? I'm not certain. Perhaps the universe of Howard Hughes was too gargantuan and forbidding for Father to grasp. More likely he discounted Howard's stature because he'd left Texas and had been favored by a big grubstake from his family. And maybe Father's cavalier treatment of Howard Hughes was his way of teaching me that money and glamour aren't everything.

20

Memorable Moments

DURING THE DEPRESSION and World War II and afterward, as the country entered the Cold War and headed toward another hot one in Korea, I experienced quite a few boyhood moments that stick in my mind. So here comes a collection of freeze-frames about episodes that still make me smile—or ponder. They'll tell you a bit more about the place and the times.

Virginia Sandel was the first girl (besides my very young sister) whom I got to know fairly well. We were in junior high school together and I wasn't shy with Virginia, as I was with girls in general—very shy in fact. Virginia was different because she wasn't available. She was very pretty, a freckle-faced redhead, physically mature, with the kind of figure that turned heads. Alas, she was the "steady" of my good friend Richard Smith, Jr., and they eventually got married. For a while, the three of us hung out together.

Virginia was a scholar and ranked all the way at the

head of our class. She looked upon her achievements as a necessity because she was absolutely determined to go to college, for which she would need a full scholarship. So she figured that it was essential for her to get almost straight A's, and she did.

I was about twelve when I first knew Virginia, and I still wasn't awfully preoccupied with the idea of needing to go to college. I wasn't the greatest student. More advanced math, for instance, might as well have been Hindustani. Not only couldn't I comprehend it, I couldn't grasp what it was for. Why was it necessary to bust my head over this stuff?

Virginia told me.

"You always say you want to be a reporter," I remember her chiding me. "There's no way you're going to be a reporter unless you go to college."

Coming from Virginia, by then almost an older sister to me, this lecture was food for thought. It was also the first time in my history with young women that I paid attention to their brains. And I did have a history of sorts.

My first crush, Jeannette Sessions in the third grade, was the prettiest and most popular girl in the class. I couldn't resist competing for her attention. Mrs. Simmons, our principal, a fan of King Arthur and male chivalry, tried to tame the boys and recruit them into some semblance of knighthood. So I carried Jeannette's books a few times, even though she lived on a street in the real Heights, far from my own home. The chivalry didn't take. Jeannette found too many other book carriers.

At thirteen, I had a sobering experience with Rachel. She was another school beauty, dark-haired with olive skin, very gentle, a little like a mini-version of my mother. It was the time when I was feeling like an outcast because of my bout with rheumatic fever, and Rachel was sweet to me, although I also picked up that she had a certain firmness about her.

Rachel and I would go to have a Coke now and then,

that was all. I never could psyche myself up sufficiently to ask her out for a movie.

The moment of truth came later, when I was feeling better and was getting on a Heights bus. The driver, in uniform, had his arm around the waist and hips of a dark-haired girl in shorts. I was profoundly shocked to see that it was Rachel. I had thought of her as a schoolgirl. The bus driver had obviously viewed her differently. A year or so later they were married.

For better or worse, my leaps toward beauty would not cease. In ninth grade I again developed something of a hang-up on the most popular girl within theoretical reach. She was a cheerleader and definitely the cheerleader type. Her name was evocative: Bebe Hooks. I dreamed of carrying *her* books, an impossible dream. She was much too much in demand. This time I didn't mind. It had dawned on me that I was still too awkward with girls. It was good that I didn't have to appear in that stunted condition before the great Bebe Hooks.

When I was fourteen, the monthly school dances began. By then Mother had taught me the rudimentary dance-floor skills. Still, I couldn't see myself summoning the courage actually to ask a girl to dance. The first time I went to a dance I did have a good time, albeit as a bystander. I sat through the whole event, wistfully listening to the last number, "Let Me Call You Sweetheart." I didn't get near enough to call any girl anything.

I brought up my problem with my peers, and one of them, Frank Ring, proved the perfect consultant. He was a tall boy, secure in his early maturity, and known as our jitterbug king. I was especially eager to know precisely how close one could hold a girl. Frank gave me the word. The main move, he said, was to take charge. And there was nothing wrong about the bodies touching. I should mention for context that our first ninth-grade dances were about as loose as the Congress of Vienna.

During the second dance, Frank walked halfway across the floor with me for support and I actually sidled up to a very tall, dark-haired girl—one of the class beauties, naturally—and I actually asked her to dance! I felt like one of those knights that Mrs. Simmons back in grade school had hoped I would turn out to be.

We danced. I did not faint. I did not stumble. The minimal steps seemed to come to me all right. I was, however, struck dumb. Luckily, my partner—Doris Ewing, I think it was—picking up that I wasn't exactly Mr. Smooth, initiated the conversation, which went fine. I was back on preferred territory: words.

There's nothing boys need more than approval from their fathers, and my dad was never stingy with his. Like Mother, he was a true believer in the power of praise.

Anytime I brought home a good report card, he made a ritual of the occasion. I gave the report to Mother after school, she handed it to Dad before supper, and he would beam and break into a marvelously redundant recital: "Good, very good," he'd start out as he began to scan my grades, and then: "Very good, excellent!" and his smile would turn two miles wide, plenty big enough for me to bask in.

Whenever I had mowed the lawn, a job I detested but had to do twice a week, Father would walk around to inspect the yard in detail. Usually he'd say, "Good job." Then he'd add with emphasis, "We *finish* jobs!" I translated this to mean, "You and I don't leave jobs half finished, the way some people do. We Rathers think alike."

My choice of career baffled him at first. Journalism? What exactly was that and how could a man make a decent living at something so vague? If Danny was going to insist on going to college, why couldn't he become a lawyer or a doctor or something else that was solid?

He came around as soon as I was "on the radio." Radio

was a vital source of knowledge, so Father was proud of me and said so. It helped for me to give him a running account of my earnings. He considered them remarkable even back in the late 1950s, as indeed did I.

Father never earned more than twelve thousand dollars a year, and for many years I believed I'd never crack the $10,000 barrier, which was every young man's dream. Behold, by 1959 I was making $10,800! This was by way of holding three jobs: working as a staff newsman at a local radio station and as reporter for two news services. My total take also included extra fees for play-by-play sportscasting.

My time was spread so thin that I wasn't watching much television, and I almost made the mistake of turning down a local TV job on KHOU-TV, Houston's Channel 11. A friend, Bob Levy, talked me into it, thank heaven. This time I held only one job, not three, and I started at $10,900 a year. That was in 1960. In December 1961, after some hurricane coverage had caught CBS's eye, I signed on with the network for $18,000 a year. Just before I actually started working with CBS News in March, my father and I talked. He was so proud.

"Dan, you're in a different league now, a whole different world," he said. "It's a world I don't know or understand. But gawdamighty, boy, I think you'll make $25,000, maybe $35,000 a year before you're through! And I'll tell you something else, son: This is an important job, important work." His awed tone gave me the most fantastic lift. It would have been hard to tell whose chest was stuck out more, his or mine. That was in March.

In May 1962 my father died at the age of fifty-two. He was killed in a head-on car collision as he drove to work early one morning. It happened on Shepherd Drive, not far from our old watermelon-stand lot.

A sixteen-year-old kid lost control of a huge concrete truck he was driving; the truck swerved across the center line onto Dad's side of the street. My father died instantly, in freshly ironed khakis with a red bandanna folded neatly in his hip pocket.

My mother died in Houston, 1968. She had had the beginnings of what were described as "early signs of stroke." It was decided that surgery was necessary. She never really recovered from it. That's the official cause of death. (She was fifty-eight.) My own view is that she never came back from the shock of my father's death and the loneliness that followed, that she actually died of a broken heart—one she would never let show.

She marveled at the places I went, the things I saw, what I was experiencing. She believed (and sometimes said) that it all just proved again "how much was possible with hard work and God's grace." She worried much about my traveling during the worst of the civil rights time. She recognized what my coverage of the Kennedy assassination meant in terms of my acceptance as a professional. When I covered the White House in 1964 she fretted that perhaps I was being too tough on President Johnson—after all, he was a Texan. When I went to London she loved it. *That* was "big time," capital "B," capital "T," with her (besides, she knew I had wanted to go to Vietnam instead and was pleased that I hadn't been allowed to).

She was opposed to my going to Vietnam when I did, "or any other time," worried that I would not make it back alive. But she understood. She visited us in London, helped Jean with the children there while I was away covering the war. When I came back from 'Nam in 1966, back through London, then back to the White House, she was beginning to be ill.

Later, near death (although I did not know it), she admonished me, "About yesterday, no tears. About tomorrow, no fears."

*   *   *

Little plays and other theatrical undertakings were common in school, at church, in backyards and garages. My young friends and kinfolk and neighbors may have thought they spotted a little yen to perform in me early on. Was this a bid for approval by my peers? Maybe.

Anyway, it's beyond dispute that at about eight or nine I appointed myself impresario of a theatrical troupe that went into action on the dirt floor of our garage. In addition to the usual suspects—Georgie Hoyt and Homer Bredehoft—I was able to dragoon some of the neighborhood girls into the act. Ellen Hoyt, Georgie's sister, was a good sport about it and so was Betty McManus, the prettiest girl in our surroundings. Tommy Snyder helped. So did Roy Fahey.

Walt Disney was our guiding light and *Snow White* was our big hit presentation. We used a flour sack for the star's cape and sometimes our shortage of personnel led to a cast reduction from seven dwarves to three or four. Nevertheless, the audience received us warmly. Perhaps this was because we charged no admission. We could usually count on a gaggle of children and two or three mothers.

For the life of me, I can't recall which one of the dwarves' parts was mine to enact. Was I Sneezy? Doubtful. I didn't have that many colds. Was I Dopey? I certainly hope not. I do remember that we also produced the Heights Annex version of *Pinocchio* and that I played the part of Gepetto, the father, and puffed around wearing some sort of itchy homemade mustache.

The role called for me to send Pinocchio off to school and instruct him to be a good boy and not to lie. Everybody knows how much good that did. I did like being the cast's elder statesman.

Most of all, I loved the applause, even of this audience that neither paid nor was subject to Nielsen ratings. Looking back on it and reflecting, I no doubt loved the approval. Children do, even those who never let on. When my fellow performers and I launched into a finale of "Zip-A-Dee-Doo-Dah" and the spectators started clapping and whistling, life was good.

Not only were more Americans closer to the land in the 1930s and forties, more were closer with (and knew more about) animals, too: horses, cows, mules, chickens, and especially dogs. Cats as pets grew in popularity as the country grew more urban in the 1950s, sixties, and seventies. In earlier parts of the century, dogs were the most popular household pets. In our neighborhood some people had cats; everybody had a dog.

When I was eight, the family mourned the loss of Buck. It was an awful day.

We had a dog named Blackie, too, a mongrel that looked like a shelty and was everybody's pet. But Buck was special because he was Dad's alone and the love he had for Buck was a thing to behold. Something more than affection went on between those two. Buck brought out the teacher that was dormant in Dad. He was Professor Higgins to Buck's Eliza Doolittle.

The loving relentlessness of a Higgins was indeed required to coax the all too latent hunter in Buck. Dad had felt the need for a bird dog, but real bird dogs were expensive and so he negotiated a trade—for a tool? a used tire?—and brought home Buck as a pup, a few weeks old. He was a supposedly full-bred pointer, but doubts developed early on about Buck's antecedents.

A bird dog was supposed to heel and point and retrieve and to perform his duties with a hunter's zeal, to be at one with his master on the prowl. Evidently Buck lacked the requisite fever in the blood. He wasn't exactly retarded, but he displayed what today we would charitably call a "learning disability." I think he was plain too good-natured.

Dad felt challenged. He would teach Buck. I think he

had visions of himself setting forth like the kind of gentleman hunter he had read about in a copy of *Outdoor Life* in
the barbershop.

He fed Buck personally. He bought a book on dog
training and lavished the same energy on this dog that he
invested in coming to terms with the slide rule. I watched
him spend endless hours teaching Buck to heel. It was a
frustrating campaign; fortunately it was impossible to get
mad at Buck. He was too sweet.

And he was so thin that his ribs stood out. His head was
long, his tail was white with big brown spots. And cuddly!
Buck invented cuddly. He loved everybody and licked your
toes. Regrettably, he didn't seem to enjoy the woods all that
much and remained slow even at retrieving. He was just too
friendly to enact the martial role he had been assigned to fill
in life. Characteristically, Father never gave up, and after
four years of unflagging effort Buck had been transformed
into a reasonably competent bird dog.

Father took him everywhere on troubleshooting trips
and, to make sure he wouldn't ever be left behind, Buck
slept under Dad's company car, Houston Pipeline's 1939
Ford coupe. One morning Dad was leaving for work and we
heard heartbreaking yelps of pain. Dad had backed out over
Buck.

There couldn't have been a more desperate lifesaving
effort if Buck had been human. Mother rushed to get several
blankets to wrap around him. Our rubber hot-water bottle
kept him warm. Buck was in shock and kept whimpering. A
lay animal expert lived in the neighborhood and I was deputized to get him. Father didn't go to work for half a day, and
when Buck inevitably died he was severely shaken.

We held a funeral for Buck in the vacant lot out in back.
Father's eyes were rimmed with tears. Up to his own death,
he never again backed out a car without walking around it
first, and when he taught me to drive he made sure I followed the same routine.

What shook me most was the effect of Dad's mistake on himself. He was a forgiving man, but he couldn't forgive himself. I'd never seen him vulnerable, and I couldn't remember that he had ever made a big mistake before.

The mobility of rank-and-file Americans exploded during and after World War II. Before the war, a trip of two hundred miles was a big adventure and a major expense for most families. It was for ours. . . .

Texas was one hundred years old in 1936, when I was five, and therefrom hangs a memory that is only vicariously mine. It really belongs to my parents, but I heard about it in so much glowing detail and so often over the years that I felt I'd been with them on the grand adventure of their lives.

My parents were spirited armchair travelers, especially my father. I used to hear his ruminations about transatlantic crossings on huge, luxurious ocean liners like the *Normandie* with a lot of swell folks in expensive clothes. The *Normandie*, launched in 1932, was the world's largest, more than a thousand feet long. It was also the most elegant; every first-class cabin was done in an entirely different decor. Alas, Father only glimpsed its huge bow on cheery travel posters.

Truth to tell, the three-or-four-day outing to the 1936 Texas Centennial in Fort Worth and Dallas was the peak of my parents' live travel experience in all their years. It was their second honeymoon, their passage through the big time. Of course they had no money for a lot of restaurant meals, so Mother cooked for days ahead, packing lots of jars into white flour sacks for the 250-mile train journey. Their belongings filled a cheap suitcase, then called a "grip." I don't recall where they put up; it must have been a very cut-rate rooming house.

The payoff in thrills made Mother and Father burble whenever they reminisced, for the Centennial wasn't merely Texas-sized. It was a double-whammy, a twin event run simultaneously in Dallas *and* Fort Worth because neither city could stand to be upstaged by the other.

In Dallas, the emphasis was on culture. They offered a million-dollar Hall of State, five museums, and a new amphitheater with symphonic shell. Admiral Richard E. Byrd set up a replica of the camp he had established in Little America at the North Pole. About as low-brow as the Dallas exhibits got was a replica of Judge Roy Bean's courtroom where he administered the law as practiced "west of the Pecos."

Upstart Fort Worth ballyhooed a more down-to-earth pitch. It hired the Broadway showman Billy Rose, known as "the mighty midget" because he was little more than five feet tall, and Billy came up with the sly slogan, "Dallas for Education, Fort Worth for Entertainment." He lived up to his propaganda. His centerpiece was the Casa Manana, an unprecedented combination of amphitheater and restaurant seating four thousand people and charging $1.50 for a meal, which was a pile of money. And the centerpiece of the centerpiece was the inimitable fan dancer Sally Rand.

Sally, thirty-two and a onetime Mack Sennett dancer in Hollywood, was the most respectable scandal of the time. Three years earlier, at the Chicago World's Fair, she pulled off a sensation—and five thousand a week—with a dance of her own design that made the preachers see blue. Twirling two seven-foot ostrich fans across strategic parts of her anatomy, she swayed her allegedly nude body through Debussy's "Clair de Lune" and Chopin's Waltz in C-sharp Minor.

Ecstatic crowds climbed the walls in Chicago and again for Billy Rose in Fort Worth. Everyone claimed to be shocked. Only the preachers really were.

While Sally got the billing and the publicity, the true stars were in the big production numbers: the handpicked show girls, known as "Rose's long-stemmed American roses." Their beauty dazzled Mother and Father and everybody else.

"A thousand girls, 999 costumes," Father always said

appreciatively, probably repeating another Billy Rose slogan.

The other day I decided to read up on what finally happened to Sally Rand before her death at seventy-five in 1979. The preachers were wrong in her case because she did not seem headed for hell. Upon her retirement from dancing she went to college, received her degree, and became active in the PTA of her son's school. Gypsy Rose Lee and Madonna hit the big time in Sally's wake. She was the original.

"How high's the water, Mama?"

Johnny Cash, whom I know and like, did a song of that title in the late 1950s, and instantly my memory went back to 1935 and stories told about the great hurricane and flood that hit Houston that year.

Exactly the same question about the height of the water was repeatedly asked by my dad of my mother during the eighteen hours or so when we thought we might have to flee our house at any minute.

"It's past the field," she called out to him sometime before 4:00 A.M. on the first night, which was the worst period. That meant the flood was mighty close, and after sunup I could see the water lapping over the steps of the houses down the block. Mother and Father often told the story, etching details in my memory over the years. I was so young that about all I actually remembered was that I'd never been so scared before.

It began when it got very dark late in the afternoon and the torrential rain started pounding down. Radio bulletins caused my parents to murmur with concern. Then the electricity went off. The radio and the phone stopped working and we peered out of the windows into the darkness, seeing almost nothing. Coal oil lamps gave us light in the house, but we had no idea what was happening anywhere outside.

Pretty soon the roof started leaking onto the back

porch and we put out buckets. I helped Mother pack Father's grip because we thought we'd probably have to run to relatives four blocks away and then perhaps still farther. Father put on his foul-weather gear and piled a few burlap bags against the cement-block foundation of the house.

Eventually there was nothing left to do but wait. Mother and Father took turns watching the water in front of the house and that's when I remember Father shouting to Mother to ask about the flood level. In Johnny Cash's song, the water keeps rising up and up, which is what it also did in the Heights Annex. The Bayou never got so far out of its banks before or since.

Later it turned out that we had lived through Houston's worst flood ever. Two thirds of the county was underwater. Seven people died. Damage totalled $2.5 million. Downtown, boatmen rowed on rescue missions past the flooded ground floors of office buildings.

For us in the Heights Annex, the water crested just in time. Most homes were damaged but few were inundated.

Floods such as this and the need to create public-works jobs during the Depression led to a surge in federal and state flood-control projects, including many dams. The surge began just before World War II and was revived right after the war. We were beginning to tame the environment.

We'd never heard of pizza or yogurt. One of our best family treats was Grandma Page's stone soup. That's correct, stone soup, and I never thought there was anything odd about it.

The family was visiting in Bloomington and cash was tight all around, so Grandma would clean up a big stone and cook it with water and lots of grass, especially grass that came with seeds. I'd help and so did everybody else. We chopped up some carrots or onions and Grandma added a little Tabasco sauce.

She simmered this mix slowly, eventually bringing it briefly to a boil. It made a tasty soup. Although Grandma made no medical claims for it, I suspect in retrospect that she valued it as her private equivalent of a Jewish grandmother's chicken soup. That is: good for what ails you.

A less-austere Depression treat was vinegar pie, a Texas dessert since the middle of the nineteenth century or maybe earlier. It was a direct ancestor of lemon meringue pie, which was too fancy for us because no lemons were produced in Texas until the 1920s, and they became plentiful only after World War II. Vinegar pie was immensely popular because it was so cheap and the ingredients were few.*

When times were relatively flush—that is, whenever a pa had made a payday—two cups of sugar were used. Sour times made the pie more sour. The deed could be done with two thirds or even half a cup of sugar. Grandma Page, more often than not, used brown sugar, my mother used the white kind. Outsiders who sampled vinegar pie have told me: "Its sometimes tart and sometimes sweet, depending on the times."

A sweeter delicacy—I associate it with the tranquility of Sunday as the day was winding down—was ice cream. Few people went out to *buy* ice cream in bulk in those days, very

---

* Here is my mother's recipe as preserved by my sister, Pat:

pastry for 9-inch pie (with lattice top, optional)
1 cup cider vinegar
1¾ cups water
½ to 2 cups brown or white sugar (depending on the times)
2 T. butter
¾ cup flour (adjust if doesn't thicken)

Line a 9-inch pie plate with pastry dough. Chill while preparing the filling. Combine vinegar, water, and sugar in a saucepan. Bring to a boil and cook 3 minutes. Add butter and stir until melted. Mix flour with just enough cold water to make a smooth paste. Stir slowly into the hot butter/syrup. Cook, stirring constantly, until thickened and smooth. Pour filling into pie shell. Crimp edges of shell. Lay on lattice strips (if desired). Press ends of strips securely to edge of crust. Bake at 450° F for 10 minutes; reduce heat to 350° F and bake 25 minutes longer. Serve hot or cold. Serves 6 to 8.

Spices may be added to hot syrup—cinnamon, nutmeg, mace, or allspice (singly or in combination).

few. The word "cholesterol" was unknown. We made our own ice cream in our "ice cream freezer," with loads of cream and fresh peaches or blackberries or other local fruit, and Sunday after 6:00 P.M. was the right time for it: languid, nothing to do but slap the mosquitoes and watch the sun go down.

A few other families would come over with their kids, some still in their Sunday best. Somebody would have baked cookies, and when the tree frogs began to croak and there was some ice cream left, a boy knew that the world was a pretty satisfactory place.

For my parents, the best pause for repose would come Saturday afternoon, except from December to February, when it was too cold. In the screen porch Father built in the back of the house there was room for a little table and a couple of chairs. Mother and Dad would sit and relax out there, not saying much, sipping iced tea from quart-sized fruit jars.

Iced tea was *the* Texas drink. People swam in the stuff. Ours had a little lemon and, after I was around ten years old and we got a refrigerator, the tea contained some chips of ice. The tea was special and was called "sun tea" because it was left out for an hour or so in the sun to enhance the flavor.

Sun-tea time was another blessed occasion when my parents seemed freed of worry. Families making ice cream and sun tea are about gone from American life, replaced by a new pace and new pastimes, especially television. I'm partial to change, as I've said, but I've not forsaken the old pleasures.

In my private office at CBS, I keep a gift from writer and friend Tom Flynn that resonates with memories of my boyhood. It is a framed old-fashioned movie poster that advertises the cult classic and television perennial *Casablanca*.

My parents and I went to see it at the Majestic Theater in downtown Houston in the spring of 1943, and I had rarely known Mother and Dad to chatter with greater animation than when we emerged after being swept away by what is arguably the most famous and moving farewell scene on film: Humphrey Bogart, with his fedora tilted and his trench coat tightly belted, mutters "Here's lookin' at you, kid," and Ingrid Bergman takes off into the fog on the Lisbon plane with her resistance-hero husband, Paul Henreid, half a step ahead of the gestapo, leaving Bogie behind to fight the Nazis.

The war news stoked our excitement. The Russians had lately smashed the siege of Stalingrad. The Allies had seized their first toehold on the European mainland by storming the beaches of Italy. And, providentially, we had won the war's first significant victory by landing on November 8, 1942, in Morocco and liberating Casablanca in three days of bitter street fighting.

With its first rushed finished print, the movie opened November 26 at Warner's Hollywood Theater in Manhattan to rave reviews and standing-room audiences. It was a press agent's dream. A columnist suggested that the War Department check with the producers, Warner Brothers, before planning future invasions.

What did I know about *Casablanca* and when did I know it? The answers are: not much and mostly not until much later. To make up for this deficiency I've recently boned up with some background reading* and discovered that the Rathers' outing to the Majestic Theater was very much part of a national trend. Movies were *the* entertainment then. Some 85 million Americans saw films *every week*, the average ticket costing 25.2 cents, and twice as many movie theaters existed as do now.

What I didn't know about *Casablanca* could have filled

* Of the astoundingly voluminous literature on *Casablanca*, I most enjoyed the fortieth-anniversary essay by Lance Morrow in the December 27, 1982, issue of *Time*, appropriately entitled, "We'll Always Have Casablanca." The book *You Must Remember This: The Filming of Casablanca* by Charles Francisco (Prentice-Hall, 1980) is encyclopedic. A shorter version of the *Casablanca* story appears on pp. 82–91 of *As Time Goes By: The Life of Ingrid Bergman* by Laurence Leamer (Harper & Row, 1986).

books—and did. Certainly I didn't know that the movie was based on an unproduced play, *Everybody Comes to Rick's*, by two unknown playwrights who never did become known, Murray Burnett and Joan Allison; that Ronald Reagan had been considered for Paul Henreid's role, that filming started helter-skelter with an unfinished script; that two endings were written because nobody could figure out until the last shooting whether Bogart or Henreid should get Ingrid. Ugh!

And of course nobody could predict that *Casablanca* would never die and that many of its lines would become rooted in our culture: "Round up the usual suspects" . . . "Play it, Sam. Play *As Time Goes By*" . . . "We'll always have Paris" . . . and, always and forever, "Here's lookin' at you, kid."

In trying to dissect the durability of the film over so many years, some analysts have called it a fable about commitment and sacrifice, about the burdens of the private self in the dangerous public world. Others believe it is a wrench of nostalgia for the simpler, black-and-white times evoked in Rick's Café when the Nazi officers rise to belt out *Die Wacht am Rhein* and Rick gives the black pianist Dooley Wilson the OK to have Paul Henreid's democrats sabotage them by breaking into the Marseillaise.

As we left the Majestic in 1943, my parents knew that they had watched something much more sophisticated than their usual favorites, musicals like the Deanna Durbin songfests or swashbucklers like *Mutiny on the Bounty*. They talked about what they would do under a conqueror's pressure, to risk resistance or cooperate quietly. Suddenly, that was a question.

My father had long held forth on his disgust for traitors and his adoration of resisters like the King of Denmark. None of us Rathers had ever been much for grays when black and white would do. The inner turmoil of the Bogart, Bergman, and Henreid triangle, and especially the slow unmasking of Claude Rains, playing the collaborationist

Vichy police prefect, as a closet anti-Nazi threw a new light on the dilemma of choice-making under the gun.

After *Casablanca* Father began to see the world in subtler nuances. It was a real change in him. Thereafter, when arguments erupted about ambiguities, he would say, "Ah, but you have to allow for light and shade."

That caveat stuck with me and proved handy in TV news work.

Father went still further. It no longer sufficed that he reminded mother of Humphrey Bogart. He went out and bought a wide-brimmed hat, as worn by Bogie and Paul Henreid, and tilted it at the same angle. It was his *Casablanca* hat, to go with his new *Casablanca* vision of the world.

In the nearly half a century since my parents and I first saw *Casablanca* at the Majestic, I've viewed it perhaps a couple of dozen times in theaters and on TV. Its hold on me is strong and something always happens to draw me back to it.

In 1965 I was in Greece, covering riots and unrest. During an off-camera interview with a government minister, he, seemingly offhandedly, brought up the name of George Polk. Polk was a CBS News correspondent who vanished and was assassinated because he was a great reporter and found out too much about Communists and the Greek government back in 1948.

Suddenly, the minister riveted me with a stare and said, "I hope that *you*, Mr. Rather, will not have too much zeal!"

The thought struck me instantly: *Casablanca*! The line suggesting that one might be risking one's life by displaying too much zeal could easily have been uttered by Claude Rains, representing the fascist Vichy government, or, better yet, by Sydney Greenstreet as the slimy racketeer of the bazaars, the fat guy with his big fez.

As soon as I got back to my London headquarters I went to see the film once again and confirmed how eerily it conveys a sense of foreboding.

Even these days, when I return to the picture, I am struck by touches I'd never noticed before. The last time I was stopped short by the way the leading characters *walked* on their way to the farewell scene at the airport. I'd never before recognized how their gaits mirrored their characters and purposes.

Play it again!

21

TV? Never Heard of It!

THERE ARE some people who heard of television in the 1930s. I'm not sure I learned at the time that radios with little screens were on display at the New York World's Fair in 1939. Recently I read somewhere that there were supposed to have been several thousand sets in operation in New York around then. I find that hard to accept. What would these premature fans have been watching? There was no organized programming of any kind.

For the Rather family, the curtain went up a full decade later, in 1949. I remember the scene. We were on a shopping trip, ambling through the appliance section of a department store, and were bowled over by a stunning sight. People were watching a ball game on a tiny screen. It was live, not a movie, black and white of course, and they called it television. It was a measure of our isolation in the hinterlands—not some particular backwardness on the part of my family—that we were barely familiar with the term.

I remember we watched the ball game for around

fifteen to twenty minutes in order to let the enormity of this contraption sink in. It was too farfetched to think we would one day own one of these things. Instead, we were concerned with how this novelty worked and why. There is something unforgettable about being in, sort of, on the birth of a revolution. It freezes your perspective. I guess that's why I find it not totally believable that at my fishing camp today I have a TV dish giving me access to 103 different channels.

Ever spellbound by anything involving electricity, Father briefed us on the theory of how TV functioned. He had come across some articles on the subject in his *Popular Mechanics* magazines and also drew on his expertise in radio. He could repair radio tubes. He taught me Morse code when I was ten or eleven and together we built a send/receive Morse set and a one-station radio in his garage workshop.

And still, TV remained just a contraption. It was not, so to say, in our field of vision. Most certainly it wasn't among our priority longings. We would have been impressed with a rocket ship, but it would hardly have occurred to us to save for one. We were working for a new car, our first truly unused vehicle, which finally materialized as a shiny 1952 Chevrolet.

It isn't mysterious why people found it so easy to get along without a device as dainty as a Muntz TV. The early sets didn't much resemble today's. The better ones were very expensive: around three hundred pre-inflation dollars for a receiver with a picture tube that didn't explode like a toy balloon. That was a fortune, not to mention the cost of the repair people, who used to drop by with the frequency of milkmen. Not to worry. Nobody in the Heights Annex owned a TV and no neighborhood pressure was building to get one, not even by the time my parents acquired a set in 1957 or 1958.

There was still hardly anything to watch, anyway. Entrepreneurs like Houston's sainted jillionaire, Jesse Jones, dismissed television as gadgetry with no future. He warned his investor friends to stay out of it, so Houston had only one station until 1956. One of my good friends, the late newscaster Douglas Edwards, pioneered on CBS with *Douglas Edwards and the News* in 1948, but only five eastern stations carried it. Forget Texas.

Also, it's often overlooked that nobody really needed television. We had radio, which we loved and were addicted to. That loyalty lasted for a long time. Right into the sixties, news magazines carried sections called "Radio—TV," not the other way around. Radio was *the* recreation and pain-killer of the Depression era. By the mid-1930s, an estimated 27.5 million American families (out of a total 32 million) owned a radio, a greater proportion than had indoor plumbing or electricity.

Number one on our family hit parade—and for years his show was the top-rated in the country—was Jack Benny; I mean the radio comedian as he practiced his art long before he made the switch to television. He went on the air every Sunday night, sponsored by Jell-O, which paid him $350,000 a year, and he convulsed us, especially Father. My dad was a prime sucker for any gags whatsoever, and the slightest reference to Benny's stinginess, which was totally fictional, turned him upside down.

I recall the one about Jack and his wife, having had dinner with Jimmy Stewart and his wife, watching the waiter bring the check.

"I'll take it," says Benny reluctantly.

"Oh no," says Jimmy, "I'll take it."

"I couldn't let you do that."

"I'd feel better if I paid the check," says Jimmy Stewart.

"Oh, well, Jimmy, if your health is involved . . ."

Or take the night Jack felt a gun shoved into his ribs. A holdup man snarled, "Your money or your life!"

There was a pause, a very, very long pause.

"Come on, hurry up," says the holdup man.

"I'm thinking it over," says Benny.

This line, perhaps Benny's most famous, was historic, clocking over two minutes of not quite continuous laughter. The gales rose and rose and stopped and then resumed.

I think the appeal of the gags about miserliness had a lot to do with the reality of the Great Depression. When everybody is broke, thrift is a virtue by necessity.

Benny taught me the importance of superior diction. Grandma Page often commented on how easy he was to understand. And his pauses! Benny was the grand master of the grand pause. I found myself listening for his delivery, and when I went on TV many years later I never forgot that television is also importantly an oral medium. Actually, some of Benny's gags worked better without pictures. At least I enjoyed conjuring up my own.

Throughout the many turbulent news days of childhood, beginning in the late 1930s, radio was our lifeline. I grew up on European crises, and all of us were glued to the tinny sound of our static-infested little radio above the sink in our kitchen window.

Would there be war? For years the question hung like a cloud over our dining table. Since Father and Uncle John were forever enmeshed in discussions about the prospects abroad, the isolation of my life was pierced by an odd ray. New York was on the moon, but, thanks to Edward R. Murrow, the voice of CBS News and later my idol, London came alive in our kitchen on Prince Street.

"This is London," Murrow's doomful, throaty sign-on, was as present as our saying grace, and we also never got our full fill of the other newscasters and commentators who were household names to every child: H. V. Kaltenborn (whom we didn't care for), William Shirer, Raymond Graham Swing, Eric Sevareid, and a few others.

At the time of the Munich Pact in late September 1938, the news grew electrifying. Bulletins kept interrupting regular programming from earliest morning through late at night. Would the Allied troops march to oppose Hitler's threat against Czechoslovakia? This was the time when I learned about "appeasement" and its attendant maneuvers—concepts still invoked more than fifty years later during President George Bush's early propaganda war against Iraq's Saddam Hussein.

The Munich controversy had its counterpart in our kitchen. Father thought that Hitler could not be appeased, that he would inevitably go to war, then or a little later. Uncle John, not unreasonably, argued that the world's memories of the ten million lives lost in World War I (which had ended only twenty years earlier) would restrain all sides, even Hitler, the mad corporal with the silly-looking mustache.

Unfortunately, Uncle John's thinking proved too idealistic, and so we listened disgustedly to hear appeasement in action, step by step, on our kitchen radio. The lambs volunteered for the slaughterhouse. Early in the afternoon of September 29, the Allied delegation, led by the long, owlish British Prime Minister, Neville Chamberlain, in wing collar and black suit, walked stiffly into Hitler's office edifice, Munich's *Fuehrerbau*, as CBS correspondent Bill Shirer watched. It was the point of no return.

Bit by bit, we heard how Czechoslovakia was sold out by the West that day. It was Hitler's show from the start. He yelled insults about the defenseless Czechs. He beat his fist against the palm of his other hand. Reasoned discussion was impossible. It was not a negotiation, it was chaos, and at 12:30 A.M. on the thirtieth a protocol approving the dismemberment of Czechoslovakia was ready for signature in four languages. Hitler left the *Fuehrerbau* swaggering, brushing past Bill Shirer, still making notes for his broadcasts.

At Heston Airport the following afternoon, Chamberlain emerged from his plane carrying what became the most notorious umbrella in history, his talisman, forever the symbol of appeasement. In the other hand, he grasped the meaningless document he and Hitler had signed.

"I've got it," the Prime Minister shouted, "I've got it!"

A bit later, he appeared on the balcony of No. 10 Downing Street and spoke the misguided words for which he is best remembered: "I believe it is peace in our time."

The crowd shouted, "Good old Neville!" and sang, "For he's a jolly good fellow."

Our kitchen radio put us there. It was quite a history lesson.

The commanding authority of radio was devastatingly demonstrated exactly a month later. The war scare was still on. People had remained jittery. In Britain, gas masks were being distributed to the populace. And at 8:00 P.M. Eastern time on Sunday, October 30—appropriately and not coincidentally, the event had been scheduled for Halloween, my birthday—CBS dropped a bombshell. It began to broadcast *War of the Worlds* by H. G. Wells, as modernized by Orson Welles, an ambitious actor, producer, and theatrical genius, then all of twenty-three years old.

Six million listeners were stunned to hear an orchestra make way for an announcer who said: "Ladies and gentlemen, we interrupt our program of dance music to bring you a special bulletin." Professors at two university observatories, he continued, had observed "several explosions of incandescent gas, occurring at regular intervals on the planet Mars."

Building up tension with the help of further "bulletins" and "interviews" with "authorities," the program informed the audience at 8:38 P.M. that poisonous gas had begun to spread across the East Coast. It was reaching Manhattan. Hordes of Martian invaders with "tentacles" had materialized, their skin glistening, their V-shaped mouths dripping saliva from rimless lips.

"Now the first Martian reaches the shore," said an announcer allegedly broadcasting from atop a New York skyscraper. "He stands watching, looking over the city. His steel, owlish head is even with the skyscrapers. He is waiting for the others. Now they're lifting their metal hands. This is the end now, people in the streets see it. They're running towards the East River . . . thousands of them dropping in like rats."

At least one million people believed enough of this hodgepodge to become "frightened or disturbed." So concluded a Princeton professor, Hadley Cantril, who analyzed the program's impact in a detailed academic study. Denials didn't help to diminish the panic, not even when they became emphatic.

Walter Winchell, the columnist, told his fans in his regular 9:00 P.M. radio show on another network, "Mr. and Mrs. America, there's no cause for alarm. America has *not* fallen. I repeat: America has *not* fallen." No matter. The next morning, the *New York Times* front-page headline did justice to the events: "Radio Listeners in Panic, Taking War Drama as Fact."

Indeed, highways in some areas had become clogged with fleeing cars. Some people wrapped their heads in wet towels to guard against the poison gas. In Newark, a fatalistic housewife got out some leftovers from Sunday dinner and told her nephew: "We may as well eat this chicken—we won't be here in the morning."

Where was I, the future reporter, while this was crashing around all about us? I'm embarrassed to admit that I haven't the faintest idea. I know that it was my birthday and that for some reason I didn't hear the program. I do recall the morning after. A lot of excitement was still agitating the neighborhood. Some people were outraged by the hoax. Many had accepted the drama as real but didn't want to admit they had been taken in. My impression is that my parents belonged to that last group.

That wouldn't have been surprising. Like television today, radio was all too real. And we were a lot more innocent.

Sports were a family passion, baseball in particular, and again our beloved radio picked us up and dropped us smack-dab into the middle of the action, never mind the absence of any pictures. Houston was a Cardinals town, our Buffaloes being their farm team, and the big leagues seemed awfully far away, though not invariably so.

I remember the fourth game of the 1941 World Series as if it were yesterday. The Yankees were playing the Brooklyn Dodgers at Ebbets Field and the odds on a Yankee victory stood at one to five. At the top of the ninth inning, the Bums held a four-to-three lead. Hugh Casey, the mighty Casey, was pitching. At 4:45 P.M., Tommy Henrich was the Yankees' final hope.

Meyer Berger, the great *New York Times* columnist, then still writing sports, caught the moment in poetry:

There was ease in Casey's manner as he stood there in the box.
There was pride in Casey's bearing from his cap down to his sox.
And when, responding to the cheers, he took up his trouser's sag,
No stranger in the crowd could doubt, he had them in the bag. . . .
Pale as the lily, Henrich's lips; his teeth were clenched in hate.
He pounded with cruel violence his bat upon the plate.
And now Great Casey held the ball, and now he let it go.
And Brooklyn's air was shattered by the whiff of Henrich's blow. . . .

In fact, Henrich missed the ball by a foot. But it also eluded Mickey Owen, the Dodgers catcher. Stunned, Henrich for one second failed to realize what had happened. Then, bat still in hand, he ran for first and made it. The Yankees won seven to four and Meyer Berger captured the joy and the sorrow:

In Hunts Point men are laughing, on the Concourse children shout
But there is no joy in Flatbush. Fate had knocked their Casey out.

Listening to the game in the Heights Annex, our hearts stood still. Although we were unburdened by partisanship, our world had stopped. Radio had done it again.

*   *   *

If Edward R. Murrow occupies a specially venerated niche in the echo chamber of my memory, I insist that this is not only because Murrow carried the flag of CBS, my future employer. He seemed to personify the American presence at its most eloquent.

In Murrow's vocabulary, Winston Churchill, reporting on the disastrous evacuation of Dunkerque, became "Britain's tired old man of the sea." When the bombs began to fall near Murrow in London, he described his "most undignified" but recommended position: "flat on the ground, facedown, mouth slightly open, and hands covering ears." By then our family was listening on a big box of a radio in the living room.

Through Murrow's clipped and somber tones, I "saw" the face of war, absorbed it by ear, without pictures, very graphically, beginning at the age of seven or eight. Murrow painted pictures with words and sounds. My mother loved it that he held a microphone close to the ground so you could hear footsteps on the sidewalk. By then I knew what a reporter was, reinforced by Murrow referring to himself as "this reporter."

He was a live extension of our newspapers and he placed us at the scene of action long before the blitz turned London into the front line. His voice resounds through my memories of the Austrian *Anschluss*, the dive-bombing of Poland and Rotterdam. At first the British Air Ministry refused him permission to broadcast live from a London roof while an air raid was in progress. Finally he appealed to Churchill personally, who approved, and shortly the familiar voice crackled across the Atlantic:

> I'm standing on a rooftop looming out over London. . . . I think probably in a minute we shall have the sound of guns in the immediate vicinity. The lights are swinging over in this general direction now. You'll hear two explosions. There they are! I should think in a few

minutes there may be a bit of shrapnel around here.
Coming in, moving a little closer all the while. . . . The
searchlights now are feeling almost directly overhead.
Now you'll hear two bursts a little nearer in a moment.
There they are! That hard stony sound.

That hard stony sound. Murrow didn't need television
to make his mark.

22

Almost a Dropout

WITHOUT COACH LAMAR CAMP I might never have made it very far out of Father's ditch. That's not the kind of coaching one forgets, even when it happens to have nothing to do with sports.

One of my pivotal moments arrived when I was fifteen and had just started out at John H. Reagan High School. I was not Rhodes scholar material. My best average barely hit B-minus. I could never fathom algebra, not any of it, and that was considered the test, the dividing line between blue collar and college material.

I remember the family discussions after supper. The issue was never formally phrased; it didn't have to be. The question was obvious and fateful: What's Danny going to do with his life?

My mother, the incurable optimist, had never wavered in her determination: I absolutely *had* to go to college. Today we'd say she was projecting, seeing me as the fulfillment of her own college dream of long ago. I'm not so sure about that. I think she merely wanted me to have the chance and believed that the family ought not to be a brake on my escape from the Heights Annex.

My father, the realist, didn't oppose the college track for me. He simply couldn't figure out how we'd pay for it even if I could get some assistance from a scholarship. Nor do I think he could visualize having a son who was a college man. It was a dream too far, and perhaps not worth the struggle, not in the perspective of the family's immediate, unpostponable needs.

Our finances were still limp; there was rarely any cash to spare. If I dropped out of school, I could bring in meaningful money and that meant more than dollars. It was one of the verities of the time that children, especially boys, were supposed to contribute to the household. That meant quitting school, which many of my buddies from the neighborhood were doing.

Was I different? I wasn't certain. Another arbiter would be helpful.

Enter Coach Lamar Camp, one of the Big Daddies of the community, unquestionable and unquestioned. He was the head high school coach, and that doesn't begin to suggest the scope of his power, not for a time and place when sports were the way, often the only way, to whisk teenagers like me out of places like Prince Street.

Coach Camp presided at the pinnacle of a formidable feeder system. Six or eight elementary schools and two junior highs pumped talent into his pool of potential winners. He could veto football careers for men, cheerleader dreams for women. To us he was the ultimate judge and holder of values.

If the Heights, quintessentially on the wrong side of the tracks, was a "show me" place and "tough" was probably its controlling word, Lamar Camp personified the term and defined its generally accepted varieties. There was plain, ordinary tough; then street tough; then prison tough. There was no place for phony tough.

It's possible that in looking back upon Coach Camp through the lenses of a teenager, I'm exaggerating his status as an authority figure. But I don't think so. All adults of my acquaintance were equally awed by him. Over the years, he'd raised too many winning football teams. He was our Bear Bryant, our Woody Hayes, our entry to the world where winning wasn't everything but the only thing.

At first glance, Coach Camp looked his part, with the shoulders of an Abrams tank, weighing in at 220 pounds, six feet one inch tall, automatically commanding any landscape he chose to enter. But—surprise!—he was knock-kneed, he lisped, he stuttered. Which is surely why he spoke so little. Coach Camp lent the word "taciturn" a new depth. You could be around him for half a day and never hear him utter a syllable.

He didn't have to. We knew he had played football in college, in the navy, and in the semipro industrial leagues, that he had also been a boxing champion in the navy and had boxed in the Golden Gloves. This man knew how to win, and he could do it with teams that weren't supposed to make the grade because the community's best football material had already gotten away from him by drifting into the work force.

Tough? I'd seen Coach lift a 230-pound tackle by his jersey, and when Camp did open his mouth, there could be no argument about his meaning.

"The name of the game is 'Knock'!" he would lisp. "As in 'knock-somebody-DOWN'! Your job is to line up in front of the other guy. It doesn't matter how big he is or how fast. I'm not interested in your excuses. Your job is to *knock him down!*"

If this caused somebody to move his head, Coach Camp's voice would rise.

"I saw you looking over there! You don't need to do that! Just knock him down, that's your job!"

Coach Camp was not so fierce about running or passing. Blocking and tackling were his passions, and, God, did he believe in practice! Hour after hour, we blocked, we tackled, and I still hear his lispy voice ringing in my ear with his war cry, "The name of the game is *knock!*"

Drinking and smoking were capital crimes to the coach. Banishment from the team was the penalty. As with all of his rules, these restrictions were upheld by community opinion in the Heights, in part because the coach was known for making his dicta stick—if necessary by direct action. He believed, in sports as in life, in keeping things simple.

One autumn he caught four boys smoking *and* drinking beer and kicked them off the football team. The boys were upset and got hold of their older brothers. In the dark, after four hours of practice, Coach Camp was heading back to Fourteenth Street with his whistle around his neck when seven or eight people walked up to him and one, without a word, hit him on the side of his face.

Coach Camp wheeled around, decked him, and then, one by one, all the others. According to the account I received, the bad guys were stacked like cord wood. Whereupon Coach lisped at them, "What the hell you lookin' at?"

This was the type of self-help that got you respect in the Heights.

The coach knew how to size up character, and if you were his kind of player he could occasionally muster mercy. Red Mitchell was of the right kind, small but explosive. He played guard and he was a brawler, having learned the skills from his father, who owned a wrecking truck. In the Heights, a car wreck and a football had a central characteristic in common. You had to fight for it.

It figured that Red Mitchell was a discipline problem, and I remember one occasion when the coach caught him smoking. Red had to watch the next game from the sidelines.

It was a difficult game. With seconds left to play, our opponents were on our two yard line, two yards from the winning score.

"Send me in!" wailed Red, tugging at the sleeve of the coach.

Coach Camp ignored him.

"Send me in, Coach!" Red wailed again. "I won't smoke no more!"

The coach relented at this cri de coeur. Red stopped them.

The story was told and retold around the Heights for years. It held up our community banner of crime and punishment, justice and redemption, not to speak of smoke-free living, ages before anybody heard of the lung-cancer risk in cigarettes.

I don't want to leave the impression that Coach Camp was a champion of street fighting. He did value scrappers such as Red Mitchell and "Racehorse" Haynes, who would grow rich as a criminal defense lawyer (see Chapter 2). Tactics generally lacked finesse in the Heights. I saw people grabbed by the skull who had their noses broken against a wall.

Coach Camp preferred to channel violence into the boxing ring, and his recruiting tactic was simplicity itself, as always. He invited one of our natural sluggers into the ring, decked him before the kid could see what was coming, whereupon Camp would inquire politely, "Wouldn't you like to learn how to do that?"

Having picked up the essentials of boxing earlier from my neighbor, Mr. Bredehoeft, I was delighted to get graduate lessons from Coach Camp. He added to my skills, no question, but mostly he reinforced the requirement for heart, lots of heart, which meant getting up when you were down, no matter what.

"You've got to get up!" the coach lisped. "You've got to

clear your head and get up! And you must remember never
to give up!"

It is one of life's supreme lessons, all the more valuable
considering who and where Coach Camp was teaching and
when he was teaching it.

He coached the Reagan High School Bulldogs before,
during, and after the war, from the mid-1930s and the
depths of the Depression to the late 1950s. When he died of
natural causes my first thought was of what he had once said
when one of his favorite professional boxers had died suddenly: "Stand over him and start counting. He'll get up."

From the early 1930s to this day, as I've mentioned, most
able-bodied Texas males have been reared with the idea that
they must be football heroes, not just play but be good at it.

Would I be playing football in high school? No career
opportunity in later years tantalized me more. It was a very
open question. Obviously, I lacked heft. But I was agile, I
could catch. So it came down to this: Did I have enough
heart?

By the grace of the football gods, Coach Camp did not
grade the potential of candidates for his teams by applying
the rule of genetics. That was the technique of my earlier
coach, my nemesis, Mr. Kivel. Kivel thought he could judge
you at a glance. You either "had it" or you didn't.

For all his purported simplicity, Coach Camp, whether
he knew it or not, leaned to the investigative methods of
sociology and psychology. Like a typical Texan, he judged
you by the look in your eye, the shake of your hand, and the
pumping of your heart. Camp tried to look inside you. Did
you have the fighting heart of a Red Mitchell, raised on his
daddy's wrecker truck? That was the ultimate test.

The selection for the teams—A Team, B Team, first
string, second string, third string—was occasion for ceremony. We candidates were rounded up under a huge oak
tree in a corner of the playing field. Cheerleaders did their

stuff. A band played. The assistant coaches warmed us up with inspirational pep messages. Everything attended the appearance of the coach.

And finally the Sphinx came out and spoke!

Quietly, not too fluently, the coach read from his notes, running down each position on each team, every decision momentous in somebody's life, and beyond appeal.

I'm not sure Coach Camp had any idea who I was. I did hear later that I'd found a supporter in the assistant coach, Leroy "Stump" Ashmore. I guess Coach Ashmore had subjected my heart to examination and had not found it wanting. Anyway, that day under the oak tree with the band blaring out, it was announced that in my first year I'd be playing third string on the B Team. It was like being appointed Anchorman in heaven. Friends Linwood Jackson, Dan Winship, and Jeannine Blankenship congratulated me.

By the time of our family discussions about my dropping out of school, Coach Camp knew who I was. Stump Ashmore kept him briefed, and Stump knew how I burned to play, how badly I needed this validation of myself. And they were mourning their losses by then, great talent like my buddy George Hoyt, who had to leave Reagan High in the tenth grade. How they hated to see Georgie go!

I had just dressed for practice and was walking to the practice field, pensive. I still see the spot in my mind. It was on a grassy area, and Coach Camp caught up with me from behind. He never stopped. He spoke no more than two sentences and moved right on. I don't remember his words, but he was saying I ought to stay in school. It's a little hard to believe in retrospect, but I'm positive that this was enough to make me join my mother's side. I *had* to go to college.

23

Moving On at Last

M Y ASCENT out of the ditch began on a Greyhound bus. Mother and I were off to college. The year was
1950 and we were going by bus because we still had the 1938
Oldsmobile and there was a serious question whether it
could withstand the trip to Huntsville, Texas, seventy-five
miles to the north. Earlier, I had hitchhiked there to see the
football coach at Sam Houston State Teachers College, the
nearest small school, and on my return I'd sold Father on
the proposition that I had been offered a football scholarship.

This was neither a total lie nor did it bear much resemblance to the truth.

"I'd be glad to have you come out" was all the coach had
said, no more and no less.

The bus trip was unforgettable. I remember how
Mother and I were all but bursting with exhilaration and
tension and apprehension at the unknown. There was no
mistaking Mother's pride in the moment. A son was off to

college! It was a notable first for the Rathers. And yet: Was
Danny really going to get into school? In particular, would
there be enough money?

Mother had brought along two twenty-five-dollar U.S.
savings bonds that she would cash in Huntsville. The family
had paid $18.75 each for these "war bonds." It was a patri-
otic act to buy them because they would finance the war. You
were only supposed to cash them in an emergency. At the
time of our college emergency the bonds were not worth
much more than we'd paid for them, and this presented a
grave problem.

We knew that I would need twenty-five dollars to enroll,
plus fifteen for student-activity fees. The bonds would barely
cover those items. What we didn't know was whether there
would be other fees. And where would I stay? The regular
dormitories were much too expensive. I was hoping to bed
down in the athletic dorm, but that was far from a sure thing.

Between long silences, we talked about these imponder-
ables on the bus, and I was relieved but not surprised to
gather that Mother was as determined as I was: Our mission
wouldn't fail. I couldn't have felt more strongly supported.

In the dean's office in Huntsville, Mother let me do the
talking, even though I saw that she was literally biting her lip.
The dean sized us up quickly and correctly. He didn't know
about my football plans or the athletic dorm. He did direct
us to the rooming house that was the least expensive and
whose owners were the most sympathetic to impecunious
students. Indeed, they didn't need to be paid until the end of
the month, when I would have earned some money from odd
jobs, and after that I paid for my board by working in the
kitchen.

It was a fragile existence, and I knew I had a lot more
hurdles still to overcome. Fortunately, I didn't know the
odds, which is so often an incomparable advantage. If all
difficulties were known at the outset of a long journey, most
of us would never start out at all. In our blessed ignorance,

Mother and I could afford to feel triumphant over my first step out of the ditch, and we did.

I was trying to hang on as a brand-new freshman at Sam Houston State Teachers College on the strength of the football "scholarship" that was no scholarship at all. It turned out to be a sequence of unceremonious tryouts, revocable week by week at the pleasure of the coach, T. F. "Puny" Wilson, all six feet seven inches of him, a one-time All-American.

The day was at hand when I suspected that my trial time was up. I was supposedly playing end and all of one afternoon Puny had the opposition run one power sweep after another in my direction. This meant that the ball was given to one of their players and *all* the rest were supposed to knock me out of the way. I was convinced that my staying in school depended on my passing this test. And staying in school was the only way for me to stay out of the ditch.

I held my own at least tolerably well for the first couple of downs. Then they were knocking me past the cinder track. And pretty soon I landed over the fence and then in the next county.

When the ordeal was all over, Coach Puny thumped his bear arm around my shoulder and issued his verdict.

"Son," he said, "I watched ya out thar the whole time t'day. And I wanna tell ya sumptun' I hope'll stay with ya the rest of your life. 'Cause if it does, it'll be of no small value to you. You're little." Pause. "And you're *yellow!*" (He said "yeller," of course.)

That was a defining moment, all right, a one-sided definition anyway. I *was* little by football standards, no doubt about that. I measured six feet and always said that I weighed 167 pounds, which was an outrageous lie. I weighed 155, a fly among elephants. Was I also "yeller"? Absolutely not! I simply hadn't been given the opportunity to show how great I was at *catching* the ball. So I told myself.

I also decided that Coach Puny wasn't challenging my

manhood. All he wanted was for me to go away, which was the one move I wouldn't make. While I had to forget about the "scholarship," I kept coming out for football year after year, like a dog that was banished but wouldn't stay away. I played almost not at all, but I wouldn't give in altogether. That I'd really have considered "yeller." I had been beaten but not defeated.

By cutting off my so-called scholarship, Coach Puny had crushed a dream; eliminated my chance at housing in the athletic dorm; and I might have been driven out of college altogether. As it turned out, however, the coach had done me an immeasurable service. To stay in school, I latched on to an apprentice sportscaster's spot at a little radio station, and my obsession with football abated sufficiently so I could shift my attentions to where they would do me the most good for the long run—my journalism courses.

I can't claim that I felt spurred on to greater things when Coach Puny called me yellow. I did feel challenged. And I remembered the solace of a saying I was taught by my grandma Page: "Strong timber does not grow at ease. The stronger the breeze, the stronger the trees."

24

The Making of a Reporter—II

THESE DAYS it may not be widely believed, but it's true that I was shy as a boy. I was respectful of authority, perhaps too respectful. However anyone wants to view it, when I said "Yessir" to my father and "Yes ma'am" to my mother, I was being my deferential self. I certainly didn't care for stressful confrontations. When I ducked my duty badgering money out of slow-paying customers on my newspaper route, I was doing what came naturally.

At Love Elementary School, this reluctance was recognized and my sainted principal, Mrs. Simmons, went to work on it. I still hear her lecturing me on how to meet and greet people. It went like this:

"Stand up, look 'em in the eye, shake hands, and *speak up!*" The handshake was to be firm, the speaking up unmistakable.

Grappling with my peers and my coaches as I grew older, I made headway against my timidity, but not enough to qualify for a reporting career. In my freshman college year at Sam Houston State Teachers College in Huntsville, Texas, another of my revered role models, Hugh Cunningham, my journalism instructor, sent me out to conduct interviews for practice. Often I didn't go on these jobs and ducked behind alibis instead.

Cunningham told me straight out I wasn't aggressive enough. If I was going to realize my dream, I was going to have to become considerably more assertive. Today he'd probably say he never intended for me to go as far in that direction as I have.

Cunningham, a most persuasive teacher, coaxed me out of my early inhibitions. By the time I reached college, this was no longer a hard task for me because my drive to be a reporter had become so overwhelming. Also, I discovered other attributes in myself that came in handy.

I took to anything new just because it was new. Unlike a lot of people, I never experienced newness as threatening. Newness meant excitement. When I first heard of the Zephyr streamliner or of dirigible airships I was turned on by the very unfamiliarity of these innovations. The same characteristic of freshness still thrills me about the day's news. To me, a magic dimension of tonight's newscast is that I couldn't have delivered it yesterday.

Anyone who has followed these pages to this point will know, moreover, that I'm addicted to stories and storytelling. It's a family tradition. My mother was wonderful with Bible stories, an affinity that she inherited from my grandma Page. Grandma was still reading to-be-continued stories to me years after I could read for myself. Stories are a fever in the Rather blood.

It helped that I took to *words* at a very early age. I loved words dearly. I polished them in my mind and aloud and adopted some like pets. This wasn't so strange because certain words had talismanic appeal for my parents. My mother thought that "meadow" was the most beautiful word in the English language. Although the field beyond Prince Street was mostly weeds, Mother loved calling it a "meadow." I think it was the calmness of the sound that pleased her, along with the restful, bucolic mental picture it evoked.

Father's favorite word was "courage" and it became my pet word, too. It had a mental exclamation mark behind it. Father liked the word's definition, its look and its sound. No doubt the word also delivered deep personal meanings to him. I think Father used it as an incantation, a one-word pep talk to buck up himself as well as others when the going got rough or when extra effort was called for. "Courage!" was what he said to me when I embarked on my summer brush-cutting job following my bout with rheumatic fever. The word served as a supplication and a cry to arms.

I picked up on it early and used it for years as a saluta-tion or adios when I wrote personal notes to friends. Some time ago I aired it for a while as a signature at the end of the evening news. Newspaper critics began giving me hell about it. A few viewers wrote to say it puzzled them. Some network executives thought it was a bit melodramatic. There was less here than met the ear. It had simply occurred to me that Father's old injunction might provide a heartening, distinc-tive way to sign off broadcasts.

The concept of courage also interests me for broader reasons, and President Kennedy did a great job probing its many varieties in his book, *Profiles in Courage*. He found courage "a magnificent mixture of triumph and tragedy," and this was his bottom line: "A man does what he must—in spite of personal consequences, in spite of obstacles and dangers and pressures—and that is the basis of all human morality."

I've never achieved goals so lofty. Nor do I realistically ever expect to, but I do still savor the word. Nonetheless, I've been forced to sense that my use—some insist upon saying "misuse"—of it involved me in a good deal more than mem-ories, exhortation, and semantics.

To be more direct: However it may have seemed, I

never used it on the air as any signal of concern or to create any mystery. I just thought it might be a nice signature for the *Evening News*, a good, positive way to end the broadcast each night. I was wrong.

Another wonderful thing about words was that I was never at a loss for them. Since early on, I was always pretty glib and insatiably inquisitive. Of course all children are little question machines. "Why" is every kid's middle name. I don't wish to be immodest, but—to hear my parents tell it—my capacity to bore in with questions and questions and questions, questions about anything at all, seemed to them extraordinary. They generally encouraged curiosity, and I didn't feel stifled. There were times, however, when they told me to go away for a while and give them respite.

My aunt Marie, my father's sister (now Mrs. Hartzell Sherrill), recognized and encouraged my memory ability early. She praised me mightily when I remembered instantly where Grandma Rather had left a ring long ago and retrieved it. It was like doing card tricks. The Boy Scout oath I learned to repeat in little over a minute. I rattled off the Gettysburg Address, all of it, in no time and sang our Baptist hymns nonstop, with spirit and without an open hymn book. This was remarked upon. Our normal service ran for about one hour and fifteen minutes. Some twenty minutes of this were devoted to the sermon. The rest was hymn singing, which added up to one whale of a lot of hymns. I knew them all by heart. I still do. My memory's not super, but it's OK.

My memory became a key element in the final direction of my career choice. Perhaps it was crucial in differentiating myself from my father.

I've mentioned his near-religious fervor for electricity. "The future is electricity" is a motto he drilled into me like a mantra. I was like the impressionable young man in the film *The Graduate* who had the word "Plastics!" whispered into his ear like a command or a prayer.

So when Father and I built our own radio and our Morse set and I quickly memorized the Morse code, it became clear to me what was happening between him and me. To my father, the medium, radio, was the message! To me, the medium was not the message, it was merely the medium. The message was the thing to go after. That was substance. And messages were what I'd be dealing with as a reporter. It further strengthened my determination to make it into college and on beyond, up beyond Father's ditch.

Once I had landed at Sam Houston State, it quickly developed that my memory was money in the bank. I got a part-time job as a sportscaster on the college radio station because I could quickly memorize how I was supposed to open up each game. It became clear that, to me, radio broadcasting was like reeling off captions for mental pictures. I possessed a kind of television of the mind. I had no difficulty "watching" Jarring John Kimbrough on the football field, "seeing" his slight hesitation ... and ... then making up an entire game, play by play, all out of my head.

Later, when I applied for work in Houston television, my interviewers sat me down in front of a camera and said, "Do a newscast." Just like that. Well, I'd done several newscasts already on radio that day, so I rattled off one more on camera. The bosses were impressed. In fact, they shut me off. Could be they feared I'd go on forever.

Eye contact with the viewers was the prized hat trick of those days. Few could manage it. There was no TelePrompTer then, so the newscasters were reading awkwardly from scripts, looking up rarely and only briefly. My ability to memorize helped me to achieve eye contact with few lapses.

When Bill Leonard at CBS eventually decided to give me Walter Cronkite's job, it was partly because I was a glutton for homework and because I was able to retrieve bits or sequences of information from my mind fast and without much effort. Don't get me wrong: I do not have a photographic memory, such as those whizzes who can memorize all the cards played from a deck at the blackjack table. And I've known plenty of others who could memorize scripts better than I.

I once watched Winston Burdett of CBS learn twelve pages of script in less than thirty minutes and deliver it flawlessly. This took a lot of swagger out of me. Still, I'm proud of what my memory can deliver, especially at the time of the acid test, elections, that sacrament of democracy.

CBS puts out an internal election handbook—up to 250 pages of facts and statistics—before each major election day. I use my spare time for a few days beforehand to memorize the book. Then I know plenty about the elections, and that's part of what I get paid for. Since the flow of election news is no flow at all but really a series of lurches, a lot of pauses have to be filled with "ad-libbing," which is no art; a lot of it is regurgitation from the handbook.

I developed a great love for politics and like to think that Father would be proud if he could see me cover elections. He was the one who stimulated my affection for the political process because he took it so seriously. He disdained people who didn't register and failed to vote. It made him angry. He studied issues and candidates as if his life depended on them and scribbled his own detailed notes, which he took along with him into the polling booth.

It may be impossible to overemphasize the impact of comic books on American children from the time they were first popularized in the late 1930s until nationwide television took hold in the 1950s. Given that and the enchantment with newness I got from my father, I was bound to tumble under the spell of a phenomenon that appeared on the horizon with meteor-like suddenness and bowled over the kids of my generation. That was Superman.

While the magnificent fellow is still with us in distant incarnations, it is difficult to convey his gargantuan original appeal almost from the moment he hit the cover of *Action*

Comics in June 1938. You'd have thought every youngster in America was longing to worship precisely such a schizoid hero.

It was as if his dual identity doubled his seductive powers over us. As an extraterrestrial in tights and cape, he whooshed through the air like a jet and packed the muscle of a tank division. He could do anything. His very approach made spirits soar: "It's a bird! It's a plane! It's *Superman!*"

It was comforting that this exalted being had an earthly side. One could identify with him when he stepped meekly out of a phone booth as Clark Kent, the "mild-mannered reporter" for the *Daily Planet*, modestly attired, badgered by an unsympathetic boss, and spooked by the irony of having constantly to compete with himself for the love of Lois Lane, the girl of his dreams.

Superman's success was of staggering proportions. By 1941, he appeared as a comic strip in more than a hundred newspapers with a combined circulation of nearly twenty-five million. Within ten weeks after his first appearance as a radio serial, his program had become the most popular children's show in history. By 1943, Superman had helped push sales of comic books to eighteen million a month. The movie serial was one of the most lucrative ever.

Two myopic Cleveland teenagers, Jerry Siegel and Joe Shuster, were responsible for this bonanza. It's a fabulous story. They were science-fiction addicts and shy with girls. They haunted the movies on Saturday afternoons. They too had gone to an Alexander Hamilton Junior High School. And they had to scramble after a dollar.

"I am lying in bed counting sheep when all of a sudden it hits me," so Siegel would remember Superman's birth. "I conceive a character like Samson, Hercules and all the other strong men I ever heard tell of rolled into one. Only more so. I hop right out of bed and write this down. . . ." History was made, although it took the boys six years to earn their first

$150. When they started out they were so poor that Shuster made his drawings on wrappings and the back of wallpaper.

For my pals and me in the Heights Annex, Superman was a particularly revolutionary advent because our everyday heroes were conventional cowboys, grim men stuck on horseback like Hopalong Cassidy. They were straight arrows, adventurers restrained by rousing creeds. You could tell these immortals by their brave horses, their huge hats, tight lips, and golden hearts.

"A cowboy never takes unfair advantage, even of an enemy," says Gene Autry's code, still hung up framed on my CBS office wall. And: "A cowboy is clean about his person in thought, word and deed." Tough to do on your best days, impossible most days. Still it's worth shooting for, and it keeps those Saturday afternoons in the old Heights Theater alive on the back trails of my mind.

Superman was curious competition for the old western worthies. Here was a new, new idol, again an adventurer, again a straight arrow, not even in need of basic horse transportation. This guy could fly and pull other miracles out of his cape. That opened new vistas of hero worship. Yes, and this mighty personage had chosen to be a reporter, of all professions, exactly what I was going to be! Without my knowing it, this may have been another early tug in the direction of my future life's work.

I had better clarify that my preoccupation with heroes and hero worship wasn't exceptional. It was largely another sign of our innocent times. We hungered for demigods and tended to give full faith and credit to their virtue. Cynicism was still pretty alien to us. I have no survey to prove it, but I'd bet that far more kids than now believed in Santa Claus then.

Along with church, school, the civic club, and Putney's store, the barbershop was among the community's most important gathering places. Women had their "beauty parlors," men had barbershops. "Hairstyling" was hardly even a word then; neither was "unisex."

Indirectly and incongruously, my journalistic ambition was further coaxed along by the Fourteenth Avenue Barbershop. This lively and popular establishment had a black-and-white checkerboard tile floor, one chair, one spittoon, and was my neighborhood's bastion of masculinity. It offered no facials, no "styling," no frills beyond rose hair oil, which cost "extree" and was therefore mostly shunned. Of course the place tolerated no females and vice versa.

"Get your haircut and then get out, pronto," Mother said when she found out that I used to like hanging around there. She rated barbershops as only slightly less threatening to my innocence than pool halls and beer joints. Not too much to my detriment, I suppose, I was enthralled and drank in the boisterous banter of baseball, football, and politics, the raw language and rawer jokes.

The barbershop also charmed me because it was my only access to the *Police Gazette*. The *Police Gazette*? I doubt that many males under fifty remember this earthy and specialized tabloid. It was too untamed to bring home—the forerunner of scandal sheets like *Confidential* but a good deal less manicured. This was my open sesame to the adult world beyond the Heights of murder scenes, gunfire, dead bodies, danger, betrayal, all manner of blood and guts, live-or-die situations, crimes so bizarre that one's breakfast was not secure.

I was riveted reading every story the *Police Gazette* could dredge up. It strengthened my sense that reporters dealt up close with real life—life as it is rather than as people would like it to be. In later years while covering the police beat, the civil rights movement, the Kennedy assassination, and wars in Vietnam and the Persian Gulf, I have often remembered those hours spent reading the *Police Gazette* in the old Fourteenth Avenue Barbershop. Remembered, and smiled.

"Courage!"

Years ago a professor wrote a book deploring people who are "other directed." He meant people who didn't develop minds of their own.

There is another side to the coin called other people, and that's listening and remembering. I mean listening to people who have useful thoughts about you, even if painful. I think of Grandma Page's wisdom, "The stronger the breeze, the stronger the trees." I've been through a lot of rough breezes. Grandma was right about what they can do for you.

Or take that network fellow, a small, glib guy given to snap judgments, who said I wasn't anchor material. He hadn't picked up on that other maxim of mine: Things aren't always what they seem. His judgment of me was an important spur, a knockdown that helped me grow. I'm grateful to him.

As I go back over these pages, I'm glad once again that I listened to people around me: Father, who urged, "Courage!" and "You don't quit!" And Mrs. Simmons with her injunction, "Stand up, look 'em in the eye, shake hands, and *speak up!*"

I'm happy I grew up in the times and places and with the parents, relatives, kids, teachers, coaches, bosses, and heroes who populate my memories.

About yesterday: no tears. About tomorrow: no fears.

I remember.